Keith Markham qualified as a Solicitor in 2001 and now works as a freelance consultant.

After beginning his career in private practice, in 2004 he moved in-house at the BGL Group, a major insurance intermediary that includes comparethemarket.com among its brands. During his time there Keith advised extensively on all areas of data protection. He also conducted contract negotiations of a complex nature, often with major blue chip companies.

In 2007, Keith joined BPP Professional Education, one of Europe's leading providers of professional development training. He worked there as both an in-house lawyer dealing with data protection and commercial contracts and also as a presenter of training courses before going freelance in 2009.

Drawing on his considerable experience Keith has designed and delivered a wide variety of training for BPP, MBL and other providers as well as for his own clients in the commercial law field. In particular, he teaches topics relating to data protection and commercial contracts to lawyers and non-lawyers alike. He also provides consultancy services to an increasing number of clients in those fields.

A Practical Guide to the General Data Protection Regulation (GDPR) 2nd Edition

A Practical Guide to the General Data Protection Regulation (GDPR)
2nd Edition

Keith Markham
LLB Hons
Solicitor (non-practising)
Freelance Consultant

Law Brief Publishing

Published 2020 by Law Brief Publishing, an imprint of Law Brief Publishing Ltd
30 The Parks
Minehead
Somerset
TA24 8BT

www.lawbriefpublishing.com

Paperback: 978-1-912687-76-3

To my wife and children, whose complete lack of interest in the GDPR allowed me to keep some perspective while writing this book.

FOREWORD

The latest edition of Keith's book is a timely and practical publication that is ideal for any professional lawyer, Data Protection Officer, Privacy Manager or Compliance Professional responsible for compliance with the UK Data Protection Act 2018 and the GDPR. Not only does the author explain the law and its practical applications but also gives useful examples and templates that are essential to anyone advising in this area.

Robert Bond
Partner and Notary Public
Bristows LLP

PREFACE

In the two years since the first edition of this book was completed there have been a number of significant developments in this area of law and this is reflected in a series of additional chapters devoted to topics such as data protection impact assessments, compensation and, inevitably, Brexit. My principal aim remains to provide a resource to lawyers and non-lawyers alike so that they can navigate the often treacherous waters of data protection compliance with increased confidence. To that end I have sought to summarise the key issues in a succinct and accessible fashion, and I have also included a series of worked examples in part B to illustrate the practical approach that needs to be taken to this topic. The law is as stated on 31st January 2020.

Keith Markham
January 2020

CONTENTS

PART A

OVERVIEW OF THE GDPR

This section of the book sets out a summary of the main provisions of the GDPR. Each chapter focusses on a different issue and, having outlined the key content, concludes with a series of practical steps to be considered by the reader.

The chapters are as follows:

1. Introduction to the GDPR
2. Principles and accountability
3. Data protection impact assessments
4. Controllers and processors
5. Processing conditions
6. Exemptions
7. Rights of data subjects
8. Right of access
9. Marketing
10. Security
11. International transfers
12. Data protection officers
13. Enforcement
14. Compensation
15. Brexit

CHAPTER ONE
INTRODUCTION TO THE GDPR

The General Data Protection Regulation ('GDPR') came into force on 25th May 2018 and transformed the data protection landscape across the European Economic Area by introducing a series of important changes that affect controllers and processors alike. This book seeks to outline the key provisions together with a series of practical steps that need to be taken to ensure compliance with the rules in a common sense, risk focussed manner.

1.1 Key phrases

When considering the topics covered in this book, I suggest that you bear the following five phrases in mind:

1.1.1 Evolution not revolution

The Information Commissioner's Office ('ICO') has been at pains to stress that the GDPR and the DPA 2018 do not represent wholesale change in the rules relating to data protection, rather what is being implemented is intended to build on the existing regime and take into account the development of new technologies.

1.1.2 Common sense

Not typically a phrase associated with this legislation, it is essential to use common sense when trying to apply the high-level principles of the GDPR to specific scenarios. Guidance is available from the ICO but even this is not always that helpful depending on the precise circumstances. From my own experience of dealing with this topic for the last ten years I can safely say that there have been times when only common sense has been able to shine a light in the sometimes dark tunnel of data protection compliance.

1.1.3 Risk assessment

Therefore, although important to ensure that all aspects of GDPR are complied with, organisations should consider prioritising the steps they take by reference to the actual levels of risk they face.

1.1.4 Reasonable steps

No organisation is capable of ensuring 100% compliance with every aspect of the GDPR and therefore over the years the phrase 'reasonable steps' has become increasingly important. It is used, amongst other things, to describe the steps to be taken to ensure accuracy of information and also to rectify a data breach and remains a useful first line of defence for organisations found to be in breach of their obligations.

1.1.5 Appropriate measures

This phrase is found throughout the GDPR and essentially requires organisations to take into account a number of the matters referred to above and decide on what measures will be implemented. This assessment of appropriateness is critically important for organisations seeking to comply with the GDPR so as to ensure on the one hand that they do not under-prepare but on the other hand that they do not unnecessarily gold plate their procedures.

By remembering these simple phrases organisations will be well placed to find a way through the minefield that awaits in terms of complying with GDPR.

1.2 Application of the GDPR

The GDPR applies to:

- processing of personal data by **both** controllers and processors that are established within the EU.[1]

1 Article 3(1)

- processing of personal data relating to data subjects resident in the EU by a controller not established in the EU where the processing activities are:

  (a) the offering of goods or services, irrespective of whether a payment of the data subject is required, to such data subjects in the Union; or

  (b) the monitoring of their behaviour as far as their behaviour takes place within the Union.[2]

In this case a controller established outside of the EEA is required to appoint a representative within the EEA.[3] Typically this representative shall be established in one of the Member States where data subjects, whose personal data is being processed, reside.[4]

In practice, organisations that were controllers under the DPA 1998 will continue to be controllers under the GDPR and therefore will need to comply with the changes outlined in the following chapters. Clearly, some organisations based outside of the EEA may be caught by the expanded scope of the GDPR and this needs to be dealt with on a case by case basis.

However, the biggest change has been the extension of the GDPR to cover the activities of processors and this means that from May 2018 processors have had to comply with certain specific provisions and are more likely to be the subject of enforcement action than was the case previously

2 Article 3(2)

3 Article 27(1)

4 Article 27(3)

1.3 Relationship between the GDPR and the DPA 2018

This book is largely focused on the content and application of the GDPR, however it is also important to note that, with effect from the 23rd May 2018, the Data Protection Act 2018 ('DPA 2018') came into force and exists alongside the GDPR. A summary of the content of the DPA 2018 may be found at appendix 2 and a comparison with the content of the GDPR found in appendix 1 shows that in many ways the content is very similar.

Generally in this book where the provisions of the GDPR and the DPA 2018 are essentially the same I will only focus on the GDPR. However, where the DPA 2018 does set out additional provisions then these will be referred to directly; for example in the areas of exemptions and enforcement.

1.4 ICO's Guidance

The ICO has produced a detailed guidance note in respect of the GDPR which can be accessed here:

https://ico.org.uk/for-organisations/guide-to-data-protection/guide-to-the-general-data-protection-regulation-gdpr/

This document contains a large number of sections dealing with individual topics and I provide details in each chapter of this book as to how to access each relevant section. The ICO is also in the process of updating its existing guidance and again I provide links in each chapter to the relevant documents. Unless stated otherwise, any reference to the 'ICO's Guidance' is a reference to the relevant section of this document.

The intention in each chapter of this book is to summarise the ICO's guidance in a bite sized format while pointing readers in the direction of more detailed resources that are available if necessary.

1.5 Brexit

At the time of writing, there remains considerable uncertainty as to the precise format that Brexit will take. Clearly a no deal Brexit will have a considerable impact on a number of GDPR related issues and I set out a summary of the current advice as well as steps to take in chapter 15.

1.6 Summary

In summary, although the key definitions remain largely the same it is important to note that the application of the GDPR is wider than that of the DPA 1998 and this is particularly significant for organisations that act as processors as their obligations have been increased significantly. Detail of these key changes are set out in the following chapters.

CHAPTER TWO
PRINCIPLES AND ACCOUNTABILITY

2.1 Introduction

The basic architecture of the DPA 1998, in terms of principles, remains largely unchanged in the GDPR and DPA 2018. The most significant development however has been the introduction of the concept of 'accountability'. Each of these issues will now be discussed in turn.

2.2 Principles

The GDPR is structured around a series of principles that are largely the same as those found in the DPA 1998 and I set out a brief summary of them below:

2.2.1 1st principle – lawfulness, fairness and transparency

> *'data to be processed lawfully, fairly and in a transparent manner in relation to the data subject'*

Essentially this principle requires controllers to have a 'lawful basis' in place to justify their processing of personal data. This issue will be discussed in more detail in chapter 5.

2.2.2 2nd principle – purpose limitation

> *'data to be collected for specified, explicit and legitimate purposes and not further processed in a manner that is incompatible with those purposes; further processing for archiving purposes in the public interest, scientific or historical research purposes or statistical purposes shall, in accordance with Article 89(1), not be considered to be incompatible with the initial purposes'*

This issue has not typically attracted much attention either from controllers or from supervisory authorities. In practice all that is required is for controllers to inform data subjects at the outset of their relationship that the personal data collected will be used for purposes that are specified and lawful. If any changes are proposed subsequently, the controller would have to contact the data subjects and inform them of the changes and of their ability to object, albeit in practice this occurs very rarely.

Of more interest to most controllers is the question as to what constitutes a specified and lawful purpose and I set out some suggestions below that are based on purposes suggested by the ICO:

- Accounts and records
- Staff management
- Provision of goods or services
- Provision of advice
- Credit checking
- Marketing
- Market research

This information would normally be provided to data subjects in the privacy statement required by articles 13 and 14 which is discussed in more detail in chapter 7.

2.2.3 3rd principle – data minimisation

> *'data collected to be adequate, relevant and limited to what is necessary in relation to the purposes for which they are processed'*

At the time of first collection of a data subject's personal data it can be tempting for controllers to embark on a wide-ranging exercise to gather as much personal data as possible. Unsurprisingly, there have always been limits as to the extent of such an exercise and the application of a certain amount of common sense is likely to avoid any major infringements.

Ultimately, if challenged by the ICO, any controller would have to demonstrate why the collection of the disputed personal data was necessary. If the personal data collected was necessary for the provision of goods or services of one type or another then this should be a formality. However, collection of special categories data such as religious belief or sexual orientation is likely to be more difficult to justify unless the controller has a particular requirement to access such information, for example to carry out equality monitoring.

Example

A data subject wishes to purchase a book from a well-known website. In order to facilitate this purchase the only personal data required from the data subject will be; name, contact details, delivery address, payment details and details of the item ordered. Anything else would be a breach of this principle.

2.2.4 4th principle – accuracy

> *'data to be accurate and, where necessary, kept up to date; every reasonable step must be taken to ensure that personal data that are inaccurate, having regard to the purposes for which they are processed, are erased or rectified without delay'*

Clearly no controller can ever be 100% accurate in terms of the personal data it collects. Therefore, it is important to note that if personal data is found to be inaccurate controllers are to take reasonable steps to erase or rectify without delay. This will typically be in response to a request for erasure or rectification of which more detail to follow in chapter 7.

Of course, controllers would be well advised to take reasonable steps at the time of collection of the personal data so as to minimise errors. Such reasonable steps could include asking the data subject to:

- repeat key information to the controller's employee – eg if providing information via the telephone
- check information carefully before submitting it to the controller – eg via a form on a website
- provide a document with key information written on it so that this could be copied by the controller's employee – eg if the data subject is physically present

Ultimately the nature of any reasonable steps would largely be dictated by the sensitivity of the personal data be collected as well as the consequences that could follow if it was collected incorrectly.

Example

A data subject is due to undergo an operation and the details of the operation need to be communicated to the surgery team. In this case the utmost care should be taken to transmit this information accurately and this is likely to involve several checks prior to the operation taking place

2.2.5 5th principle - storage limitation

> *'data to be kept in a form which permits identification of data subjects for no longer than is necessary for the purposes for which the personal data are processed; personal data may be stored for longer periods insofar as the personal data will be processed solely for archiving purposes in the public interest, scientific or historical research purposes or statistical purposes in accordance with Article 89(1) subject to implementation of the appropriate technical and organisational measures required by this Regulation in order to safeguard the rights and freedoms of the data subject'*

The phrase *'no longer than necessary'* has always caused lawyers to raise an eyebrow given that no further guidance is provided within the GDPR as to precisely what this might mean. In practice controllers need to ensure that they have a data retention policy in place which summarises the personal data held, the length of time it is held for and also a justification for this.

Example

A law firm establishes a data retention policy with the following features:

Type of personal data	Time period	Justification
Client files	6 years following file closure	SRA Rules Defence or exercise of legal claims
Complaint files	6 years following file closure	LeO / SRA Rules Defence or exercise of legal claims
Application forms (unsuccessful candidates)	6 months following unsuccessful application	Defence or exercise of legal claims Consideration for another suitable position
Payroll files	7 years following end of employment	HMRC Rules
Personnel files	6 years following end of employment	Defence or exercise of legal claims

Of course, there may be exceptions to these general rules. Perhaps the best example would be a wills file which hopefully should not need to be consulted for many years following the drafting of the will but would need to be retained until such time as it was required for probate purposes.

The other main consideration is ensuring that such a policy is actually implemented in practice. Many is the firm or organisation that I have visited in recent years where employees are either blissfully ignorant of such a policy or have yet to apply it to the content of the cupboard under the stairs.

This issue will be discussed further in chapter 7 in the context of requests for erasure.

2.2.6 6th principle – integrity and confidentiality

> *'data shall be processed in a manner that ensures appropriate security of the personal data, including protection against unauthorised or unlawful processing and against accidental loss, destruction or damage, using appropriate technical or organisational measures'*

This principle is of the utmost importance, not least because a serious breach could well lead to the imposition of a civil monetary penalty and therefore it is discussed at great length in chapter 10.

2.2.7 Missing principles

Data protection aficionados will no doubt be aware that the DPA 1998 contained a total of eight principles and therefore two principles appear to have vanished post GDPR. In fact, the missing principles relating to the rights of data subjects and transfers of personal data outside of the EEA have been retained elsewhere in the GDPR at articles 12-22 and 44-50 respectively.

2.3 Registration Fees

Under the DPA 2018 most controllers are still required to pay a registration fee to the ICO[1]. The details of this are set out in the Data Protection (Charges and Information) Regulations 2018 as follows:

Tier One – Micro-organisations

£40.00 (£35.00 if controllers set up an annual direct debit) Maximum turnover of £632,000 or no more than ten members of staff.

Tier Two – SMEs

£60.00 – this is payable by controllers whose annual turnover exceeds £630,000 but is less than £36million or no more than 250 members of staff

Tier Three – Large organisations

£2,900.00 – this is payable by controllers that do not meet the criteria of either tiers 1 or 2.

Two important points to note are that some controllers are exempt and that there is no such thing as a group notification and therefore all controllers that fall within any of the three tiers must be registered accordingly.

Failure to pay the relevant fee can result in the levying of a civil monetary penalty which according to the aforementioned regulations is payable as follows:

- Tier One - £400.00
- Tier Two - £600.00
- Tier Three - £4,000.00

---

1 s137 DPA 2018

Note however that the ICO reserves the right[2] to increase the amount payable up the statutory maximum under s158 of the DPA 2018 which is capped at:

> *'150% of the highest charge payable by a controller in respect of a financial year in accordance with the regulations, disregarding any discount available under the regulations.'*[3]

In practice this leads to a potential maximum penalty of £4,350.00.

Since May 2018 the ICO has been active in pursuing controllers who have not paid the appropriate registration fee and has issued hundreds of notices of intent requiring controllers to pay up failing which a civil monetary penalty will be issued. As of yet it appears that every controller has ultimately paid up without the need for further enforcement action.

Controllers wishing to check if they are exempt and/or register should consult the following link:

https://ico.org.uk/for-organisations/data-protection-fee/

2.4 Accountability

Despite the obvious similarities referred to above there is one major difference between the DPA 1998 and the GDPR and this is the concept of 'accountability' that is introduced under the GDPR.

> *'the controller shall be responsible for, and be able to demonstrate compliance with, paragraph 1 ('accountability').*[4]*'*

---

2 ICO Regulatory Action Policy p28

3 s158(3) DPA 2018

4 Article 5(2)

In practice this means that the controller is responsible for and must be able to demonstrate compliance with the principles set out above.[5] The need to demonstrate compliance is more onerous than what was required under the DPA 1998.

The GDPR suggests five ways in which controllers can comply with the accountability principle.

2.4.1 Implement appropriate technical and organisational measures

The GDPR uses this phrase in respect of various topics including measures to be taken to ensure security of personal data. The ICO Guidance suggests that this will include:

- creation and review of internal data protection policies,
- staff training, and
- internal audits of processing activities

2.4.2 Maintain relevant documentation on processing activities[6]

The GDPR requires controllers, and where applicable their representatives, to maintain a record of their processing activities that shall contain the following information:[7]

(a) the name and contact details of the controller and, where applicable, the joint controller, the controller's representative and the data protection officer;

(b) the purposes of the processing;

(c) a description of the categories of data subjects and of the categories of personal data;

5 Article 5(2)

6 Article 30

7 Article 30(1)

(d) the categories of recipients to whom the personal data have been or will be disclosed including recipients in third countries or international organisations;

(e) where applicable, transfers of personal data to a third country or an international organisation, including the identification of that third country or international organisation and, in the case of transfers referred to in the second subparagraph of Article 49(1), the documentation of appropriate safeguards;

(f) where possible, the envisaged time limits for erasure of the different categories of data;

(g) where possible, a general description of the technical and organisational security measures referred to in Article 32(1).

The GDPR also requires processors and where applicable their representatives to maintain a record of all categories of processing activities carried out on behalf of a controller including:[8]

(a) the name and contact details of the processor or processors and of each controller on behalf of which the processor is acting, and, where applicable, of the controller's or the processor's representative, and the data protection officer;

(b) the categories of processing carried out on behalf of each controller;

(c) where applicable, transfers of personal data to a third country or an international organisation, including the identification of that third country or international organisation and, in the case of transfers referred to in the second subparagraph of Article 49(1), the documentation of appropriate safeguards;

(d) where possible, a general description of the technical and organisational security measures referred to in Article 32(1).

---

8 Article 30(2)

In both cases the records are to be in writing, including in electronic form,[9] and shall be made available to the ICO on request.[10]

However, where an organisation has less than 250 employees then the requirements of paragraphs 1 and 2 will only apply if the processing is:[11]

- likely to result in a risk to the rights and freedoms of data subjects,
- the processing is not occasional, or
- the processing includes special categories of data as referred to in Article 9(1) or personal data relating to criminal convictions and offences referred to in Article 10[12]

Apart from the requirements set out above there is no prescribed format for this document and therefore controllers and processors have a degree of flexibility as to how they will retain this document. As always, the best advice is to try and incorporate this document within existing documents.

2.4.3 Appoint a data protection officer[13]

The GDPR states that both controllers and processors are required to appoint a data protection officer in certain circumstances. This role and its precise characteristics are discussed in more detail in chapter 12.

9 Article 30(3)
10 Article 30(4)
11 Article 30(5)
12 Article 30(5)
13 Article 37(1)

2.4.4 Implement measures that meet the principles of data protection by design and data protection by default[14]

The GDPR contains this phrase and it is one that has been present in data protection circles for a number of years. The ICO suggests that the following ideas are characteristic of a 'design and default' approach:

- Data minimisation (only collecting information from data subjects that you actually need);
- Pseudonymisation (holding information in a way that does not readily identify the data subjects affected);
- Transparency (providing information to data subjects at the outset about what information you collect, what you will use it for, who you will share it with and what rights they have); and
- Creating and improving security features on an ongoing basis (taking into account technological developments)

In deciding what steps to take, the controller is able to take into consideration the:

- Technological state of the art
- Cost of implementation
- Nature, scope, context and purposes of processing
- Varying likelihood and severity for rights and freedoms of natural persons

In practice this means two things:

First, that the approach taken will vary considerably from one controller to another. Some controllers will have significant financial resources while others will not. Some will be processing large amounts of special categories data about large numbers of data subjects while others may

14 Article 25

only be processing basic personal data about their own employees. All of these matters need to be taken into account in deciding on an approach that is appropriate in the context in which the processing is taking place.

Secondly, it is essential for data protection issues to be discussed at the beginning of any project involving personal data rather than leaving them until the end. If issues are raised at an early stage then data protection considerations can be built in as part of the architecture of what is planned. If they are left until the last moment then this is likely to lead to frustration and delay for all involved.

2.4.5 Data protection impact assessments[15]

Finally, the GDPR suggests that controllers may wish to carry out a data protection impact assessment. These documents are discussed in more detail in chapter 3.

2.5 Summary

In summary then, there is considerable continuity between the principles of the DPA 1998 and the principles of the GDPR. The main change is the introduction of the concept of accountability which requires controllers and processors to be more proactive in demonstrating compliance with the applicable rules. In order to do this there are several steps that controllers and processors can take.

2.6 Practical steps:

- Consider how you will comply with the accountability principle
- Review and revise all data protection related policies and procedures

15 Article 35

- Consider the content and detail of existing records relating to data processing
- Appoint a data protection officer if required
- Consider implementation of a 'design and default' approach
- Use data protection impact assessments where appropriate

CHAPTER THREE
DATA PROTECTION IMPACT ASSESSMENTS

3.1 Introduction

As has been noted in chapter 2, one of the ways that controllers can fulfill their accountability obligations is to carry out a data protection impact assessment ('DPIA') prior to commencing processing of personal data in a new way. This chapter set out a summary of the circumstances in which a DPIA must be carried out as well as a summary of the methodology to be followed.

3.2 Guidance

Guidance as to how to carry out a DPIA may be obtained from the following two documents:

EDPB Guidelines on data protection impact assessments and determining whether processing is 'likely to result in a high risk' for the purposes of Regulation 2016/679 ('EDPB Guidance')

http://ec.europa.eu/newsroom/article29/item-detail.cfm?item_id=611236

ICO – Data Protection Impact Assessments ('ICO Guidance')

https://ico.org.uk/for-organisations/guide-to-the-general-data-protection-regulation-gdpr/data-protection-impact-assessments-dpias/

The ICO Guidance also refers to a sample template document ('ICO Template') that can be used but is not compulsory. This is available here:

https://ico.org.uk/media/about-the-ico/consultations/2258461/dpia-template-v04-post-comms-review-20180308.pdf

A copy of this document is also to be found at appendix 4.

3.3 What is a DPIA?

The ICO Guidance states that DPIAs are designed to help controllers systematically analyse, identify and minimise the data protection risks of a project or plan. Furthermore, it is one of the ways in which controllers can assess and demonstrate how they comply with their GDPR obligations.

The purpose of a DPIA is not to eradicate all risk, but it is intended to help controllers minimise and determine whether or not the level of risk is acceptable in the circumstances, taking into account the benefits of what they want to achieve.

In addition, they are designed to be a flexible and scalable tool that can be applied to a wide range of sectors and projects. The complexity and time taken will vary from one project to another but ultimately there must be a level of rigour in proportion to the privacy risks arising.

3.4 When is a DPIA required?

There are several scenarios when carrying out a DPIA is compulsory and I set out a summary of these below. They can also be used on a voluntary basis if thought appropriate.

3.4.1 General Rule – Article 35(1)

> *Where a type of processing in particular using new technologies, and taking into account the nature, scope, context and purposes of the processing, is likely to result in a high risk to the rights and freedoms of natural persons, the controller shall, prior to the processing, carry out an assessment of the impact of the envisaged processing operations*

on the protection of personal data. A single assessment may address a set of similar processing operations that present similar high risks

(i) Meaning of 'high risk':

The EDPB Guidelines set out nine criteria which may act as indicators of likely high-risk processing:

- Evaluation or scoring.
- Automated decision-making with legal or similar significant effect.
- Systematic monitoring.
- Sensitive data or data of a highly personal nature.
- Data processed on a large scale.
- Matching or combining datasets.
- Data concerning vulnerable data subjects.
- Innovative use or applying new technological or organisational solutions.
- Preventing data subjects from exercising a right or using a service or contract.

The EDPB Guidelines go on to say that in most cases, a combination of two of these factors indicates the need for a DPIA. However, this should not be regarded as a strict rule and controllers may be able to justify a decision not to carry out a DPIA if they are confident that the processing is nevertheless unlikely to result in a high risk. However, the reasoning for such a decision must be documented. Furthermore, in some cases, a DPIA may be required if only one factor is present and it would be good practice to do so in any event.

(ii) Meaning of 'new technologies':

The ICO Guidance notes the following points in respect of 'new technologies'

- 'new technologies' is not defined in the GDPR except for recital 91 which states that this concerns new developments to the state of technological knowledge in the world at large, rather than technology that is new to the controller.

- using technology to process personal data in novel or unexpected ways is likely to be inherently more risky than using technologies that are tried and tested, as the practical implications will not yet be fully understood. For example, the application of artificial intelligence or machine learning within processing operations.

- what is regarded as a new technology may vary by sector to sector, depending on the maturity of its use in that area.

- if the proposed technology is new to an organisation but has been used before by others a DPIA is still recommended

The EDPB Guidance also suggests that:

- the concept of new technologies includes the innovative application of existing technologies to process data in new ways or for new purposes

- if controllers are planning to use technology they have not used before, even if it is not brand new, it is recommended that they still do a DPIA. The technology itself may have been tested by others, but the controller needs to ensure that it understand the risks and implements it in the most privacy-friendly way – and it may still be considered a 'new technology' if the controller is actually using the existing technology in a new or innovative way.

- controllers may be able to rely to some extent on any earlier DPIAs carried out on existing technologies by the developer or by another controller who has already put it to use, but it is important to add on an assessment of the controller's own specific implementation plans including the specific nature, scope, purposes and context of the proposed processing.

3.4.2 Specific Scenarios – Article 35(3)

In addition to the general rule article 35(3) of the GDPR sets out three scenarios where a DPIA must be carried out:

Scenario 1:

- *a systematic and extensive evaluation of personal aspects relating to natural persons which is based on automated processing, including profiling, and on which decisions are based that produce legal effects concerning the natural person or similarly significantly affect the natural person;*

ICO Guidance example – credit checking

Scenario 2:

- *processing on a large scale of special categories of data referred to in Article 9(1), or of personal data relating to criminal convictions and offences referred to in Article 10; or*

ICO Guidance example – dating website

Scenario 3:

- *a systematic monitoring of a publicly accessible area on a large scale.*

ICO Guidance example – usage of automatic number plate recognition technology in a public car park

As can be seen from these three scenarios there are a number of key phrases that need to be understood and unfortunately none of them are defined in the GDPR. However, some guidance is available from other sources and I set out a summary below:

(i) Meaning of 'extensive'

The EDPB's guidance on Data Protection Officers[1] notes that the term 'extensive' implies that the processing covers a large area, involves a wide range of data or affects a large number of individuals.

(ii) Meaning of 'systematic'

The EDPB's guidance on Data Protection Officers notes that this has the following characteristics:

- occurs according to a system;
- is pre-arranged, organised or methodical;
- takes place as part of a general plan for data collection; or
- is carried out as part of a strategy

(iii) Meaning of 'significantly affect'

The EDPB's guidance on Profiling[2] states the following:

- it is something that has a noticeable impact on an individual and can affect their circumstances, behaviour or choices in a significant way

- a legal effect is something that affects a person's legal status or legal rights. A similarly significant effect might include some-

1 http://ec.europa.eu/information_society/newsroom/image/document/2016-51/wp243_en_40855.pdf

2 https://ico.org.uk/for-organisations/guide-to-data-protection/guide-to-the-general-data-protection-regulation-gdpr/individual-rights/rights-related-to-automated-decision-making-including-profiling/

thing that affects a person's financial status, health, reputation, access to services or other economic or social opportunities.

- decisions that have little impact generally could still have a significant effect on more vulnerable people, such as children.

(iv) Meaning of 'large scale'

Again, the GDPR does not contain a definition of large-scale processing, but the ICO's Guidance suggests that when deciding whether processing is on a large scale you should consider:

- the number of individuals concerned;
- the volume of data; · the variety of data;
- the duration of the processing; and
- the geographical extent of the processing

Examples of large-scale processing include:

- a hospital (but not an individual doctor) processing patient data;
- tracking individuals using a city's public transport system;
- a fast food chain tracking real-time location of its customers;
- an insurance company or bank processing customer data;
- a search engine processing data for behavioural advertising; or
- a telephone or internet service provider processing user data.

However, individual professionals processing patient or client data are not processing on a large scale.

3.4.3 ICO List – Article 35(4)

Finally, article 35(4) of the GDPR states that:

> *The supervisory authority shall establish and make public a list of the kind of processing operations which are subject to the requirement for a data protection impact assessment pursuant to paragraph 1.*

The ICO has now produced such a list and this is set out in the ICO Guidance. The key point to note is that, unlike the matters contained on the 'high risk' list in the EDPB Guidance, the ICO Guidance states that a DPIA must be carried out in the event that only **one** of the following matters can be identified.

(i) New technologies:

Processing involving the use of new technologies, or the novel application of existing technologies (including AI).

(ii) Denial of service:

Decisions about an individual's access to a product, service, opportunity or benefit which is based to any extent on automated decision-making (including profiling) or involves the processing of special category data.

(iii) Large-scale profiling:

Any profiling of individuals on a large scale.

(iv) Biometrics:

Any processing of biometric data.

(v) Genetic data:

Any processing of genetic data other than that processed by an individual GP or health professional, for the provision of health care direct to the data subject.

(vi) Data matching:

Combining, comparing or matching personal data obtained from multiple sources.

(vii) Invisible processing:

Processing of personal data that has not been obtained direct from the data subject in circumstances where the controller considers that compliance with Article 14 of the GDPR would prove impossible or involve disproportionate effort.

(viii) Tracking:

Processing which involves tracking an individual's geolocation or behaviour, including but not limited to the online environment.

(ix) Targeting of children or other vulnerable individuals:

The use of the personal data of children or other vulnerable individuals for marketing purposes, profiling or other automated decision-making, or if you intend to offer online services directly to children.

(x) Risk of physical harm:

Where the processing is of such a nature that a personal data breach could jeopardise the health or safety of individuals

As stated above controllers must carry out a DPIA to assess the risk even if only one of these matters has been identified. Of course, the fact that a DPIA is carried out does not mean that there will always be a high risk.

Furthermore, the ICO encourages controllers to think carefully about doing a DPIA for:

- any other processing that is large scale, involves profiling or monitoring, decides on access to services or opportunities, or involves sensitive data or vulnerable individuals.

- any major new project involving the use of personal data even if there is no specific indication of likely high risk

3.4.4 EDPB Opinion

On 25th September 2018 the EDPB reviewed the ICO list and issued an opinion which can be found at:

https://edpb.europa.eu/sites/edpb/files/files/file1/2018-09-25 opinion_2018_art._64_uk_sas_dpia_list_en.pdf

The EDPB criticised the approach taken by the ICO and suggested that the following should not, on their own, automatically require a DPIA to be undertaken:

- New technologies
- Biometrics
- Genetic data
- Tracking

It remains to be seen what the outcome of this dispute will be.

3.4.5 Exceptions

The ICO Guidance states that controllers may not have to carry out a DPIA if:

(a) the controller is processing on the basis of legal obligation or public task. However, this exception only applies if:

- the controller has a clear statutory basis for the processing;
- the legal provision or a statutory code specifically provides for and regulates the processing operation in question;
- the controller is not subject to other obligations to complete DPIAs, such as those required by Cabinet Office for consideration of information governance risks or requirements derived from specific legislation, such as Digital Economy Act 2017;
- a data protection risk assessment was carried out as part of the impact assessment when the legislation was adopted. This may not always be clear, and in the absence of any clear and authoritative statement on whether such an assessment was conducted the ICO recommends that controllers err on the side of caution and conduct a DPIA to ensure they consider how best to mitigate any high risk.

(b) The Controller has already done a substantially similar DPIA. Controllers need to be confident that they can demonstrate that the nature, scope, context and purposes of the processing are all similar.

(c) The ICO issues a list of processing operations that do not require a DPIA. This list has not yet been created.

3.5 Content of a DPIA

A DPIA requires the following steps to be undertaken:

Step 1	**Identify the need**
Step 2	**Describe the processing**
Step 3	**Consider consultation**
Step 4	**Necessity and proportionality**
Step 5	**Identification and assessment**
Step 6	**Risk reduction measures**
Step 7	**Sign-off and record outcomes**
Steps 8-9	**Integration and review**

As has been previously stated the level of detail and complexity of the DPIA is likely to vary taking into consideration the type of personal data that is being processed as well as the scale and complexity of what is being done. However, regardless of the complexity my recommendation is that you use the ICO's sample template as your starting point and then expand on this as appropriate.

I will now consider each of the steps in turn. Please note that in addition to this chapter there is a worked example of a data protection impact assessment which can be accessed in Part B of this book.

Step 1 – Identify the need

This first stage requires a controller to analyse whether the proposed processing is caught by any of the following:

- EDPB's 'high risk' list
- Three specific scenarios from GDPR Article 35(3)
- ICO's list

Step 2 – Describe the processing

This step can potentially be quite time consuming but an accurate description of what is proposed is essential in terms of the risk analysis that must then be carried out in later stages.

(i) The **nature of the processing** is what you plan to do with the personal data. This should include, for example:

- how you collect the data;
- how you store the data;
- how you use the data;
- who has access to the data;
- who you share the data with;
- whether you use any processors;
- retention periods;
- security measures;
- whether you are using any new technologies;
- whether you are using any novel types of processing; and
- which screening criteria you flagged as likely high risk.

(ii) The **scope of the processing** is what the processing covers. This should include, for example:

- the nature of the personal data;
- the volume and variety of the personal data;
- the sensitivity of the personal data;
- the extent and frequency of the processing;
- the duration of the processing;
- the number of data subjects involved; and
- the geographical area covered.

(iii) The **context of the processing** is the wider picture, including internal and external factors which might affect expectations or impact. This might include, for example:

- the source of the data;
- the nature of your relationship with the individuals;
- the extent to which individuals have control over their data;
- the extent to which individuals are likely to expect the processing;
- whether they include children or other vulnerable people;
- any previous experience of this type of processing;
- any relevant advances in technology or security;
- any current issues of public concern; and
- in due course, whether you comply with any GDPR codes of conduct (once any have been approved under Article 40) or GDPR certification schemes.
- whether you have considered and complied with relevant codes of practice.

(iv) The **purpose of the processing** is the reason why you want to process the personal data. This should include:

- your legitimate interests, where relevant;
- the intended outcome for individuals; and
- the expected benefits for you or for society as a whole.

Step 3 – Consider consultation

Having completed step 2 the next step requires controllers to consider consulting interested parties. The ICO's Guidance suggests that the following should be consulted where appropriate:

- Data processors

- Relevant internal stakeholders – eg those responsible for information security
- Existing contacts (eg existing customers or employees)

The ICO's Guidance also suggests that you should consult any relevant independent experts such as IT experts, sociologists or ethicists but notes that there is no specific requirement to do this.

Furthermore, if a controller plans to collect the personal data of individuals not yet identified it may need to carry out a general public consultation process or more specific research to ascertain the views of such groups.

Ultimately though, it is important to note that the controller's DPIA decision does not have to agree with the views of those consulted but, if it is at odds with their views, the controller need to document its reasons for disregarding them.

Step 4 – Necessity and proportionality

Clearly the controller will need to be able to justify what is planned and this requires an assessment of necessity and proportionality. In particular, the EDPB Guidance states that a series of matters should be reviewed and I summarise these below:

- your lawful basis for the processing;
- how you will prevent function creep;
- how you intend to ensure data quality;
- how you intend to ensure data minimisation;
- how you intend to provide privacy information to individuals;
- how you implement and support individuals rights;
- measures to ensure your processors comply; and
- safeguards for international transfers.

Step 5 – Identification and assessment

The next step requires controllers to assess whether any risk identified risk is a high risk. The ICO Guidance makes the following key observations:

- both the likelihood and severity of the possible harm need to be considered
- harm does not have to be inevitable to qualify as a risk or a high risk
- it must be more than remote, but any significant possibility of very serious harm may still be enough to qualify as a high risk
- a high probability of widespread but more minor harm might still count as high risk

This then leads to an objective assessment of the risk and the ICO suggests that a structured matrix is used to think about likelihood and severity of risks. Furthermore, the ICO sets out a series of factors that should be considered when assessing risk and it is important to note that they include the possibility of physical, emotional or material harm or damage.

Describe the source of risk and nature of potential impact on individuals. Include associated compliance and corporate risks as necessary	**Likelihood of harm**	**Severity of impact**	**Overall risk**
	Remote, possible or probable	**Minimal, significant or severe**	**Low, medium or high**

Note that the final decision as to the level of risk requires controllers to use the matrix set out below.

Severity of impact	**Serious Harm**	**Low Risk**	**High Risk**	**High Risk**
	Some Impact	**Low Risk**	**Medium Risk**	**High Risk**
	Minimal Impact	**Low Risk**	**Low Risk**	**Low Risk**
		Remote	**Reasonable Possibility**	**More likely than not**
		Likelihood of harm		

Step 6 – Risk reduction measures

The ICO Guidance sets out a series of measures for reducing risk which include:

- deciding not to collect certain types of data;
- reducing the scope of the processing;
- reducing retention periods;
- taking additional technological security measures;
- training staff to ensure risks are anticipated and managed;
- anonymising or pseudonymising data where possible;
- writing internal guidance or processes to avoid risks;
- adding a human element to review automated decisions;
- using a different technology;
- putting clear data sharing agreements into place;

- making changes to privacy notices;
- offering individuals the chance to opt out where appropriate; or
- implementing new systems to help individuals to exercise their rights.

Assuming that certain medium or high risks have been identified it is then necessary to see whether the application of some of these measures may reduce the risk in question to a more acceptable level. The ICO suggests that the following table can be used to record the information and the controller's assessment.

Risk	Options to reduce or limit risk	Effect on risk	Residual risk	Measure approved
		Eliminated, reduce or accepted	Low, medium or high	Yes/no

Step 7 – Sign-off and record outcomes

Having completed step 6 it remains for controllers to record their conclusions. The ICO's Guidance states that the following matters should be recorded:

- what additional measures the controller plans to take;
- whether each risk has been eliminated, reduced, or accepted;
- the overall level of 'residual risk' after taking additional measures; and
- whether the controller needs to consult the ICO.

Of particular importance is the ICO's observation that it is not necessary to eliminate every risk. In her guidance she notes that even a high risk may be deemed as acceptable in the light of the benefits of processing and the difficulties of mitigation. Nevertheless, if there is still a high risk controllers are required to consult the ICO before going ahead with the proposed processing.

The ICO's Guidance then requires that the controller's DPO be consulted as to whether the processing is compliant. If the DPO says that the processing is not compliant the controller can still proceed but needs to record its reasons, together with any reasons for going against the views of individuals or other consultees, in the following suggested format.

Item	**Name/date**	**Notes**
Measures approved by		Integrate actions back into project plan, with date and responsibility for completion
Residual risks involved		If accepting any residual high risk, consult the ICO before going ahead
DPO advice provided		DPO should advise on compliance, step 6 measures and whether processing can proceed
Summary of DPO advice		
DPO advice accepted or overruled by:		If overruled you must explain your reasons

Comments		
Consultation response overruled by:		If your decision departs from individuals' views, you must explain your reasons
Comments		
This DPIA will be kept under review by:		The DPO should also review ongoing compliance with DPIA

Steps 8-9 – Integration and review

Having completed the DPIA the ICO's Guidance suggests the following actions be carried out: by controllers:

- integrate the outcomes of your DPIA back into your project plans.
- identify any action points and who is responsible for implementing them
- monitor the ongoing performance of the DPIA and, if necessary, repeat the process before your plans are finalised.
- where a controller has decided to accept a high risk, either because it was not possible to mitigate or because the costs of mitigation were too high, it needs to consult the ICO before it can go ahead with the processing

- keep the DPIA under review, and repeat it if there is a substantial change to the nature, scope, context or purposes of the processing.

Finally, the ICO suggests that, as a matter of good practice, controllers should publish their DPIA so as to aid transparency and accountability (sensitive information can be redacted out)

3.6 Consultation with the ICO – Article 36(1)

As has been seen above, controllers are required to assess the level of risk posed by the proposed processing. In the event that a high risk is identified that cannot be mitigated then the controller is required to consult the ICO before commencing the proposed processing. The ICO will then provide written advice typically within eight weeks but in more complex cases this could increase to a period of fourteen weeks. The ICO will either permit the processing to proceed or alternatively can issue a formal warning not to process the data or even ban the processing entirely.

3.7 Summary

DPIAs clearly are here to stay and represent an additional burden for controllers in terms of ensuring compliance with the GDPR and the DPA 2018. However, as the ICO has been keen to stress they do not require a one size fits all approach and can be scaled and tailored accordingly depending on the complexity and sophistication of what is proposed. Furthermore, they are in practice an extremely good way of documenting your processes and are useful both in terms of implementing procedures internally as well as dealing with external enquiries from the ICO.

3.8 Practical steps

- familiarise yourself with the ICO's Guidance
- download the sample template form

- advise colleagues of the type of scenarios where a DPIA must be carried out
- consider using a DPIA even where it may not be a legal requirement to do so

CHAPTER FOUR CONTROLLERS AND PROCESSORS

4.1 Introduction

Although the GDPR generally places greater emphasis on the responsibility of processors for their actions it still places certain obligations on controllers to ensure that they have a data processing contract in place with any processor that they use. This chapter sets out a brief summary of the key issues. Further information can be obtained from the following sources:

Guide to the GDPR – Controllers and processors

https://ico.org.uk/for-organisations/guide-to-data-protection/guide-to-the-general-data-protection-regulation-gdpr/key-definitions/controllers-and-processors/

https://ico.org.uk/for-organisations/guide-to-data-protection/guide-to-the-general-data-protection-regulation-gdpr/controllers-and-processors/

Contracts and liabilities between controllers and processors

https://ico.org.uk/for-organisations/guide-to-data-protection/guide-to-the-general-data-protection-regulation-gdpr/contracts-and-liabilities-between-controllers-and-processors-multi/

4.2 Key Definitions:

There are four types of organisation that need to be considered in this chapter.

4.2.1 Controller

> *means the natural or legal person, public authority, agency or other body which, alone or jointly with others, determines the purposes and means of the processing of personal data; where the purposes and means of such processing are determined by Union or Member State law, the controller or the specific criteria for its nomination may be provided for by Union or Member State law;*[1]

4.2.2 Processor

> *means a natural or legal person, public authority, agency or other body which processes personal data on behalf of the controller;*[2]

4.2.3 Joint Controller

This phrase is not defined in the GDPR but the ICO makes the following comments about joint controllers in her guidance notes:

> *Controllers can determine the purposes and means of processing alone, or jointly with others – as a joint controller. Article 26(1) of the GDPR states that where two or more controllers jointly determine the purposes and means of processing, they shall be* ***joint controllers****.*
>
> *Joint controllers decide the purposes and means of processing together – they have the same or shared purposes. Controllers will not be joint controllers if they are processing the same data for different purposes.*

4.2.4 Sub-processor

This term is also not found in the GDPR but the ICO's guidance suggests that typically it is taken to mean an organisation to whom the processor wishes to sub-contract some or all of the processing.

---

1 Article 4(7)

2 Article 4(8)

4.3 Determining whether an organisation is a controller or a processor

According to the ICO, organisations are not by their nature either controllers or processors. Rather it is important to consider:

- the personal data
- the processing activity that is taking place
- who is determining the purposes and the manner of the processing

In particular the ICO recommends that you ask which organisation decides:

- to collect personal data in the first place;
- the lawful basis for doing so;
- what types of personal data to collect;
- the purpose or purposes the data are to be used for;
- which individuals to collect data about;
- whether to disclose the data, and if so, to whom;
- what to tell individuals about the processing;
- how to respond to requests made in line with individuals' rights; and
- how long to retain the data or whether to make non-routine amendments to the data.

The ICO notes that all of these decisions can only be taken by the controller and if an organisation makes any of these decisions it will be a controller. However, the ICO states that within the terms of controller – processor contract a processor may decide all or any of the following:

- what IT systems or other methods to use to collect personal data;

- how to store the personal data;
- the details of the security measures to protect the personal data;
- how it will transfer the personal data from one organisation to another;
- how it will retrieve personal data about certain individuals;
- how it will ensure it adheres to a retention schedule; and
- how it will delete or dispose of the data.

These lists are not intended to be illustrative rather than exhaustive

The key point to note is that the processor may be allowed a certain amount of freedom to decide how to carry out certain activities on the controller's behalf but it cannot take any of the overarching decisions such as what types of personal data to collect or what the personal data will be used for. Such decisions must only be taken by the controller.

Having set out the key principles let us now turn to a series of practical examples.

4.3.1 Controller Organisations

As a general rule, controller organisations will include the following:

- All employers in respect of their employees' personal data
- All providers of goods and services in respect of their individual customers' or clients' data

The following organisations with whom a controller may wish to share personal data are also likely to be controllers:

- Government Departments
- HMRC
- Regulators
- Local Authorities

- Experts – barristers; accountants; medical experts
- Financial institutions

4.3.2 Processor Organisations

As a general rule, the following organisations may well be considered as processors to the extent that they are implementing the instructions of a controller:

- Cloud storage providers
- E-mail screening providers
- Telephony service providers (including call centre operators in some cases)
- Shredding service providers
- Marketing companies (assuming their role is to send out communications on behalf of a controller)

4.3.3 ICO Examples

In her guidance notes the ICO provides the following examples in terms of the distinction between controllers and processors:

> *A bank hires an IT services firm to store archived data on its behalf – having ensured that the IT firm has given sufficient guarantees about the security of its systems and processes. The bank will still control how and why the data is used and determine its retention period. In reality the IT services firm will use a great deal of its own technical expertise and professional judgement to decide how best to store the data in a safe and accessible way. However, despite this freedom to take technical decisions, the IT firm is still not a data controller in respect of the bank's data – it is a processor. This is because the bank retains exclusive control over the purpose for which the data is processed, if not exclusively over the manner in which the processing takes place*

A private company provides software to process the daily pupil attendance records of a state-maintained school. Using the software, the company gives attendance reports to the school.

The company's sole purpose in processing the attendance data is to provide this service to the school. The school sets the purpose – to assess attendance. The company has no need to retain the data after it has produced the report. It does not determine the purposes of the processing, it merely provides the processing service. This company is likely to be a processor.

4.4 Obligations of controllers and processors

As stated in chapter 1, the GDPR has increased the level of obligations that apply to the processor and, drawing on extracts from the ICO's Guidance, I summarise these and contrast them with those applicable to the controller below:

Obligation	Controller	Processor
Compliance with the data protection principles:	*you must comply with the data protection principles listed in Article 5 of the GDPR.*	N/A
Individuals' rights:	*you must ensure that individuals can exercise their rights regarding their personal data, including the rights of access, rectification, erasure, restriction, data portability, objection and those related to automated decision-making.*	N/A

Security:	*you must implement appropriate technical and organisational security measures to ensure the security of personal data.*	*you must implement appropriate technical and organisational measures to ensure the security of personal data, including protecting against accidental or unlawful destruction or loss, alteration, unauthorised disclosure or access.*
Choosing an appropriate processor:	*you can only use a processor that provides sufficient guarantees that they will implement appropriate technical and organisational measures to ensure their processing meets GDPR requirements. This means you are responsible for assessing that your processor is competent to process the personal data in line with the GDPR's requirements. This assessment should take into account the nature of the processing and the risks to the data subjects.*	N/A
Processor contracts:	*you must enter into a binding contract or other legal act with your processors, which must contain a number of compulsory provisions as specified in Article 28(3).*	*you must enter into a binding contract with the controller. This must contain a number of compulsory provisions, and you must comply with your obligations as a processor under the contract.*

Controller's instructions	*N/A*	*you can only process the personal data on instructions from a controller (unless otherwise required by law). If you act outside your instructions or process for your own purposes, you will step outside your role as a processor and become a controller for that processing.*
Sub-processors:	*N/A*	*you must not engage another processor (ie a sub-processor) without the controller's prior specific or general written authorisation. If authorisation is given, you must put in place a contract with the sub-processor with terms that offer an equivalent level of protection for the personal data as those in the contract between you and the controller.*
Notification of personal data breaches:	*you are responsible for notifying personal data breaches to the ICO and, where necessary, other supervisory authorities in the EU, unless the breach is unlikely to result in a risk to the rights and freedoms of individuals. You are also responsible for notifying affected indi-*	*if you become aware of a personal data breach, you must notify the relevant controller without undue delay. Most controllers will expect to be notified immediately, and may contractually require this, as they only have a limited time in which to notify the supervisory authority (such as the ICO).*

	viduals (if the breach is likely to result in a high risk to their rights and freedoms).	*You must also assist the controller in complying with its obligations regarding personal data breaches.*
Notification of potential data protection infringements:	*N/A*	*you must notify the controller immediately if any of their instructions would lead to a breach of the GDPR or local data protection laws.*
Accountability obligations:	*you must comply with the GDPR accountability obligations, such as maintaining records, carrying out data protection impact assessments and appointing a data protection officer.*	*you must comply with certain GDPR accountability obligations, such as maintaining records and appointing a data protection officer.*
International transfers:	*you must comply with the GDPR's restrictions on transfers of personal data outside the EU.*	*the GDPR's prohibition on transferring personal data outside the EEA applies equally to processors as it does to controllers. This means you must ensure that any transfer outside the EEA is authorised by the controller and complies with the GDPR's transfer provisions.*
Appointing a representative within the	*if you are based outside the EU but offer services to or monitor individuals inside the EU, you may need to*	*if you are based outside the EU but are involved in offering services to or monitoring individuals inside the*

European Union:	*appoint a representative in the EU.*	*EU, you may need to appoint a representative in the EU.*
Co-operation with supervisory authorities:	*you must cooperate with supervisory authorities (such as the ICO) and help them perform their duties.*	*you are also obliged to cooperate with supervisory authorities (such as the ICO) to help them perform their duties.*
Data protection fee:	*you must pay the ICO a data protection fee unless you are exempt*	N/A

Further detail about the nature of these obligations is provided throughout this book but suffice it to say that the controller still bears considerably greater responsibility for compliance with the GDPR and the DPA 2018 than is borne by the processor.

4.5 Controller – Processor Contracts

Against this background, it is hardly surprising that whenever a controller uses a processor the GDPR requires that a contract is put in place between the two parties. If a processor sub-contracts any or all of the processing to sub-processor then a contract must also be put in place.

The ICO has produced detailed guidance which can be accessed at:

https://ico.org.uk/for-organisations/guide-to-data-protection/guide-to-the-general-data-protection-regulation-gdpr/accountability-and-governance/contracts/

This guidance contains the following checklist as to the content of controller – processor agreements:

The contract (or other legal act) must set out details of the processing including:

- the subject matter of the processing;
- the duration of the processing;
- the nature and purpose of the processing;
- the type of personal data involved;
- the categories of data subject;
- the controller's obligations and rights.

The contract or other legal act must include terms or clauses stating that:

- the processor must only act on the controller's documented instructions, unless required by law to act without such instructions;
- the processor must ensure that people processing the data are subject to a duty of confidence;
- the processor must take appropriate measures to ensure the security of processing;
- the processor must only engage a sub-processor with the controller's prior authorisation and under a written contract;
- the processor must take appropriate measures to help the controller respond to requests from individuals to exercise their rights;
- taking into account the nature of processing and the information available, the processor must assist the controller in meeting its GDPR obligations in relation to the security of processing, the notification of personal data breaches and data protection impact assessments;

- the processor must delete or return all personal data to the controller (at the controller's choice) at the end of the contract, and the processor must also delete existing personal data unless the law requires its storage; and

- the processor must submit to audits and inspections. The processor must also give the controller whatever information it needs to ensure they are both meeting their Article 28 obligations.

In summary, the GDPR requires the parties to have such a contract in place. Many of the provisions are relatively standard in nature but particular care needs to be taken in respect of the controller's documented instructions. As long as the processor is careful to follow these then primary responsibility for what happens under the contract will rest with the controller. However, once the processor decides to process personal data outside the controller's instructions, it will be acting as a controller in its own right for that element of its processing.

4.6 Can an organisation be a controller and a processor of personal data?

The ICO's guidance note states that it possible to be both a controller and a processor of personal data in certain circumstances and highlights the following key considerations:

- *Processors that provides services to other controllers are very likely to be a controller for some personal data and a processor for other personal data*

- *It is not possible to be both a controller and a processor for the same processing activity – the personal data must be being processed for different purposes*

- *You may be processing some personal data as a processor for the controller's purposes and only on its instruction, but also process that same personal data for your own separate purposes.*

- *If you are a processor, you should remember that as soon as you process personal data outside your controller's instructions, you will be acting as a controller in your own right for that element of your processing.*

- *If you are acting as both a controller and processor, you must ensure your systems and procedures distinguish between the personal data you are processing in your capacity as controller and what you process as a processor on another controller's behalf.*

- *If some of the data is the same, your systems must be able to distinguish between these two capacities, and allow you to apply different processes and measures to each.*

- *If you cannot do this, you are likely to be considered a joint controller rather than a processor for the data you process on your client's behalf.*

4.7 Joint controllers:

Article 26(1) of the GDPR states that:

> *'Where two or more controllers jointly determine the purposes and means of processing, they shall be joint controllers.'*

The ICO's Guidance then provides three examples of such a scenario:

> *Scenario 1*
>
> *A bank contracts a market-research company to carry out some research. The bank's brief specifies its budget and that it requires a satisfaction survey of its main retail services based on the views of a*

sample of its customers across the UK. The bank leaves it to the research company to determine sample sizes, interview methods and presentation of results.

The research company is processing personal data on the bank's behalf, but it is also determining the information that is collected (what to ask the bank's customers) and the manner in which the processing (the survey) will be carried out. It has the freedom to decide such matters as which customers to select for interview, what form the interview should take, what information to collect from customers and how to present the results. This means the market-research company is a joint controller with the bank regarding the processing of personal data to carry out the survey, even though the bank retains overall control of the data because it commissions the research and determines the purpose the data will be used for.

Scenario 2

A luxury car company teams up with a designer fashion brand to host a co-branded promotional event. The companies decide to run a prize draw at the event. They invite attendees to participate in the prize draw by entering their name and address into their prize draw system at the event. After the event, the companies post out the prizes to the winners. They do not use the personal data for any other purposes.

The companies will be joint controllers of the personal data processed in connection with the prize draw, because they both decided the purposes and means of the processing.

Scenario 3

A property management company maintains student halls of residence for the landlord, the university. The company enters tenancy agreements with the students on the university's behalf and chases any rent arrears. It collects the rent and passes it to the university after taking a commission.

The company is a joint controller of the tenancy-related information, including regarding rental payments. It decides what information it needs from the residents to set up and manage the tenancies but will share this data with the university.

Assuming that a joint controller relationship does exist, the ICO summarises the position regarding the obligations of joint controllers in the following terms:

4.7.1 Obligations of joint controllers:

You need to decide with your fellow joint controllers who will carry out which controller obligation under the GDPR. However, regardless of those arrangements, each controller remains responsible for complying with all the obligations of controllers under the GDPR.

4.7.2 Transparent arrangement:

Joint controllers are not required to have a contract, but you must have a transparent arrangement that sets out your agreed roles and responsibilities for complying with the GDPR. The main points of this arrangement should be made available to individuals. We recommend that you include this in your privacy information.

4.7.3 Individuals' rights:

In particular, you must decide (and be transparent about) how you will comply with transparency obligations and individuals' rights. You may choose to specify a central point of contact for individuals. However, individuals must remain able to exercise their rights against each controller.

In summary, whether a relationship between two parties is characterised as controller-processor relationship or a joint controller relationship will have a profound impact on the obligations of the parties. Clearly, care needs to be taken at the outset of any relationship to clarify its precise nature and thereafter to ensure that this is adequately reflected in any necessary documentation.

4.8 Sub-processors

It is commonplace for processors to sub-contract all or part of their obligations to a sub-processor. However, there are certain considerations to be borne in mind and I summarise the ICO's views below:

4.8.1 Obtaining authorisation from the controller

The original processor must first obtain written authorisation from the controller before proceeding to appoint a sub-processor. Such authorisation may be granted in either a general or specific format.

(i) General authorisation

In practice this means that:

- the controller pre-approves a list of potential sub-processors; or
- the controller approves a list of criteria that you can use to select and appoint a sub-processor.

Once general authorisation has been obtained, the processor must inform the controller if it wishes to make any changes to either of the aforementioned points and must allow the controller a chance to object. Details of the proposed changes should be provided in writing together with a cut -off date for receipt of objections from the controller. The controller should also respond in writing citing its objections (if any).

(ii) Specific authorisation

This simply means that the controller must approve the particular sub-processor for the particular proposed processing operation.

(iii) Terms of appointment

If written authorisation is granted a sub-processor may be appointed by a processor subject to a contract being put in place between the two parties. The terms of the contract that relate to matters specified in Article 28(3) of the GDPR must provide an equivalent level of protection for the personal data being processed to that contained in the controller-processor agreement.

4.9 Responsibility for non-compliance

Given the complexity that can arise in respect of data processing agreements it is essential for there to be clarity about responsibility for compliance with the GDPR and the DPA 2018. I set out below a summary of the different levels of responsibility for compliance

4.9.1 Controllers

Controllers are responsible for their own compliance with the GDPR and the DPA 2018 and for that of their processors. If using a processor Article 28(1) of the GDPR states that:

> *'Where processing is to be carried out on behalf of a controller, the controller shall use only processors providing **sufficient guarantees** to implement appropriate technical and organisational measures in such a manner that processing will meet the requirements of this Regulation and ensure the protection of the rights of the data subject.'*

The following key points should be borne in mind:

- supervisory authorities can investigate and take enforcement action
- individuals can bring claims for compensation directly against a controller where either material or non-material damage is caused to them

- controllers will not be liable for damage resulting from a breach of the GDPR where they can prove they were not in any way responsible for the event giving rise to the damage.

- where other parties were involved in the processing (ie joint controllers or processors) then the individual can claim against all parties.

- if a controller has to pay the full compensation it can then seek to recover all or part of the amount from the other parties, to the extent that they are at fault

4.9.2 Processors

Processors are required to comply with their contractual obligations and if they fail to meet those obligations or they act outside of or in contravention of the controller's documented instructions they may be liable to enforcement action or compensation.

Furthermore, where a processor is authorised by a controller to sub-contract all or any of the processing to a sub-processor the processor does not become a controller in its own right but does remain liable to the controller for the compliance of any sub-processor it uses. However, if a sub-processor is at fault, then under article 82(5) the controller may claim back compensation from the processor for the failings of the sub-processor. Of course it is then open to the processor to then claim compensation back from the sub-processor.

The following key points should be borne in mind:

- supervisory authorities can investigate and take enforcement action

- processors may be liable to the controller for breach of contract

- processors will not be liable for damage resulting from a breach of the GDPR where they can prove they were not in any way responsible for the event giving rise to the damage.
- where other parties were involved in the processing (ie joint controllers or processors) then the individual can claim against all parties.
- if a processor has to pay the full compensation it can then seek to recover all or part of the amount from the other parties, to the extent that they are at fault
- individuals can bring claims for compensation directly against a processor where either material or non-material damage is caused to them. However, a processor will only be liable for the damage if:
    - it has failed to comply with GDPR provisions specifically relating to processors; or
    - it has acted without the controller's lawful instructions or against those instructions.

4.9.3 Joint Controllers

Joint controllers can be held liable for non-compliance in the same way as a single controller. In practice this means that:

- supervisory authorities can investigate and take enforcement action
- individuals can bring claims for compensation directly against a joint controller where either material or non-material damage is caused to them
- a joint controller will not be liable for damage resulting from a breach of the GDPR where they can prove they were not in any way responsible for the event giving rise to the damage.

- where other parties were involved in the processing (ie other joint controllers or processors) then the individual can claim against all parties.
- if a joint controller has to pay the full compensation it can then seek to recover all or part of the amount from the other parties, to the extent that they are at fault

4.9.4 Sub-processors

Sub-processors will be liable for any damage caused by their processing in the following circumstances:

- if they have failed to comply with the GDPR obligations imposed on processors or
- if they have acted contrary to the controller's lawful instructions, relayed by the processor, regarding the processing

Sub-processors may also be liable to a processor where they have failed to comply with their obligations under the terms of their contract.

4.10 Summary

As in many other areas, the GDPR has introduced a series of refinements to the structure put in place under the DPA 1998. It provides greater clarity about the relationships between controllers and processors and also recognises the increasing usage of sub-processors. However, the need to clearly define the status of each party has the potential to create problems. Even where detailed guidance from the ICO now exists it is not uncommon for parties to spend an inordinate amount of time arguing about who the controller is and who the processor is and, increasingly, whether they are in fact joint controllers. Given that ultimately any such decision would have to come from the ICO this can lead to a degree of uncertainty that is far from helpful.

As with all things GDPR related perhaps the best way through the impasse is to deploy a little common sense allied with an approach focussed on risk and I set out below some steps that may be of assistance

4.11 Practical steps

Controllers:

- review what data processing agreements you have in place and whether you need to enter into any new ones
- review what guarantees of security you have in place
- consider whether you need to amend an existing agreement to comply with the requirements of the GDPR
- consider inserting an indemnity in your controller-processor agreement in respect of enforcement action and claims for compensation
- carry out regular audits of the processor's activities

Joint Controllers

- decide with your fellow joint controllers who will carry out which controller obligation under the GDPR
- document your agreed roles and responsibilities for complying with the GDPR in a transparent fashion – preferably in the form of an agreement
- ensure that the main points of this arrangement are made available to data subjects in your privacy information
- specify a central point of contact for data subjects

Processors:

- review what data processing agreements you have in place
- consider whether you are acting in accordance with the controller's instructions
- familiarise yourself with your increased obligations under the GDPR
- review any proposed indemnity in detail to ensure it merely reflects the position set out in the GDPR
- ensure that any indemnity you agree to in the controller-processor agreement is replicated in any sub-contracting arrangements
- obtain a general written authorisation re sub-processors at the time you enter into a controller-processor contract
- carry out regular audits of the sub-processor's activities
- ensure that any sub-processing contract contains equivalent protections to those required under article 28(3)

Sub-processors

- ensure that the processor has written authorisation in place from the controller
- ensure that the sub-processing agreement clearly sets out the controller's documented instructions
- review any proposed indemnity in detail to ensure it merely reflects the position set out in the GDPR

CHAPTER FIVE
PROCESSING CONDITIONS

5.1 Introduction

The DPA 1998 required controllers to have a lawful basis in place before proceeding to process personal data and special categories data and this concept is maintained and refined further in the GDPR. In this chapter we will examine the distinction between the rules relating to personal data and to special categories data and set out a series of practical steps to take.

Guidance in respect of this topic is available from:

Personal data

https://ico.org.uk/for-organisations/guide-to-data-protection/guide-to-the-general-data-protection-regulation-gdpr/lawful-basis-for-processing/

https://ico.org.uk/for-organisations/gdpr-resources/lawful-basis-interactive-guidance-tool/

Special categories data

https://ico.org.uk/for-organisations/guide-to-data-protection/guide-to-the-general-data-protection-regulation-gdpr/special-category-data/

https://ico.org.uk/for-organisations/guide-to-data-protection/guide-to-the-general-data-protection-regulation-gdpr/lawful-basis-for-processing/special-category-data/

Criminal offences data

https://ico.org.uk/for-organisations/guide-to-data-protection/guide-to-the-general-data-protection-regulation-gdpr/lawful-basis-for-processing/criminal-offence-data/

We will now consider each of these issues in turn,

5.2 Personal data

Under the GDPR controllers are required to have a lawful reason for processing personal data relating to data subjects and these are[1]:

- the data subject has given consent to the processing of his or her personal data for one or more specific purposes;
- processing is necessary for the performance of a contract to which the data subject is party or in order to take steps at the request of the data subject prior to entering into a contract;
- processing is necessary for compliance with a legal obligation to which the controller is subject;
- processing is necessary in order to protect the vital interests of the data subject or of another natural person;
- processing is necessary for the performance of a task carried out in the public interest or in the exercise of official authority vested in the controller;
- processing is necessary for the purposes of the legitimate interests pursued by the controller or by a third party, except where such interests are overridden by the interests or fundamental rights and freedoms of the data subject which require protection of personal data, in particular where the data subject is a child.

Under the DPA 1998 many controllers relied on consent as the lawful reason but as will be seen below the quality of the consent required under the GDPR is far higher and therefore an alternative approach is necessary. Let us now consider each possible approach in turn.

---

1 Article 6(1)

5.2.1 Consent

As mentioned above, many controllers have relied on some form of implied consent as the lawful reason for processing personal data. Good examples of this would be the following statements:

> *'by continuing with this transaction you consent to us using your personal data for the following purposes ...'*

> *'by signing this contract of employment you consent to the Company and where applicable any Group Company processing your personal data during your employment'*

Under the GDPR this is no longer be possible. The main reason for this is the change in the definition of consent and I set out a comparison of the respective definitions below:

Data Protection Directive 1995	General Data Protection Regulation
any freely given specific and informed indication of his wishes by which the data subject signifies his agreement to personal data relating to him being processed	*'consent' of the data subject means any freely given, specific, informed and unambiguous indication of the data subject's wishes by which he or she, by a statement or by a clear affirmative action, signifies agreement to the processing of personal data relating to him or her;*[2]

As can be seen, the GDPR raised the standard of consent to be obtained from the data subject by stating that the consent must be unambiguous and be a result of clear affirmative action. The two statements referred to above the table will clearly not satisfy this and therefore are invalid.

2 Article 4(11)

The GDPR also sets out four conditions for consent to be valid[3]:

- the controller shall be able to demonstrate that the data subject has consented to processing of his or her personal data.
- where consent is given in the context of a written declaration which also concerns other matters, the request for consent shall be presented in a manner which is clearly distinguishable from the other matters, in an intelligible and easily accessible form, using clear and plain language.
- the data subject must be informed at the outset that consent may be withdrawn at any time. Withdrawal of consent must be as easy as the giving of consent and it shall not affect the lawfulness of processing based on consent before its withdrawal.
- the performance of a contract, including the provision of a service, must not be conditional on consent to the processing of personal data except where this is necessary for the performance of that contract.

In summary, consent is best avoided under the GDPR as it is difficult to obtain in a compliant fashion and there are usually far more suitable alternatives available. However, if you do wish to rely upon consent, the ICO highlights the following as being key features of GDPR compliant consent:

(i) Unbundled:

This means that consent requests must be separate from other terms and conditions and consent should not be a precondition of signing up to a service unless necessary for that service.

---

3 Article 7

(ii) Active opt-in:

Pre-ticked opt-in boxes should no longer be used. Unticked opt-in boxes or similar active opt-in methods should be used instead.

(iii) Granular:

Data subjects should be given the option to consent separately to different types of processing wherever appropriate.

(iv) Named:

The controller and any third parties who are relying on the consent must be specifically named and references to particular categories of organisations will not be sufficient

(v) Documented:

Records need to be kept to demonstrate what the individual has consented to, including what they were told, and when and how they consented.

(vi) Easy to withdraw:

Data subjects need to be informed of their right to withdraw consent at any time, and how to do this. Withdrawal of consent must be as easy as it was to give consent.

5.2.2 processing is necessary for the performance of a contract to which the data subject is party or in order to take steps at the request of the data subject prior to entering into a contract;

This is likely to be effective in a large number of situations and is the most useful of the alternatives to consent. Clearly, if a customer or client wishes to benefit from goods or services the provision of a certain amount of information will be required. The same could also be said in respect of an employment relationship where an employer will need to obtain certain information initially at interview and subsequently during the period of employment.

5.2.3 processing is necessary for compliance with a legal obligation to which the controller is subject;

This is also likely to be of assistance albeit the scope will be somewhat narrower. It will certainly allow controllers to collect information so as to comply with any relevant legal or regulatory requirements, for example information to be provided to HMRC.

5.2.4 processing is necessary in order to protect the vital interests of the data subject or of another natural person;

This is only likely to be relevant in respect of health data and, as this falls within the definition of 'special categories', a further condition for processing will need to be identified (see below).

Furthermore, the GDPR suggests that

> *'Processing of personal data based on the vital interest of another natural person should in principle take place only where the processing cannot be manifestly based on another legal basis…'*[4]

The ICO's guidance provides the following example:

> *An individual is admitted to the A & E department of a hospital with life-threatening injuries following a serious road accident. The disclosure to the hospital of the individual's medical history is necessary in order to protect his/her vital interests.*

4 GDPR Recital 46

In summary, this lawful basis is only likely to apply in the event of emergency medical treatment where the patient is unable to give their consent.

5.2.5 processing is necessary for the performance of a task carried out in the public interest or in the exercise of official authority vested in the controller;

The ICO's guidance states that this can apply where the controller is carrying out either of the following functions:

- a specific task in the public interest which is laid down by law; or
- exercising official authority (for example, a public body's tasks, functions, duties or powers) which is laid down by law.

If you can show you are exercising official authority, including use of discretionary powers, there is no additional public interest test. However, you must be able to demonstrate that the processing is 'necessary' for that purpose.

Further assistance is available from s8 of the DPA 2018 which states that the public task basis will cover processing necessary for:

- the administration of justice;
- parliamentary functions;
- statutory functions
- governmental functions; or
- activities that support or promote democratic engagement.

5.2.6 processing is necessary for the purposes of the legitimate interests pursued by the controller or by a third party, except where such interests are overridden by the interests or fundamental rights and freedoms of the data subject which require protection of personal data, in particular where the data subject is a child.

This lawful basis has traditionally been seen as controversial but since the GDPR came into force it is being increasingly relied upon, particularly where it is not possible to rely on any of the previous possibilities.

The GDPR sets out a non-exhaustive list of possible legitimate interests including:[5]

- use of client data
- use of employee data
- marketing,
- fraud prevention,
- intra-group transfers
- disclosing information about possible criminal acts or security threats to the authorities.

The ICO's guidance on this topic, including a helpful checklist, may be accessed at:

https://ico.org.uk/for-organisations/guide-to-data-protection/guide-to-the-general-data-protection-regulation-gdpr/lawful-basis-for-processing/legitimate-interests/

https://ico.org.uk/for-organisations/guide-to-data-protection/guide-to-the-general-data-protection-regulation-gdpr/legitimate-interests/

5 GDPR Recital 47

In short, the key issues highlighted by the ICO in her guidance are as follows:

- *legitimate interests is the most flexible lawful basis for processing, but you cannot assume it will always be the most appropriate.*
- *it is likely to be most appropriate where you use people's data in ways they would reasonably expect and which have a minimal privacy impact, or where there is a compelling justification for the processing.*
- *if you choose to rely on legitimate interests, you are taking on extra responsibility for considering and protecting people's rights and interests.*
- *the legitimate interests can be your own interests or the interests of third parties. They can include commercial interests, individual interests or broader societal benefits.*
- *the processing must be necessary. If you can reasonably achieve the same result in another less intrusive way, legitimate interests will not apply.*
- *you must balance your interests against the individual's. If they would not reasonably expect the processing, or if it would cause unjustified harm, their interests are likely to override your legitimate interests.*
- *keep a record of your legitimate interests assessment (LIA) to help you demonstrate compliance if required.*
- *you must include details of your legitimate interests in your privacy information.*

In order to rely on legitimate interests the ICO suggests that you carry out a legitimate interests assessment before beginning processing. This contains the following three elements:

Purpose test: are you pursuing a legitimate interest?

Necessity test: is the processing necessary for that purpose?

Balancing test: do the individual's interests override the legitimate interest?

The ICO then makes the following comments about LIAs:

(i) Confidence

The ICO notes that there is no 'foolproof formula' for the outcome of the balancing test but does stress that controllers must be confident that their legitimate interests are not overridden by the risks they have identified.

(ii) Keep records

Controllers need to keep a record of the LIA and of the outcome. The ICO does not require this to be shown in a standard format but does expect controllers to be able to show their thinking, demonstrate that they have proper decision-making processes in place and justify the outcome of the LIA.

(iii) Review and refresh the LIA

The LIA should be reviewed and refreshed as appropriate, particularly if there is a significant change in the purpose, nature or context of the processing.

(iv) Consider alternatives

If there are doubts about the outcome of the LIA then the ICO suggests that it may be appropriate to look at using an alternative lawful basis. If the processing is either unexpected or high risk then legitimate interests should typically be avoided.

(v) Carry out a DPIA

However, if the LIA identifies significant risks, controllers can consider carrying out a DPIA (more details in chapter 3) to consider how the potential risks may be reduced to an acceptable level.

(vi) Example

I set out a worked example of an LIA in Part B of this book.

5.3 Special Categories

These are defined in the GDPR as being:

- personal data revealing **racial or ethnic origin**;
- personal data revealing **political opinions**;
- personal data revealing **religious or philosophical beliefs**;
- personal data revealing **trade union membership**;
- **genetic data**;
- **biometric data** (where used for identification purposes);
- data concerning **health**;
- data concerning a person's **sex life**; and
- data concerning a person's **sexual orientation**

Of course, controllers are required to ensure that their processing is lawful and this requires identification of an article 6 basis for processing as set out above. However, where controllers intend to process special category data they are required to satisfy one of the specific conditions set out in article 9 of the GDPR as summarised below:[6]

6 Article 9(2)

(a) the data subject has given explicit consent to the processing of those personal data for one or more specified purposes

(b) processing is necessary for the purposes of carrying out the obligations and exercising specific rights of the controller or of the data subject in the field of employment and social security and social protection law

(c) processing is necessary to protect the vital interests of the data subject or of another natural person where the data subject is physically or legally incapable of giving consent;

(d) processing is carried out in the course of its legitimate activities with appropriate safeguards by a foundation, association or any other not-for-profit body with a political, philosophical, religious or trade-union aim

(e) processing relates to personal data which are manifestly made public by the data subject;

(f) processing is necessary for the establishment, exercise or defence of legal claims or whenever courts are acting in their judicial capacity;

(g) processing is necessary for reasons of substantial public interest

(h) processing is necessary for the purposes of preventive or occupational medicine, for the assessment of the working capacity of the employee, medical diagnosis, the provision of health or social care or treatment or the management of health or social care systems and services

(i) processing is necessary for reasons of public interest in the area of public health

(j) processing is necessary for archiving purposes

It is important to note that these conditions are divided into three categories as follows:

Category	Conditions
GDPR only	(a), (c), (d), (e), (f)
GDPR and DPA 2018 sch 1 part 1	(b), (h), (i) or (j),
GDPR and DPA 2018 sch 1 part 2	(g)

5.3.1 GDPR only

(a) the data subject has given explicit consent to the processing of those personal data for one or more specified purposes

(c) processing is necessary to protect the vital interests of the data subject or of another natural person where the data subject is physically or legally incapable of giving consent;

(d) processing is carried out in the course of its legitimate activities with appropriate safeguards by a foundation, association or any other not-for-profit body with a political, philosophical, religious or trade-union aim

(e) processing relates to personal data which are manifestly made public by the data subject;

(f) processing is necessary for the establishment, exercise or defence of legal claims or whenever courts are acting in their judicial capacity;

Further guidance in respect of each of these requirements is available in the ICO's Guidance but I set out below more information in respect of **(f) legal claims** which is the most relevant of these factors.

(i) Legal claims

The ICO's Guidance states that the controller must show *'that the purpose of the processing is to establish, exercise or defend legal claims.'*

The meaning of 'legal claims' is said to include processing necessary for any or all of the following:

- actual or prospective court proceedings;
- obtaining legal advice; or
- establishing, exercising or defending legal rights in any other way.

In each case, the data used must be relevant and proportionate and the controller must have not have more data than is needed. The controller is also required to justify why processing of this specific data is necessary to establish, exercise or defend the legal claim.

The ICO provides the following examples to illustrate these principles:

> *An employer is being sued by one of its employees following an accident at work. The employer wants to pass the details of the accident to its solicitors to obtain legal advice on its position and potentially to defend the claim. The information about the accident includes details of the individual's injuries, which qualify as health data. The purpose of the disclosure is to establish its legal position and to defend the claim.*
>
> *A hairdresser conducts a patch test on a client to check that they will not have an allergic reaction to a hair dye. The hairdresser records when the test was taken and the results. The hairdresser is therefore processing health data about the client's allergies. Although there is no actual or expected court claim, the purpose is to establish that the hairdresser is fulfilling their duty of care to the client, and to defend against any potential personal injury claims in the event of an adverse reaction.*

5.3.2 GDPR and DPA 2018 sch 1 part 1

If a controller is relying on one of these conditions then it is necessary to meet the associated condition set out in UK law. A full list of the requirements in each case is set out in part 1 of schedule 1 of the DPA 2018.

(b) processing is necessary for the purposes of carrying out the obligations and exercising specific rights of the controller or of the data subject in the field of employment and social security and social protection law

(h) processing is necessary for the purposes of preventive or occupational medicine, for the assessment of the working capacity of the employee, medical diagnosis, the provision of health or social care or treatment or the management of health or social care systems and services

(i) processing is necessary for reasons of public interest in the area of public health

(j) processing is necessary for archiving purposes

Further guidance in respect of each of these requirements is available in the ICO's Guidance but I set out below more information in respect of (b), with particular emphasis on the employment aspect, which is the most relevant of these factors.

(i) **Processing is necessary for the purposes of carrying out the obligations and exercising specific rights of the controller or of the data subject in the field of employment**

The ICO's Guidance states that this condition will be of particular relevance to employers who are engaged in any or all of the following activities:

- checking if individuals are entitled to work in the UK;

- ensuring health, safety and welfare of employees;
- maintaining records of statutory sick pay and maternity pay; or
- deducting trade union subscriptions from payroll.

However, the following points also need to be borne in mind by controllers:

- the purpose of the processing must be to comply with employment law and this does not cover processing to meet purely contractual employment rights or obligations.

- therefore the controller must be able to identify the relevant legal right or obligation either by reference to a specific provision or by reference to an appropriate source of advice or guidance (such as a government website or to industry guidance that explains generally applicable employment obligations or rights)

- in each case, the data used must be relevant and proportionate and the controller must have not have more data than is needed. The controller is also required to justify why processing of this specific data is necessary to establish, exercise or defend the legal claim.

- an appropriate policy document must also be in place

The ICO's Guidance provides the following example:

A coach company wants to undertake random drug and alcohol testing of its drivers. As an employer, it has a health and safety obligation to ensure that its drivers are not under the influence of alcohol or drugs while working. It relies on the employment, social security and social protection condition for this processing.

If the company widens the test to include those staff that don't have a safety-critical role, it will not be able to justify that the processing of these individuals' data is necessary.

5.3.3 GDPR and DPA 2018 sch 1 part 2 – Substantial Public Interest

If you are relying on the substantial public interest condition in Article 9(2)(g), you also need to meet one of 23 specific substantial public interest conditions set out in paragraphs 6-28 of Part 2 of Schedule 1 of the DPA 2018.

The ICO states that controllers must identify which of the conditions are most relevant and should then consider what is required in each case. It is important to note the following key points:

- in some cases the substantial public interest is automatically built in
- in other cases it will be necessary to demonstrate that the specific processing is 'necessary for reasons of substantial public interest' on a case by case basis.
- the public interest can cover a wide range of principles and values relating to the public good or the best interests of society
- however, it must be real and of substance and the controller should be able to make specific rather than generic arguments about the wider benefits
- in some cases controllers will need to justify why they cannot give individuals a choice and get explicit consent for their processing
- in most cases an 'appropriate policy document' should be in place (copy available via the ICO's guidance on special category data referred to at the beginning of this chapter).

I summarise all of these matters below in the form of a table.

Conditions (Para no.)	**Show substantial public interest**	**Justify why no consent**	**Appropriate policy document**
6. Statutory and government purposes	Y	N	Y
7. Administration of justice and parliamentary purposes	N	N	Y
8. Equality of opportunity or treatment	N	N	Y
9. Racial and ethnic diversity at senior levels	N	Y	Y
10. Preventing or detecting unlawful acts	Y	Y	Y/N*
11. Protecting the public	Y	Y	Y
12. Regulatory requirements	Y	Y	Y
13. Journalism, academia, art and literature	Y	N	N
14. Preventing fraud	N	N	Y
15. Suspicion of terrorist financing or money laundering	N	N	Y
16. Support for individuals with a particular disability or medical condition	Y	Y	Y
17. Counselling	Y	Y	Y
18. Safeguarding of children and individuals at risk	Y	Y	Y
19. Safeguarding of economic well-being of certain individuals	Y	Y	Y
20. Insurance	Y	Y	Y
21. Occupational pensions	N	Y	Y

22. Political parties	N	N	Y
23. Elected representatives responding to requests	N	Y	Y
24. Disclosure to elected representatives	N	Y	Y
25. Informing elected representatives about prisoners	N	N	Y
26. Publication of legal judgments	N	N	Y
27. Anti-doping in sport	N	N	Y/N*
28. Standards of behaviour in sport	Y	Y	Y

5.3.4 Summary

In reality, most controllers will be able to avoid relying on substantial public interest and therefore it is simply a question of identifying a suitable processing condition and ensuring that this is communicated to data subjects via your privacy information.

5.4 Criminal offence data

In brief, the following points are of note:

- unlike the position under the DPA 1998, criminal offence data is not subject to the GDPR rules on special categories data and has its own separate safeguards[7]

- processing criminal offence data is only permissible where the controller has both a lawful basis under article 6 and either legal authority or official authority under article 10

---

7 GDPR Article 10

- s10(5) of the DPA 2018 states that the processing will meet the requirement in Article 10 of the GDPR for authorisation by the law of the United Kingdom or a part of the United Kingdom only if it meets a condition in Part 1, 2 or 3 of Schedule 1

- controllers should ensure that they determine the relevant condition prior to commencing processing of criminal offence data and should document this accordingly

5.5 Summary

In summary, the ICO has now produced a considerable amount of guidance in respect of processing conditions and controllers would be well advised to consult this in detail. In most cases, controllers will be able to justify their processing by reference to one or more of the processing conditions referred to above. However, the greater concerns are in respect of how these conditions will be recorded and also what information will be provided to the data subjects whose personal data, special categories data and/or criminal offences data are being processed in this way.

5.6 Practical steps

Personal data

- identify the processing conditions currently relied on

- consider the extent to which consent is relied upon and whether your current approach to consent is GDPR compliant

- consider what alternatives can be relied upon in place of consent

- carry out a legitimate interests assessment where appropriate

Special categories data and criminal offences data

- identify what special categories data you currently collect and what you are using it for
- review the processing conditions and select those which are appropriate
- determine what additional steps need to be taken in the light of the ICO's guidance
- prepare an appropriate policy document if required

CHAPTER SIX
EXEMPTIONS

6.1 Introduction

The GDPR and the DPA 2018 contain a series of exemptions from some of the rights and obligations which apply, depending on the purpose for which the personal data is being processed.

In most cases, the exemptions are the same or very similar to those found previously in the DPA 1998.

The ICO states that exemptions should be applied on a case by case basis and that those relying on them will need to be able to justify why they gave done so in a given instance. If an exemption cannot be identified, then the GDPR provision must be complied with as normal.

The ICO's guidance on exemptions can be accessed here:

https://ico.org.uk/for-organisations/guide-to-data-protection/guide-to-the-general-data-protection-regulation-gdpr/exemptions/

6.2 Processing for domestic purposes

Domestic purposes are defined by the ICO as being:

> *'personal data processed in the course of a purely personal or household activity, with no connection to a professional or commercial activity'*

The DPA 1998 contained a provision stating that processing data for such purposes was exempt from the application of that legislation. Neither the GDPR nor the DPA 2018 contain such a statement but this is not necessary because the GDPR does not apply to such processing. Consequently, if a data subject only uses personal data for such things as writing to friends and family or taking pictures for their own enjoyment, they are not subject to the GDPR.

6.3 Exemptions in the GDPR

The exemptions in the GDPR are typically built into specific provisions rather than having general application. For example, article 17 contains several exemptions to the right to erasure. These exemptions are not discussed in this chapter but instead are dealt with alongside the relevant GDPR provisions.

6.4 Exemptions in the DPA 2018

6.4.1 Overview

Schedules 2-4 of the DPA 2018 set out a series of exemptions to specific GDPR provisions. If an exemption applies then a controller or processor may not have to comply with some of the rights or obligations set out in the GDPR such as:

- the right to be informed;
- the right of access;
- dealing with other individual rights;
- reporting personal data breaches; and
- complying with the principles.

However, it is important to note that the application of each exemption is different in that some can exempt a controller or processor from all of the above and some from only some of the above.

6.4.2 Application of the exemptions

The application of each exemption is typically dependent on the purpose for which the personal data are being processed. Exemptions can be divided into two categories:

(i) Exemptions that apply because the controller or processor has a particular purpose

(ii) Exemptions that only apply to the extent that complying with the GDPR would:

- be likely to *prejudice* the purpose (e.g. have a damaging or detrimental effect on what you are doing); or
- *prevent* or *seriously impair* the controller from processing personal data in a way that is *required* or *necessary* for its purpose.

Consequently, care must be taken when applying exemptions to ensure that all the necessary requirements are complied with and they should not be applied on a blanket basis. Normally there will be a choice whether to apply an exemption or not albeit the ICO notes that sometimes there may be an obligation to rely upon it (for example if complying with the GDPR would infringe another piece of legislation).

6.4.3 Types of exemption

In this section I will summarise the broad picture, but it is important to consider each exemption on its merits.

Schedule 2 Exemptions from the GDPR
Part 1 Adaptations and restrictions based on articles 6(3) and 23(1)
1.GDPR provisions to be adapted or restricted: "the listed GDPR provisions"
2.Crime and taxation: general
3.Crime and taxation: risk assessment systems
4.Immigration
5.Information required to be disclosed by law etc. or in connection with legal proceedings

PART 4 Restrictions based on Article 23(1): restrictions of rules in Articles 13 to 15
18.GDPR provisions to be restricted: "the listed GDPR provisions"
19.Legal professional privilege
20.Self incrimination
21.Corporate finance
22.Management forecasts
23.Negotiations
24.Confidential references
25.Exam scripts and exam marks
PART 5 Exemptions etc. based on Article 85(2) for reasons of freedom of expression and information
26.Journalistic, academic, artistic and literary purposes
PART 6 Derogations etc based on Article 89 for research, statistics and archiving
27.Research and statistics
28.Archiving in the public interest
SCHEDULE 3 EXEMPTIONS ETC FROM THE GDPR: HEALTH, SOCIAL WORK, EDUCATION AND CHILD ABUSE DATA
PART 1 GDPR PROVISIONS TO BE RESTRICTED
PART 2 HEALTH DATA
PART 3 SOCIAL WORK DATA
PART 4 EDUCATION DATA
PART 5 CHILD ABUSE DATA

Clearly there are too many exemptions for us to discuss each of them in detail and therefore I summarise the exemptions that are most relevant for most organisations below. Of particular importance is the final column which details any relevant qualification.

No	Exemption	What exempted from	Qualification
Sch 2 Part 1 Para 2	**Crime and taxation** • the prevention and detection of crime; • the apprehension or prosecution of offenders; or • the assessment or collection of a tax or duty or an imposition of a similar nature.	• the right to be informed; • all the other individual rights, except rights related to automated individual decision-making including profiling; • notifying individuals of personal data breaches; • the lawfulness, fairness and transparency principle, except the requirement for processing to be lawful; • the purpose limitation principle; and • all the other principles, but only so far as they relate to the right to be informed and the other individual rights.	*The exemption only applies to the extent that complying with these provisions would be likely to* prejudice *your purposes of processing. If this is not so, you must comply with the GDPR as normal.*

Sch 2 Part 1 Para 5	**Information required to be disclosed by law or in connection with legal proceedings**	• the right to be informed; • all the other individual rights, except rights related to automated individual decision-making including profiling; • the lawfulness, fairness and transparency principle, except the requirement for processing to be lawful; • the purpose limitation principle; and • all the other principles, but only so far as they relate to the right to be informed and the other individual rights	*The exemption only applies to the extent that complying with these provisions would* prevent *you meeting your legal obligation to make personal data publicly available.*
Sch 2 Part 4 Para 19	**Legal professional privilege** This exemption applies if you process personal data: to which a claim to legal professional privilege could be maintained in legal proceedings; or	• the right to be informed; • the right of access; and • all the principles, but only so far as they relate to the right to be informed and the right of access.	

	in respect of which a duty of confidentiality is owed by a professional legal adviser to his client.		
Sch 2 Part 4 Para 21	**Corporate finance** This exemption can apply if you process personal data in connection with a corporate finance service (e.g. if you underwrite financial instruments or give corporate finance advice to undertakings) that you are permitted to provide (as set out in the Financial Services and Markets Act 2000).	• the right to be informed; • the right of access; and • all the principles, but only so far as they relate to the right to be informed and the right of access.	*The exemption only applies to the extent that complying with the provisions above would:* *be likely to affect the price of an instrument; or* *have a prejudicial effect on the orderly functioning of financial markets (or the efficient allocation of capital within the economy), and you reasonably believe that complying with the provisions above could affect someone's decision whether to:* *deal in, subscribe for or issue a financial instrument, or* *act in a way likely to have an effect on a business activity (e.g. an effect on an undertaking's capital structure, the legal or beneficial ownership of a business or asset*

			or a person's industrial strategy
Sch 2 Part 4 Para 22	**Management forecasts** This exemption can apply if you process personal data for the purposes of management forecasting or management planning in relation to a business or other activity.	• the right to be informed; • the right of access; and • all the principles, but only so far as they relate to the right to be informed and the right of access.	*The exemption only applies to the extent that compliance with the above provisions would be likely to* prejudice *the conduct of the business or activity.*
Sch 2 Part 4 Para 23	**Negotiations** This exemption can apply to personal data in records of your intentions relating to any negotiations with an individual.	• the right to be informed; • the right of access; and • all the principles, but only so far as they relate to the right to be informed and the right of access.	*The exemption only applies to the extent that compliance with the above provisions would be likely to* prejudice *the conduct of the business or activity.*
Sch 2 Part 4 Para 24	**Confidential references** • education, training or employment of an individual; • placement of an individual as a volunteer;	• the right to be informed; • the right of access; and • all the principles, but only so far as they relate to the right to be informed and the right of access.	

	• appointment of an individual to office; or • provision by an individual of any service.		
Sch 2 Part 5 Para 26	**Special purposes** • journalistic purposes; • academic purposes; • artistic purposes; or • literary purposes	• all the principles, except the security and accountability principles; • the lawful bases; • the conditions for consent; • children's consent; • the conditions for processing special categories of personal data and data about criminal convictions and offences; • processing not requiring identification; • the right to be informed; • all the other individual rights, except rights related to automated individual decision-making including profiling; • the communication of personal data	*The exemption only applies to the extent that:* *as controller for the processing of personal data, you reasonably believe that compliance with these provisions would be incompatible with the special purposes (this must be more than just an inconvenience);* *the processing is being carried out with a view to the publication of some journalistic, academic, artistic or literary material; and* *you reasonably believe that the publication of the material would be in the public interest, taking into account the special impor-*

		breaches to individuals; • consultation with the ICO for high risk processing; • international transfers of personal data; and • cooperation and consistency between supervisory authorities.	*tance of the general public interest in freedom of expression, any specific public interest in the particular subject, and the potential to harm individuals.*

Having summarised the key elements of the most relevant exemptions I set out below some examples produced by the ICO in respect of their application:

6.4.4 Examples

(i) Crime prevention

A bank conducts an investigation into suspected financial fraud. The bank wants to pass its investigation file, including the personal data of several customers, to the National Crime Agency (NCA) for further investigation. The bank's investigation and proposed disclosure to the NCA are for the purposes of the prevention and detection of crime. The bank decides that, were it to inform the individuals in question about this processing of their personal data, this would be likely to prejudice the investigation because they might abscond or destroy evidence. So the bank relies on the crime and taxation exemption and, in this case, does not comply with the right to be informed.

(ii) Information required to be disclosed by law or in connection with legal proceedings

The Registrar of Companies is legally obliged to maintain a public register of certain information about companies, including the names and (subject to certain restrictions) addresses of company directors. A director asks to exercise his right to erasure by having his name and address removed from the register. The request does not need to be complied with as it would prevent the Registrar meeting his legal obligation to make that information publicly available.

An employer receives a court order to hand over the personnel file of one of its employees to an insurance company for the assessment of a claim. Normally, the employer would not be able to disclose this information because doing so would be incompatible with the original purposes for collecting the data (contravening the purpose limitation principle). However, on this occasion the employer is exempt from the purpose limitation principle's requirements because it would prevent the employer disclosing personal data that it must do by court order

(iii) Confidential references

Company A provides an employment reference in confidence for one of its employees to company B. If the employee makes a subject access request to company A or company B, the reference will be exempt from disclosure. This is because the exemption applies to the reference regardless of whether it is in the hands of the company that gives it or receives it.

6.5 Summary

In summary, the exemptions contained in the GDPR and the DPA 2018 largely mirror those contained in the DPA 1998, both in terms of their content and application. The most important thing to stress is that they need to be applied on a case by case basis with particular care being taken when considering the extent to which the relevant GDPR requirements would be likely to prevent, seriously impair or prejudice the achievement of the processing purposes

6.6 Practical steps

- familiarise yourself with the different types of exemption
- apply them on a case by case basis
- take particular care when applying an exemption on the grounds of prejudice, prevention or serious impairment
- document carefully your reasons for relying on an exemption

CHAPTER SEVEN
RIGHTS OF DATA SUBJECTS

7.1 Introduction

One of the key aims of the GDPR and the DPA 2018 is to provide data subjects with specific rights to allow them to verify what information is held about them, what is being done with it, and then allow them to take appropriate action if necessary.

The rights of data subjects under the GDPR are as follows:

- Right to be informed[1]
- Right of access[2]
- Right to rectification[3]
- Right to erasure (be forgotten)[4]
- Right to restrict processing[5]
- Right to data portability[6]
- Right to object[7]
- Right to review automated decision making / profiling[8]

Further guidance on these rights can be accessed at:

---

1 Articles 12-14

2 Article 15

3 Article 16

4 Article 17

5 Article 18

6 Article 20

7 Article 21

8 Article 22

https://ico.org.uk/for-organisations/guide-to-data-protection/guide-to-the-general-data-protection-regulation-gdpr/individual-rights/

In this chapter, I will begin by summarising the principles that have a general application across all the rights and I will then consider each specific right in more detail.

7.2 General Principles

Article 12 sets out a series of general principles that apply to the specific rights and I summarise these below:

General Rules	Content	Applicability
Provision of information	Information shall be provided using appropriate measures and shall: • be in concise, transparent, intelligible and easily accessible form • use clear and plain language, • be in writing, or by other means, including, where appropriate, by electronic means. • be provided orally if requested, provided that the identity of the data subject is proven by other means.	**13-14**
Communications with data subjects	All communications with data subjects shall use appropriate measures and shall: • be in concise, transparent, intelligible and easily accessible form • use clear and plain language, • be in writing, or by other means,	**15-22**

	including, where appropriate, by electronic means. • be provided orally if requested, provided that the identity of the data subject is proven by other means.	
Time period	Where the data subject requests information then the applicable timeframe is as follows: • without undue delay and in any event within one month of receipt of the request. • this period may be extended by two further months where necessary, taking into account the complexity and number of the requests. • any such extension shall be communicated by the controller to the data subject within one month of receipt of the request, together with the reasons for the delay.	**15-22**
Refusal to comply	The controller may refuse to comply with a data subject's request but is required to: • inform the data subject of the reasons for not taking action; and • the possibility of lodging a complaint with a supervisory authority and seeking a judicial remedy. All this must be done without delay and at the latest within one month of receipt of the request	**15-22**

Charges	Information provided shall be provided free of charge. However, where requests from a data subject are manifestly unfounded or excessive, in particular because of their repetitive character, the controller may either: (a) charge a reasonable fee taking into account the administrative costs of providing the information or communication or taking the action requested; or (b) refuse to act on the request. The controller is required to demonstrate the manifestly unfounded or excessive character of the request.	**13-22**
Proof of identity	In the event that the controller has doubts about the identity of the person making the request they are entitled to request the provision of additional information to confirm the data subject's identity	**15-22**

The ICO's Guidance provides further clarity on each of these general rules and I set out a summary of the key points below.

7.2.1 Recognising a request

The GDPR and DPA 2018 do not specify what format a request should take. Therefore, the ICO's view is that requests can be made orally or in writing and can be made to any part of the controller's organisation. They do not need to refer to any specific right.

The ICO recommends that controllers take the following steps:

- train employees who interact regularly with data subjects so that they are able to identify such a request
- record details of the requests received
- check with the requester that the nature of their request has been understood
- keep a log of verbal requests

7.2.2 Charging a fee

The general rule is that controllers cannot charge a fee for dealing with a request.

The only exception is that a 'reasonable fee' may be charged for the administrative costs of dealing with a request that is *'manifestly unfounded or excessive'*. Such a fee is to be based on the administrative costs of complying with the request and data subjects must be advised promptly of the need to pay the fee.

Controllers are not required to comply with such a manifestly unfounded or vexatious request until the fee has been received. If the fee is not received the controller can decline to deal with the request.

7.2.3 Time Periods

The general rule is that requests must be complied with without undue delay and at the latest one month of receipt of the request.

The ICO's Guidance provides the following examples following recent case law:

Example

An organisation receives a request on 3 September. The time limit will start from the same day. This gives the organisation until 3 October to comply with the request.

If this is not possible because the following month is shorter (and there is no corresponding calendar date), the date for response is the last day of the following month.

If the corresponding date falls on a weekend or a public holiday, you have until the next working day to respond.

This means that the exact number of days you have to comply with a request varies, depending on the month in which the request was made.

Example

An organisation receives a request on 31 March. The time limit starts from the same day. As there is no equivalent date in April, the organisation has until 30 April to comply with the request.

If 30 April falls on a weekend, or is a public holiday, the organisation has until the end of the next working day to comply.

For practical purposes, if a consistent number of days is required (eg for operational or system purposes), it may be helpful to adopt a 28-day period to ensure compliance is always within a calendar month.

7.2.4 Exceptions to the one-month rule

The one-month time period can be extended in the following two scenarios:

(i) Incomplete request

If, on receipt of the request, the controller decides that it will charge a fee and/or requires further information to confirm the requester's identity, then the one month period will be calculated in respect of the date on which the fee and/or the further information is received by the controller.

(ii) Complexity and/or volume

If the request is complex, or if the controller has received a number of requests from the data subject, then the controller may decide to extend the time period by a further two months. However, the controller must inform the data subject of its decision and the reasons for it within one month of receiving the request.

7.2.5 Requests for identification

Clearly, the controller should take care to confirm the identity of the person making the request. Consequently, controllers are entitled to request further information that is necessary and proportionate taking into account the nature and usage of the data held by the controller. If further information is required the controller must inform the data subject about this as soon as possible.

7.2.6 Reasons for refusal

There are a number of reasons for a controller to refuse to comply with a request from a data subject, namely:

- failure to provide confirmation of identity
- failure to pay a reasonable fee
- if a general exemption applies
- if a specific exemption applies
- if the request is manifestly unfounded

- if the request is vexatious

The first two reasons have already been discussed in this chapter and the third reason was discussed in chapter 6. Specific exemptions will be discussed later in this chapter and therefore in this section we will focus our attention on the following reasons:

(i) Request is manifestly unfounded

The ICO's guidance states that a request may be manifestly unfounded if:

- *'the individual clearly has no intention to exercise their right. For example an individual makes a request, but then offers to withdraw it in return for some form of benefit from the organisation; or*

- *the request is malicious in intent and is being used to harass an organisation with no real purposes other than to cause disruption. For example:*

- *the individual has explicitly stated, in the request itself or in other communications, that they intend to cause disruption;*

- *the request makes unsubstantiated accusations against you or specific employees;*

- *the individual is targeting a particular employee against whom they have some personal grudge; or*

- *the individual systematically sends different requests to you as part of a campaign, eg once a week, with the intention of causing disruption.'*

The ICO further states that:

'This is not a simple tick list exercise that automatically means a request is manifestly unfounded. You must consider a request in the context in which it is made, and you are responsible for demonstrating that it is manifestly unfounded.

Also, you should not presume that a request is manifestly unfounded because the individual has previously submitted requests which have been manifestly unfounded or excessive or if it includes aggressive or abusive language.

The inclusion of the word "manifestly" means there must be an obvious or clear quality to it being unfounded. You should consider the specific situation and whether the individual genuinely wants to exercise their rights. If this is the case, it is unlikely that the request will be manifestly unfounded.

You must be able to demonstrate to the individual why you consider the request is manifestly unfounded and, if asked, explain your reasons to the Information Commissioner.'

(ii) Request is excessive

The ICO's guidance states that a request may be excessive if:

- *it repeats the substance of previous requests; or*
- *it overlaps with other requests.*

However, it depends on the particular circumstances. It will not necessarily be excessive just because the individual:

- *makes a request about the same issue. An individual may have legitimate reasons for making requests that repeat the content of previous requests. For example, if the controller has not handled previous requests properly;*

- *makes an overlapping request, if it relates to a completely separate set of information; or*
- *previously submitted requests which have been manifestly unfounded or excessive.*

You must be able to demonstrate to the individual why you consider the request is excessive and, if asked, explain your reasons to the Information Commissioner.

7.2.7 Refusing to comply with a request

In the event that an exemption applies controllers may refuse to comply either wholly or partly with a request. Care should be taken to consider each exemption in detail as many of them have a series of specific requirements and/or qualifications.

Where a controller does decide that an exemption applies then it must provide the following information to the data subject without undue delay and within one month of receipt of the request:

- the reasons for not taking action;
- the data subject's right to make a complaint to the ICO or another supervisory authority; and
- the data subject's ability to seek to enforce this right through a judicial remedy.

This information should also be provided if a controller requests a reasonable fee or needs additional information to identify the individual.

Ultimately, it is important to note that the onus is on the controller to explain its reasons to the data subject and the ICO as appropriate.

7.3 Specific Rights

In this section we will look at each of the specific rights in turn.

7.3.1 Right to be informed

Information provided to data subjects by controllers must be in intelligible form using clear and plain language adapted to the data subject (particularly where dealing with a child).[9] It will usually be provided using a privacy notice with the emphasis being on transparency as to how personal data is used.

(i) Direct Collection: (Article 13)

Where personal data are collected directly from the data subject the controller shall, at the time when personal data are obtained, provide the data subject with all of the following information:

(a) Basic Information[10]

- the identity and the contact details of the controller and, where applicable, of the controller's representative;
- the contact details of the data protection officer, where applicable;
- the purposes of the processing for which the personal data are intended as well as the legal basis for the processing;
- where the processing is based on point (f) of Article 6(1), the legitimate interests pursued by the controller or by a third party;
- the recipients or categories of recipients of the personal data, if any;

9 Article 12(1)

10 Article 13(1)

- where applicable, the fact that the controller intends to transfer personal data to a third country or international organisation and the existence or absence of an adequacy decision by the Commission, or in the case of transfers referred to in Article 46 or 47, or the second subparagraph of Article 49(1), reference to the appropriate or suitable safeguards and the means by which to obtain a copy of them or where they have been made available.

(b) Further information[11]

The controller shall, at the time when personal data are obtained, provide the data subject with the following further information necessary to ensure fair and transparent processing:

- the period for which the personal data will be stored, or if that is not possible, the criteria used to determine that period;
- the existence of the right to request from the controller access to and rectification or erasure of personal data or restriction of processing concerning the data subject or to object to processing as well as the right to data portability;
- where the processing is based on point (a) of Article 6(1) or point (a) of Article 9(2), the existence of the right to withdraw consent at any time, without affecting the lawfulness of processing based on consent before its withdrawal;
- the right to lodge a complaint with a supervisory authority;
- whether the provision of personal data is a statutory or contractual requirement, or a requirement necessary to enter into a contract, as well as whether the data subject is obliged to provide the personal data and of the possible consequences of failure to provide such data;

11 Article 13(2)

- the existence of automated decision-making, including profiling, referred to in Article 22(1) and (4) and, at least in those cases, meaningful information about the logic involved, as well as the significance and the envisaged consequences of such processing for the data subject.

(c) Processing for additional purposes[12]

'Where the controller intends to further process the personal data for a purpose other than that for which the personal data were collected, the controller shall provide the data subject prior to that further processing with information on that other purpose and with any relevant further information as referred to in paragraph 2.'

(d) Final qualification[13]

'Paragraphs 1, 2 and 3 shall not apply where and insofar as the data subject already has the information.'

(ii) Indirect Collection (Article 14)

Where personal data has not been obtained directly from the data subject then the controller shall provide the data subject with the following information:

(a) Basic information[14]

- the identity and the contact details of the controller and, if any, of the controller's representative;

- the contact details of the data protection officer, where applicable;

12 Article 13(3)

13 Article 13(4)

14 Article 14(1)

- the purposes of the processing for which the personal data are intended as well as the legal basis for the processing;
- the categories of personal data concerned;
- the recipients or categories of recipients of the personal data, where applicable;
- where applicable, that the controller intends to transfer personal data to a recipient in a third country or international organisation and the existence or absence of an adequacy decision by the Commission, or in the case of transfers referred to in Article 46 or 47, or the second subparagraph of Article 49(1), reference to the appropriate or suitable safeguards and the means to obtain a copy of them or where they have been made available.

(b) Further information[15]

In addition to the information referred to in paragraph 1, the controller shall provide the data subject with the following information necessary to ensure fair and transparent processing in respect of the data subject:

- the period for which the personal data will be stored, or if that is not possible, the criteria used to determine that period;
- where the processing is based on point (f) of Article 6(1), the legitimate interests pursued by the controller or by a third party;
- the existence of the right to request from the controller access to and rectification or erasure of personal data or restriction of processing concerning the data subject and to object to processing as well as the right to data portability;
- where processing is based on point (a) of Article 6(1) or point (a) of Article 9(2), the existence of the right to withdraw

15 Article 14(2)

consent at any time, without affecting the lawfulness of processing based on consent before its withdrawal;

- the right to lodge a complaint with a supervisory authority;
- from which source the personal data originate, and if applicable, whether it came from publicly accessible sources;
- the existence of automated decision-making, including profiling, referred to in Article 22(1) and (4) and, at least in those cases, meaningful information about the logic involved, as well as the significance and the envisaged consequences of such processing for the data subject.

(c) **Time of provision of above information**[16]

- within a reasonable period after obtaining the personal data, but at the latest within one month, having regard to the specific circumstances in which the personal data are processed;
- if the personal data are to be used for communication with the data subject, at the latest at the time of the first communication to that data subject; or
- if a disclosure to another recipient is envisaged, at the latest when the personal data are first disclosed.

(d) **Processing for additional purposes**[17]

'Where the controller intends to further process the personal data for a purpose other than that for which the personal data were obtained, the controller shall provide the data subject prior to that further processing with information on that other purpose and with any relevant further information as referred to in paragraph 2.'

---

16 Article 14(3)

17 Article 14(4)

(e) Exemptions[18]

Paragraphs 1 to 4 shall not apply where and insofar as:

- the data subject already has the information;
- the provision of such information proves impossible or would involve a disproportionate effort, in particular for processing for archiving purposes in the public interest, scientific or historical research purposes or statistical purposes, subject to the conditions and safeguards referred to in Article 89(1) or in so far as the obligation referred to in paragraph 1 of this Article is likely to render impossible or seriously impair the achievement of the objectives of that processing. In such cases the controller shall take appropriate measures to protect the data subject's rights and freedoms and legitimate interests, including making the information publicly available;
- obtaining or disclosure is expressly laid down by Union or Member State law to which the controller is subject and which provides appropriate measures to protect the data subject's legitimate interests; or
- where the personal data must remain confidential subject to an obligation of professional secrecy regulated by Union or Member State law, including a statutory obligation of secrecy.

Further guidance is available at:

https://ico.org.uk/for-organisations/guide-to-data-protection/guide-to-the-general-data-protection-regulation-gdpr/individual-rights/right-to-be-informed/

I set out some relevant extracts below:

18 Article 14(5)

What methods can we use to provide privacy information?

There are a number of techniques you can use to provide people with privacy information. You can use:

A layered approach *– short notices containing key privacy information that have additional layers of more detailed information.*

Dashboards *– preference management tools that inform people how you use their data and allow them to manage what happens with it.*

Just-in-time notices *– relevant and focused privacy information delivered at the time you collect individual pieces of information about people.*

Icons *– small, meaningful, symbols that indicate the existence of a particular type of data processing.*

Mobile and smart device functionalities *– including pop-ups, voice alerts and mobile device gestures.*

Consider the context in which you are collecting personal data. It is good practice to use the same medium you use to collect personal data to deliver privacy information.

Taking a blended approach, using more than one of these techniques, is often the most effective way to provide privacy information.

What common issues might come up in practice?

If you ***share*** *personal data with (or* ***sell*** *it to) other organisations:*

- *As part of the privacy information you provide, you must tell people who you are giving their information to, unless you are relying on an exception or an exemption.*

- *You can tell people the names of the organisations or the categories that they fall within; choose the option that is most meaningful.*
- *It is good practice to use a dashboard to let people manage who their data is sold to, or shared with, where they have a choice.*

If you ***buy*** *personal data from other organisations:*

- *You must provide people with your own privacy information, unless you are relying on an exception or an exemption.*
- *If you think that it is impossible to provide privacy information to individuals, or it would involve a disproportionate effort, you must carry out a DPIA to find ways to mitigate the risks of the processing.*
- *If your purpose for using the personal data is different to that for which it was originally obtained, you must tell people about this, as well as what your lawful basis is for the processing.*
- *Provide people with your privacy information within a reasonable period of buying the data, and no later than one month.*

If you obtain personal data from ***publicly accessible sources****:*

- *You still have to provide people with privacy information, unless you are relying on an exception or an exemption.*
- *If you think that it is impossible to provide privacy information to individuals, or it would involve a disproportionate effort, you must carry out a DPIA to find ways to mitigate the risks of the processing.*
- *Be very clear with individuals about any unexpected or intrusive uses of personal data, such as combining information about them from a number of different sources.*

- *Provide people with privacy information within a reasonable period of obtaining the data, and no later than one month.*

If you apply ***Artificial Intelligence (AI)*** *to personal data:*

- *Be upfront about it and explain your purposes for using AI.*
- *If the purposes for processing are unclear at the outset, give people an indication of what you are going to do with their data. As your processing purposes become clearer, update your privacy information and actively communicate this to people.*
- *Inform people about any new uses of personal data before you actually start the processing.*
- *If you use AI to make solely automated decisions about people with legal or similarly significant effects, tell them what information you use, why it is relevant and what the likely impact is going to be.*
- *Consider using just-in-time notices and dashboards which can help to keep people informed and let them control further uses of their personal data.*

(iii) Example

In order to illustrate this issue further I have set out an example of a high-level privacy statement in Part B of this book

7.3.2 Right of access

This right is discussed in more detail in chapter 8.

7.3.3 Right to rectification[19]

Under the DPA 1998, rectification could only be ordered by the court pursuant to an application by the data subject in either of the two following circumstances:

- the court was satisfied that the personal data held by the controller was inaccurate; or

- the court was satisfied that the data subject had

  (a) suffered damage by reason of any contravention by a data controller of any of the requirements of this Act in respect of any personal data, in circumstances entitling him to compensation under section 13, and

  (b) that there was a substantial risk of further contravention in respect of those data in such circumstances,

Such an order could also extend to other personal data that expressed an opinion based on the inaccurate data and the court also had the power to order that the data was substituted with a statement of the true facts. Furthermore, the court could order that third parties in possession of the inaccurate data be notified of this.

The GDPR makes it easier for a data subject to obtain rectification by removing the need for a court order. Instead the data subject has the right to obtain from the controller the rectification of inaccurate personal data concerning him or her. Further guidance is available at:

https://ico.org.uk/for-organisations/guide-to-data-protection/guide-to-the-general-data-protection-regulation-gdpr/individual-rights/right-to-rectification/

---

19 Article 16

7.3.4 Right to Erasure

Under the DPA 1998, erasure was only possible in the circumstances referred to above in respect of rectification. The GDPR makes it easier for a data subject to obtain the erasure of their personal data in certain circumstances, namely where:[20]

- the personal data are no longer necessary in relation to the purposes for which they were collected or otherwise processed;
- the data subject withdraws consent on which the processing is based according to point (a) of Article 6(1), or point (a) of Article 9(2), and where there is no other legal ground for the processing;
- the data subject objects to the processing pursuant to Article 21(1) and there are no overriding legitimate grounds for the processing, or the data subject objects to the processing pursuant to Article 21(2);
- the personal data have been unlawfully processed;
- the personal data have to be erased for compliance with a legal obligation in Union or Member State law to which the controller is subject;
- the personal data have been collected in relation to the offer of information society services referred to in Article 8(1).

In reviewing such a request the controller is entitled to take into account the available technology and the cost of implementation.

Where the controller is required to erase the personal data then it is also required to take reasonable steps to inform other controllers who are

20 Article 17(1)

processing the personal data that the data subject has requested erasure.[21]

Controllers must comply with such a request except where retention of the personal data is necessary:[22]

- for exercising the right of freedom of expression and information;
- for compliance with a legal obligation which requires processing by Union or Member State law to which the controller is subject or for the performance of a task carried out in the public interest or in the exercise of official authority vested in the controller;
- for reasons of public interest in the area of public health in accordance with points (h) and (i) of Article 9(2) as well as Article 9(3);
- for archiving purposes in the public interest, scientific or historical research purposes or statistical purposes in accordance with Article 89(1) in so far as the right referred to in paragraph 1 is likely to render impossible or seriously impair the achievement of the objectives of that processing; or
- for the establishment, exercise or defence of legal claims.

Further guidance is available at:

https://ico.org.uk/for-organisations/guide-to-data-protection/guide-to-the-general-data-protection-regulation-gdpr/individual-rights/right-to-erasure/

I set out some relevant extracts below:

21 Article 17(2)

22 Article 17(3)

Do we have to erase personal data from backup systems?

If a valid erasure request is received and no exemption applies then you will have to take steps to ensure erasure from backup systems as well as live systems. Those steps will depend on your particular circumstances, your retention schedule (particularly in the context of its backups), and the technical mechanisms that are available to you.

You must be absolutely clear with individuals as to what will happen to their data when their erasure request is fulfilled, including in respect of backup systems.

It may be that the erasure request can be instantly fulfilled in respect of live systems, but that the data will remain within the backup environment for a certain period of time until it is overwritten.

The key issue is to put the backup data 'beyond use', even if it cannot be immediately overwritten. You must ensure that you do not use the data within the backup for any other purpose, ie that the backup is simply held on your systems until it is replaced in line with an established schedule. Provided this is the case it may be unlikely that the retention of personal data within the backup would pose a significant risk, although this will be context specific.

More information on what the ICO means by 'putting data beyond use' is available from their old guidance under the 1998 Act on deleting personal data (this has not yet been updated post-GDPR). I set out a series of extracts below:

https://ico.org.uk/media/for-organisations/documents/1475/deleting_personal_data.pdf

What the DPA says

The DPA does not define 'delete' or 'deletion' – but a plain English interpretation implies 'destruction'. In the days of paper records it was relatively easy to say whether information had been deleted or

not, for example through incineration. The situation can be less certain with electronic storage, where information that has been 'deleted' may still exist, in some form or another, within an organisation's systems.

Deletion and archiving

There is a significant difference between deleting information irretrievably, archiving it in a structured, retrievable manner or retaining it as random data in an un-emptied electronic wastebasket. Information that is archived, for example, is subject to the same data protection rules as 'live' information, although information that is in effect inert is far less likely to have any unfair or detrimental effect on an individual than live information.

However, the ICO will adopt a realistic approach in terms of recognising that deleting information from a system is not always a straightforward matter and that it is possible to put information 'beyond use', and for data protection compliance issues to be 'suspended' provided certain safeguards are in place:

(i) information has been deleted with no intention on the part of the data controller to use or access this again, but which may still exist in the electronic ether.

For example, it could be waiting to be over-written with other data. This information is no longer live. As such, data protection compliance issues are no longer applicable. (A parallel situation might be a bag of shredded paper waste. Although it may be possible to re-constitute the information from the fragments, this would be extremely difficult and it is unlikely that the organisation would have any intention of doing this.)

(ii) information that should have been deleted but is in fact still held on a live system because, for technical reasons, it is not possible to delete this information without also deleting other information held in the same batch.

In cases like this the organisation holding the information may be prohibited by law from using it in the same way that it might use live information. This could happen if a court has ordered the deletion of information relating to a particular individual but this cannot be done without deleting information about other individuals held in the same batch.

Putting information 'beyond use'

The ICO will be satisfied that information has been 'put beyond use', if not actually deleted, provided that the data controller holding it:

- *is not able, or will not attempt, to use the personal data to inform any decision in respect of any individual or in a manner that affects the individual in any way;*
- *does not give any other organisation access to the personal data;*
- *surrounds the personal data with appropriate technical and organisational security; and*
- *commits to permanent deletion of the information if, or when, this becomes possible.*

We will not require data controllers to grant individuals subject access to the personal data provided that all four safeguards above are in place. Nor will we take any action over compliance with the fifth data protection principle.

It is, however, important to note that where data put beyond use is still held it might need to be provided in response to a court order. Therefore data controllers should work towards technical solutions to prevent deletion problems recurring in the future.

In summary, the position regarding erasure is somewhat more nuanced than may have been thought. Clearly, there is a need to erase information contained in backup systems as well as in live systems but the ICO's Guidance does allow a degree of leeway in terms of how far controllers are expected to go with this. As always, it is a matter of deciding on a specific approach and being able to justify this if, and when, challenged.

7.3.5 Right to restriction of processing:

Under the DPA 1998 there was no specific right to restriction but there was a right to 'block' processing in the same circumstances as those outlined above in respect of rectification and erasure.

Under the GDPR, a data subject has the right to obtain from the controller restriction of processing in any of the following circumstances:[23]

- the accuracy of the personal data is contested by the data subject, for a period enabling the controller to verify the accuracy of the personal data;
- the processing is unlawful and the data subject opposes the erasure of the personal data and requests the restriction of their use instead;
- the controller no longer needs the personal data for the purposes of the processing, but they are required by the data subject for the establishment, exercise or defence of legal claims;
- the data subject has objected to processing pursuant to Article 21(1) pending the verification whether the legitimate grounds of the controller override those of the data subject.

In each case personal data may only be processed:[24]

- with the data subject's consent; or
- for the establishment, exercise or defence of legal claims; or
- for the protection of the rights of another natural or legal person

23 Article 18(1)

24 Article 18(2)

Finally, a controller must inform a data subject who has obtained restriction of processing before the restriction of processing is lifted.[25]

More guidance can be obtained at:

https://ico.org.uk/for-organisations/guide-to-data-protection/guide-to-the-general-data-protection-regulation-gdpr/individual-rights/right-to-restrict-processing/

7.3.6 Right to data portability:

The right to data portability allows individuals to obtain and reuse their personal data for their own purposes across different services. It allows them to move, copy or transfer personal data easily from one IT environment to another in a safe and secure way, without hindrance to usability.[26]

The right only applies:[27]

- to personal data an individual has provided to a controller;
- where the processing is based on the individual's consent or for the performance of a contract; and
- when processing is carried out by automated means.

The right to data portability is subject to the transfer being technically feasible[28] and care should also be taken of the information to be transmitted also contains personal data relating to others.[29]

More guidance can be obtained at

25 Article 18(3)

26 Article 20(1)

27 Article 20(1)

28 Article 20(2)

29 Article 20(4)

https://ico.org.uk/for-organisations/guide-to-data-protection/guide-to-the-general-data-protection-regulation-gdpr/individual-rights/right-to-data-portability/

Guidance on the issue of data portability has also now been produced by the European Data Protection Board and is available on their website at:

http://ec.europa.eu/newsroom/just/item-detail.cfm?item_id=50083

7.3.7 Right to object

This right is most commonly associated with objections to using personal data for marketing purposes and this issue will be dealt with in chapter 9. In this section, we will focus on other areas where this right can be applicable. Guidance is available at:

https://ico.org.uk/for-organisations/guide-to-data-protection/guide-to-the-general-data-protection-regulation-gdpr/individual-rights/right-to-object/

I set out a summary of the key points below:

(i) What is the right to object and when does it apply?

Article 21 allows individuals to object to the processing of some or all of their personal data at any time. Whether the right to object applies depends on the purposes and lawful basis for processing.

(ii) Direct marketing

Where the personal data is being used for marketing purposes then individuals have an absolute right to object to such processing.

(iii) Processing based upon public task or legitimate interests

An individual can also object where a controller is relying on one of the following lawful bases:

- 'public task' (for the performance of a task carried out in the public interest),
- 'public task' (for the exercise of official authority vested in you), or
- legitimate interests.

In order to do so, an individual must give specific reasons for their objection based upon their particular situation.

However, it is important to note that the individual does not have an absolute right in these circumstances, and that a controller can refuse to comply if:

- the controller can demonstrate compelling legitimate grounds for the processing, which override the interests, rights and freedoms of the individual; or
- the processing is for the establishment, exercise or defence of legal claims.

(iv) Demonstrating compelling legitimate grounds

When deciding whether there are compelling legitimate grounds which override the interests of an individual, controllers must consider the reasons why the individual has objected to the processing of their data. If the objection is on the grounds of the processing causing substantial damage or distress (eg the processing is causing them financial loss), then the ICO suggests that the grounds for this objection will have more weight.

Ultimately, the controller must balance its own legitimate grounds with the individual's interests, rights and freedoms and must remember that it is the controller's responsibility to be able to demonstrate that its legitimate grounds override those of the individual.

If a controller decides not to comply with a request it must inform the individual of the following:

- the reasons for the decision
- their right to make a complaint to the ICO
- their right to seek a judicial remedy

(v) Information about the right to object

The GDPR states that individuals must be informed of the right to object at the latest at the time of first communication with them where:

- personal data is being processed for direct marketing purposes, or
- the lawful basis for processing is:
    - public task (for the performance of a task carried out in the public interest),
    - public task (for the exercise of official authority vested in you), or
    - legitimate interests.

This information must be presented clearly and separately from any other information.

7.3.8 Automated decision-making and profiling

The GDPR's provisions safeguarding individuals against the risk that a potentially damaging decision is taken without human intervention largely mirror those of the DPA 1998. However, the GDPR does introduce greater expectations where profiling is undertaken by a controller. More guidance on this topic can be obtained at:

https://ico.org.uk/for-organisations/guide-to-data-protection/guide-to-the-general-data-protection-regulation-gdpr/individual-rights/rights-related-to-automated-decision-making-including-profiling/

I set out a summary of the key points below:

(i) Definitions

Automated individual decision-making

The ICO's Guidance defines this as:

'A decision made by automated means without any human involvement.'

and suggests that examples of this could include:

- an online decision to award a loan; and
- a recruitment aptitude test which uses pre-programmed algorithms and criteria.

It does not have to include profiling but often will.

Profiling

> *'Any form of automated processing of personal data consisting of the use of personal data to evaluate certain personal aspects relating to a*

natural person, in particular to analyse or predict aspects concerning that natural person's:

- *performance at work,*
- *economic situation,*
- *health,*
- *personal preferences,*
- *interests,*
- *reliability,*
- *behaviour,*
- *location or movements.*'[30]

The ICO's Guidance provides further useful background by noting that the following information might be obtained in one or more ways:

- internet searches,
- buying habits,
- lifestyle and behaviour data gathered from mobile phones,
- social networks,
- video surveillance systems and
- the Internet of Things

and that this information is then analysed using algorithms and machine learning so as to classify people into different groups or sectors with particular emphasis on:

- finding something out about individuals' preferences;
- predicting their behaviour; and/or
- making decisions about them.

30 Article 4(4)

Obviously this can be very useful for controllers but at the same time does pose potentially significant risks for individuals.

(ii) Types of profiling

There are three types of profiling referred to in the ICO's Guidance:

- General profiling
- Decision-making based on profiling
- Solely automated decision-making, including profiling, which produces legal effects or similarly significantly affects the data subject

The ICO states that controllers can carry out profiling and automated decision-making as long as they can meet all the principles of the GDPR and have a lawful basis for the processing. However, where a controller wishes to carry out solely automated decision-making, including profiling, defined in Article 22(1) then additional safeguards and restrictions apply and these will be discussed below.

This distinction raises an important question as to how to distinguish between these types of profiling in practice. The ICO's Guidance contains the following two examples:

> *Scenario 1*
>
> *A human decides whether to agree the loan based on a profile produced by purely automated means*
>
> *Scenario 2*
>
> *An algorithm decides whether the loan is agreed and the decision is automatically delivered to the individual, without any prior and meaningful assessment by a human*

Clearly the first scenario is an example of *'decision-making based on profiling'* because there is meaningful human involvement. This cannot be said of the second scenario which is clearly an example of *'solely automated decision making'* due to the absence of meaningful human involvement.

If Article 22 does not apply then a controller can continue to carry out profiling and automated decision-making as long as they comply with the GDPR principles and the following specific matters:

- they identify and record the lawful basis for processing
- they have processes in place so individuals can exercise their rights
- they bring details of the right to object specifically to the attention of individuals

(iii) GDPR – basic rule

The basic rule is that:

> *'The data subject shall have the right not to be subject to a decision based solely on automated processing, including profiling, which produces legal effects concerning him or her or similarly significantly affects him or her.'*[31]

This rule can then be broken down into three component parts:

(a) decision based solely on automated processing, including profiling

This has already been discussed above.

31 Article 22(1)

(b) which produces legal effects concerning him or her; or

The ICO's view is that a legal effect is something that adversely affects someone's legal rights and gives the following examples of automated decisions that result in:

- cancellation of a contract;
- entitlement to or denial of a particular social benefit granted by law, such as child or housing benefit;
- refused admission to a country or denial of citizenship.

(c) similarly significantly affects him or her

The ICO notes that this is more difficult to define but could include the following decisions:

- decisions that affect someone's financial circumstances, such as their eligibility to credit;
- decisions that affect someone's access to health services;
- decisions that deny someone an employment opportunity or put them at a serious disadvantage; · decisions that affect someone's access to education, for example university admissions.

Specific examples would include:

- automatic refusal of an online credit application,
- e-recruiting practices without human intervention.

The ICO concludes by noting that these effects are not defined in the GDPR but that the underlying principle is that the decision must have a serious negative impact on an individual.

(iv) GDPR – exceptions

The exception to this rule is that article 22(1) shall not apply to the processing of personal data if the decision:

- *is necessary for entering into, or performance of, a contract between the data subject and a data controller;*
- *is authorised by Union or Member State law to which the controller is subject and which also lays down suitable measures to safeguard the data subject's rights and freedoms and legitimate interests; or*
- *is based on the data subject's explicit consent.*[32]

Furthermore, article 22(1) shall not apply to the processing of *special category personal data unless:*

- *the controller has the individual's explicit consent;* ***or***
- *the processing is necessary for reasons of substantial public interest.*[33]

(v) GDPR – safeguards

In both cases, automated decision making, including profiling, van be carried out subject to the following safeguards set out in the ICO's Guidance:

(a) DPIA

A DPIA should be carried out as this type of processing is considered high risk. Controllers should seek to identify and assess relevant risks and consider how to address them.

---

32 Article 22(2)

33 Article 22(4)

(b) Specific requirements

Controllers should:

- *provide meaningful information about the logic involved in the decision-making process, as well as the significance and the envisaged consequences for the individual;*

- *use appropriate mathematical or statistical procedures;*

- *ensure that individuals can:*
    - *obtain human intervention;*
    - *express their point of view; and*
    - *obtain an explanation of the decision and challenge it;*

- *put appropriate technical and organisational measures in place, so that you can correct inaccuracies and minimise the risk of errors;*

- *secure personal data in a way that is proportionate to the risk to the interests and rights of the individual, and that prevents discriminatory effects.*

In summary, it is essential to determine whether the profiling being carried out falls within rules set out in article 22. However, even if the profiling strictly falls outside of these rules controllers are advised to ensure they comply with the applicable articles of the GDPR and should also consider carrying out a DPIA on a voluntary basis.

7.4 Summary

As has been shown, many of the rights available under the DPA 1998 continue to be available under the GDPR. However, controllers should particularly note the changes to the rules in respect of erasure and profiling and consider what steps need to be taken to ensure compliance.

7.5 Practical steps

General principles

- update existing procedures for dealing with requests
- train customer facing staff to ensure that they are aware of these procedures
- create a database to record details of requests

Right to be informed

- consider how information is collected from and provided to data subjects
- review and revise your existing privacy statement to ensure that it is compliant

Right to erasure

- familiarise yourself with the ICO's guidance notes
- consider how much personal data is stored in backup files
- review how you can put back up data beyond use

Right to object

- review existing procedures to ensure that the right to object is clearly communicated to individuals at the time your first collect their personal data

Automated decision-making and profiling

- consider the extent to which you are carrying out automated decision-making and whether this includes profiling or not

- review what types of profiling you are carrying out and determine whether this falls under the prohibition in article 22(1) or not
- put in place appropriate safeguards where necessary

CHAPTER EIGHT
RIGHT OF ACCESS

8.1 Introduction

The right of access is set out in article 15 of the GDPR and contains the following key rights for data subjects:

- right to obtain confirmation as to whether or not personal data is being processed and where so access to that personal data and to specific information about the processing[1]
- right to be informed of safeguards concerning transfer of personal data outside of the EEA[2]
- right to obtain a copy of the personal data undergoing processing[3]

The following procedural requirements apply to dealing with these requests.

- recognition of a request
- verification of identity
- fees
- clarification
- time period

Finally, the rights are then qualified in two ways:

---

1 Article 15(1)

2 Article 15(2)

3 Article 15(3)

- the rights and freedoms of third parties must not be adversely affected[4]
- provision of information may be subject to a series of exemptions[5]

Guidance in respect of these requests may be found in the following place:

https://ico.org.uk/for-organisations/guide-to-data-protection/guide-to-the-general-data-protection-regulation-gdpr/individual-rights/right-of-access/

At the time of writing the ICO is consulting on draft right of access guidance which can be accessed here:

https://ico.org.uk/about-the-ico/ico-and-stakeholder-consultations/ico-consultation-on-the-draft-right-of-access-guidance/

The GDPR states that the reason for allowing individuals to access their personal data is so that they are aware of and can verify the lawfulness of the processing.[6] As will be seen, the GDPR retains most of the DPA 1998 requirements and therefore this right is likely to remain as contentious as ever in terms of being an excellent way to obtain information on the basis of which to pursue legal action.

4 Article 15(4)

5 Article 23

6 Recital 63

8.2 Rights of the data subject

8.2.1 Right to obtain confirmation as to whether or not personal data is being processed and where so access to that personal data and to specific information about the processing[7]

The data subject has the right to be informed by the controller of the following matters:

1. *the purposes of the processing;*

2. *the categories of personal data concerned;*

3. *the recipients or categories of recipient to whom the personal data have been or will be disclosed, in particular recipients in third countries or international organisations;*

4. *where possible, the envisaged period for which the personal data will be stored, or, if not possible, the criteria used to determine that period;*

5. *the existence of the right to request from the controller rectification or erasure of personal data or restriction of processing of personal data concerning the data subject or to object to such processing;*

6. *the right to lodge a complaint with a supervisory authority;*

7. *where the personal data are not collected from the data subject, any available information as to their source;*

8. *the existence of automated decision-making, including profiling, referred to in Article 22(1) and (4) and, at least in those cases, meaningful information about the logic involved, as well as the*

---

7 Article 15(1)

significance and the envisaged consequences of such processing for the data subject.

In practice this should merely be a formality as this information typically has to be provided by the controller to the data subject at the time of first data collection. This will normally be done via a privacy statement. Consequently, if the controller is in receipt of such a request they should merely need to provide a further copy of their existing privacy statement in order to comply.

8.2.2 Appropriate safeguards relating to transfers outside of the EEA

This issue is discussed at length in chapter 11 and therefore I will not dwell on it here. Suffice it to say that the controller would merely need to confirm to the data subject what safeguards were in place.

8.2.3 Right to obtain a copy of the personal data undergoing processing[8]

This right is the most significant by far and has given rise to innumerable arguments between data subjects and controllers. Year on year approximately 40% of complaints made to the ICO have been in respect of a failure to provide information albeit it is interesting to note that the ICO has not yet levied a single civil monetary penalty in respect of this issue. Instead disputes tend to be resolved before the courts and there have been a number of cases decided under s7 of the DPA 1998 but none to date in respect of the GDPR. Further discussion of relevant case law can be found later in this chapter.

8.3 Procedural requirements

A number of the issues discussed in this section have already been discussed at length in chapter 7. Therefore, their treatment in this chapter is rather brief unless there are specific additional considerations that require further explanation.

8 Article 15(3)

8.3.1 Recognition of a request

Requests can be made orally or in writing and do not need to refer to the right of access, nor do they need to be addressed to a particular person or part of the controller's organization.

8.3.2 Verification of identity

The controller should use all reasonable measures to verify the identity of a data subject who requests access, in particular in the context of online services and online identifiers.[9] Consequently, controllers are entitled to request further information that is necessary and proportionate taking into account the nature and usage of the data held by the controller. If further information is required, the controller must inform the data subject about this as soon as possible.

8.3.3 Fees

Usually no fee can be charged for dealing with a request for access. The only exception is where the request is manifestly unfounded or vexatious (see chapter 7 for more discussion of this topic). If a controller does decide to charge a fee then the ICO's draft guidance suggests that only reasonable administrative costs can be charged to include:

- photocopying
- printing
- postage

The fee charged must be justifiable and should be explained to the individual. No fee can be levied for the time taken to deal with the request. If a fee is to be charged then the controller must request this from the individual as soon as possible and the time period referred to below will not commence until the fee has been received.

---

9 Recital 64

8.3.4 Clarification

The issue of clarification has always been a source of controversy. The DPA 1998 allowed controllers to request clarification before proceeding to disclose personal data to an individual and this concept continues under the GDPR as follows:

> *'Where the controller processes a large quantity of information concerning the data subject, the controller should be able to request that, before the information is delivered, the data subject specify the information or processing activities to which the request relates.'*[10]

The expectations on controllers under the GDPR when responding to a SAR are high and extensive efforts should be made to find and retrieve the requested information. Controllers are expected to implement information management systems that allow information to be accessed easily.

Nevertheless, controllers have often tried to rely on this to either refuse to comply with a request or to greatly reduce the amount of information that they need to provide. Individuals have often not been in a position to provide further clarification or have not wanted to narrow down the scope of their request. This standoff has often led to a dispute between the parties.

The ICO's draft guidance deals with a number of issues relating to this topic and I summarise the key points below:

(i) Clarification of the request

Clarification can be requested where a controller holds a large amount of personal data about an individual. However, such clarification can only include a request for the following:

- details of the information

---

10 Recital 63

- details of the processing activities
- time periods
- context of processing (eg as a customer or employee)

The individual cannot be asked to narrow the scope of their request and ultimately an individual is entitled to ask for 'all the information held' about them. Therefore, if an individual refuses to provide any additional information or does not respond, a controller must still comply with their request by making reasonable searches for the information covered by the request.

The impact of this on time limits is as follows:

- the time limit is not paused whilst the controller waits for a response, so they should begin searching for information as soon as possible.

- if controllers receive a request where it is genuinely unclear whether a SAR is being made, then the time limit does not begin until they have clarified whether a SAR is being made, and what personal data is being requested. In such cases, the expectation is that the individual is contacted as soon as possible.

This represents a change in approach compared to previous guidance which suggested that the time period could be paused pending clarification. It remains to be seen if this new approach finds its way into the final guidance.

(ii) Extent of the search

Controllers are required to search all filing systems for both automated and non-automated personal data. 'Filing system' is defined in the GDPR as meaning:

> *'any structured set of personal data which are accessible according to specific criteria, whether centralised, decentralised or dispersed on a functional or geographical basis'*[11]

Information held electronically will typically be held in a filing system but where information is held in a non-electronic form (eg hard copy paper files) then controllers must decide whether this information is covered by the right of access.

However, it is important to note that under the DPA 2018 personal data held in unstructured manual records processed by public authorities is covered by the right of access.[12] This includes paper records that are not held as part of a filing system. Therefore, public authorities will have to search this information to comply with SARs.

(iii) Information included

The ICO's draft guidance also states that the right of access will apply to the following information:

(a) Archived information and back-up records

The ICO expects controllers to use the same effort to find information to respond to a SAR as they would to find archived or backed-up data for their own purposes.

(b) Information contained in emails

The contents of emails stored on a controller's computer systems, including items contained in a 'deleted items' folder are a form of electronic record to which the right of access applies. This also extends to e-mails that have been archived and removed from a live system albeit the controller is entitled to ask for further information from the individual if there is a large amount of such information.

---

11 Article 4(6)

12 s24 DPA 2018

Tellingly the ICO's draft guidance states that *'the right of access is not limited to personal data that is easy for you to provide'*.

(c) Information stored on personal computer equipment

In this case, an organisation in receipt of a SAR is only obliged to provide personal data in respect of which it is the controller. In practice, if personal data is stored on someone else's computer system the organisation will not be the controller (except where that person is a processor). The only other exception to this would be if the personal data was stored on equipment belonging to staff members or was stored in a private e-mail account of a staff member.

Many controllers place strict limits on the usage of personal devices or personal e-mail accounts. However, if a staff member is processing personal data on their employer's behalf that personal data is likely to be within the scope of a SAR albeit the purpose for which the personal data is held and its context will be of relevance. Furthermore, the ICO does not expect controllers to search the private emails or personal devices of staff members in response to a SAR unless they have good reason to believe that their staff members are holding relevant personal data.

(d) Information stored in different locations

The location or locations of the information is irrelevant. The right of access applies to personal data wherever it is stored.

(iv) Information not included

The ICO's draft guidance states that information deleted by a controller as part of general records management will not be caught by a SAR even though *'expensive technical expertise might enable it to be recreated'*. Of course it is important to remember that the DPA 2018 makes it an offence for anyone to delete information that is the subject of a SAR.[13]

8.3.5 Time Period

This issue is discussed at length in chapter 7 but suffice it to say that the standard time period to comply with a SAR is one month from receipt, subject to the following exceptions:

- the period can be extended by a further two months if the request is complex
- if a fee or proof of identity is requested then the time period will not usually commence until receipt of whatever has been requested
- if clarification is requested then the time period is not paused unless the request is genuinely unclear in which case the time will be paused until clarification is received

8.3.6 Manifestly unfounded or excessive

This issue is discussed in more detail in chapter 7.

8.4 Third party rights

The GDPR states that:

> *'The right to obtain a copy referred to in paragraph 3 shall not adversely affect the rights and freedoms of others.'*[14]

This rule was also present in the DPA 1998 and the ICO's draft guidance seems to largely reflect what was previously recommended. In the event that the proposed disclosure of personal data under a SAR

---

13 s173 DPA 2018

14 Article 15(4)

could potentially lead to the disclosure of personal data relating to another 'third party' the following procedure should be followed:

8.4.1 Does the request require the disclosure of information that identifies another individual?

When determining this, the controller should take into account the information being disclosed and any information the individual making the request may already have.

If so, then the controller may delete names or edit documents if the third-party information does not form part of the information requested.

If this is impossible to do then the controller must consider the following two questions,

8.4.2 Has the other individual consented?

The best way to justify a disclosure of third-party information is to obtain the third party's consent and therefore this should be requested where appropriate. Notwithstanding this, a controller is not legally required to ask for consent and in some cases it may not be appropriate to disclose information about the requester to the third party.

8.4.3 Is it reasonable to disclose without consent?

Obtaining third party consent may often prove to be difficult in practice as a third party may be difficult to locate or may refuse to consent. In such circumstances, the ICO states that a controller should consider whether it is reasonable to disclose the information without consent taking into account the following issues required by the DPA 2018:[15]

- the type of information that they would disclose;

15 Schedule 2, Part 3, para 16

- any duty of confidentiality owed to the third-party individual;
- any steps they have taken to try to get the third-party individual's consent;
- whether the third-party individual is capable of giving consent; and
- any stated refusal of consent by the third-party individual.

The ICO's draft guidance then proceeds to discuss the issue of confidentiality in more detail and makes the following observations:

A duty of confidence arises where information that is not generally available to the public and has been disclosed to the controller with the expectation it remains confidential.

The following relationships would generally carry with them a duty of confidence:

- Medical (doctor and patient)
- Employment (employer and employee)
- Legal (solicitor and client)
- Financial (bank and customer)
- Caring (counsellor and client)

Confidentiality should not be automatically assumed. Marking a document as 'confidential' does not ensure that it has the necessary 'quality of confidence' if the information contained is available in the public domain. On other occasions a duty of confidence may not arise for public interest reasons.

Ultimately, if an obligation of confidence does exist, the normal approach would be to obtain the third party's consent and, if this was not forthcoming, the third-party information should be withheld.

8.4.4 Other factors

The ICO suggests that two final considerations should be borne in mind before disclosing third party information.

(i) Information generally known to the individual making the request

If the third party information has previously been provided to the individual or is in the public domain then it is more likely that disclosure of this information will be reasonable. Consequently, information about a staff member who is well-known to the requester is more likely to be disclosable than information about an anonymous private individual.

(ii) Circumstances relating to the individual making the request

Controllers should weight the competing considerations of confidentiality and the importance of information to the requester. The more significant the information to the requester, the more likely it should be disclosed even in the absence of consent from the third party.

8.5 Exemptions:

As has already been discussed in chapter 6, the GDPR and the DPA 2018 set out a series of exemptions to the rights of data subjects and I set out below a list of all the exemptions that are particularly relevant to the right of access together with some examples from the ICO's Guidance as to how they might be applied.

The ICO underlines the fact that the exemptions should be applied on a case by case basis taking into account their individual requirements. Some of the exemptions are focussed on the nature of the information while others are focussed on disclosure being likely to prejudice, prevent or seriously impair the purpose for which the information is being processed.

- Crime and taxation: general

- Crime and taxation: risk assessment
- Legal professional privilege
- Journalism, academia, art and literature
- Health, education and social work data
- Management information
- Negotiations with the requester
- Confidential references
- Exam scripts and exam marks

8.5.1 Crime and taxation – general

A bank conducts an investigation into one of its customers for suspected financial fraud. During its investigation the bank receives a subject access request for all of the personal data it holds from the customer in question. The bank decides that it will withhold information in relation to the investigation because it would be likely to prejudice the investigation as the individual may abscond or destroy evidence. However, the bank is able to provide other information in response to the request which would not prejudice the investigation (for example the individual's account details and transactions).

8.5.2 Management information

The senior management of an organisation are planning a reshuffle. This is likely to involve making certain employees redundant, and this possibility is included in management plans. Before the plans are revealed to the workforce, an employee makes a subject access request. In responding to that request, the organisation does not have to reveal their plans to make the employee redundant, if doing so would be likely to prejudice the conduct of the business (perhaps by causing staff unrest before the management's plans are announced).

8.5.3 Negotiations with requester

An individual makes a claim to his insurance company. The claim is for compensation for personal injuries he sustained in an accident. The insurance company disputes the seriousness of the injuries and the amount of compensation it should pay. An internal paper sets out the company's position on these matters including the maximum sum it is willing to pay to avoid the claim going to court. If the individual makes a subject access request to the insurance company, it does not have to send him the internal paper – because doing so would be likely to prejudice the negotiations to settle the claim.

8.5.4 Confidential references

Company A provides an employment reference in confidence for one of its employees to company B. If the employee makes a subject access request to company A or company B, the reference will be exempt from disclosure. This is because the exemption applies to the reference regardless of whether it is in the hands of the company that gives it or receives it.

8.6 Responding to a request

8.6.1 Provision of information

Having decided to disclose information pursuant to such a request, a controller should consider the format in which it is provided to the data subject.

The ICO makes the following suggestions:

- when deciding what information to provide it may be easier to provide a mixture of personal data and ordinary information to the requester rather than spending lots of time selecting only personal data

- the format in which the information is provided will depend on the manner in which the requester submitted their request
- if the request was submitted electronically then a copy should be provided in an appropriate electronic format
- if the request was submitted in another format then the controller should provide the information in a commonly used format (electronic or otherwise) unless the individual reasonably requests otherwise
- the right of access is a right to information not documents[16] and therefore a controller may provide transcripts, print outs of information or extracts from documents rather than original documents themselves
- if the information provided is likely to be difficult to understand (for example because it contains jargon) then further explanation should be provided to the data subject

8.6.2 Refusing to comply with a request

As has been discussed in chapter 7 a controller wishing to refuse to comply with a request must provide the following information to the data subject:

- details of the reasons why
- the right of the data subject to make a complaint to the ICO
- the right of the data subject to seek a judicial remedy

Note that if the controller is relying on an exemption the level of detail given to the data subject will vary. If disclosing the nature of the exemption would prejudice the purpose of the exemption then any

16 Rudd v Bridle [2019] EWHC 893 (QB) Warby J

response should be more general. A good example of this would be the crime prevention exemptions.

8.7 Relevant case law

At the time of writing there is no case law specifically interpreting the provisions of the GDPR or the DPA 2018 in respect of these requests. However, there is a body of case law interpreting the provisions of the DPA 1998 which is likely to influence the courts' approach in the future and I set out below a brief summary of the key cases and their findings to date.

Durant v FSA [2003] EWCA Civ 1746 Auld LJ

Mr. Durant had made several complaints to the Financial Services Authority about his own bank. The FSA investigated the complaints and concluded that no further action was required. Mr. Durant did not accept this explanation and made two data subject access requests to the FSA requiring sight of all the personal data they held about him. The FSA disclosed all computer records pertaining to Mr. Durant but did not disclose any paper files arguing that they were outside the scope of the DPA 1998.

The Files in question were as follows:

Major Financial Groups Division systems file ("the MFGD Systems file").

A file, in two volumes, relating to the systems and controls that Barclays Bank was required to maintain and which was subject to control by the FSA. The file, which was arranged in date order, also contained a few documents relating to part of Mr. Durant's complaint against the Bank, which concerned such systems and controls.

"the MFGD Complaints file"

This related to complaints by customers of Barclays Bank about it to the FSA — the sub-dividers being ordered alphabetically by reference to the complainant's name, containing behind a divider marked "Mr. Durant" a number of documents relating to his complaint, filed in date order.

Bank Investigations Group file ("the B.I.G file"),

This was maintained by the FSA's Regulatory Enforcement Department, relating and organised by reference to issues or cases concerning Barclays Bank, but not necessarily identified by reference to an individual complainant. It contained a sub-file marked "Mr. Durant", containing documents relating to his complaint. Neither the file nor the sub-file was indexed in any way save by reference to the name of Mr. Durant on the sub-file itself.

Company Secretariat papers

A sheaf of papers in an unmarked transparent plastic folder held by the FSA's Company Secretariat, relating to Mr. Durant's complaint about the FSA's refusal to disclose to him details and the outcome of its investigation of his complaints against Barclays Bank, not organised by date or any other criterion.

Mr. Durant pursued his complaint to the Court of Appeal. The Court of Appeal duly found in the FSA's favour and considered two main issues in reaching its decision:-

(i) What is meant by "Relevant Filing System"?

This was defined in the DPA 1998 as:

> *"**relevant filing system**" means any set of information relating to individuals to the extent that, although the information is not processed by means of equipment operating automatically in response to*

instructions given for that purpose, the set is structured, either by reference to individuals or by reference to criteria relating to individuals, in such a way that specific information relating to a particular individual is readily accessible.

On considering the definition of relevant filing system the court concluded that the DPA 1998 should only apply to filing systems which contained a clear referencing system and allowed the identification of relevant information at a minimum of time and cost. The court also emphasised that for paper files to be caught by the DPA 1998 they would need to be structured in a format akin to computerised records. On these facts the court ruled that none of the four files satisfied this test and therefore Mr. Durant's claim failed.

Note that this has now been qualified by the ruling in **Dawson-Damer v Taylor Wessing [2019] EWHC 1258 (Ch)** set out below.

(ii) What is meant by "personal data"?

The Court also emphasised the need for the data concerned to relate to the data subject and was of the view that information did not become personal data merely because it mentioned the data subject by name. In order to clarify this further the court suggested a two limbed test:

(a) the information had to be significantly biographical rather than merely recording the individual's involvement in an event; and

(b) the data subject had to be the focus of the information.

In summary, the court's view was that the right to subject access under section 7 of the DPA 1998 was intended to protect personal privacy rather than be used as a fishing expedition prior to litigation.

Dawson-Damer v Taylor Wessing [2015] EWHC 2366 (Ch) Behrens J [2017] EWCA Civ 74 Arden LJ

The Dawson-Damer family were the beneficiaries of a discretionary trust settlement known as the Glenfinnan Settlement that was created for them in 1992 by the Grampian Trust Company Limited ('Grampian'). Grampian was the sole trustee and was at all times based in the Bahamas. The Glenfinnan Settlement was stated to be subject to the law of the Bahamas. Taylor Wessing and their predecessor firms had acted on behalf of Grampian since 1992.

The Dawson-Damer family began proceedings against Grampian in the Bahamas and made data subject access requests to Taylor Wessing under s7 of the DPA 1998. Taylor Wessing refused to provide any information on the grounds that one or more of the exemptions found in the DPA 1998 applied.

The following correspondence took place:

4 August 2014

Dawson-Damer's Solicitors sent subject access requests to Taylor Wessing asking for *'all data of which they are the data subject (including data in which they are identified expressly or by inference) and which is in your firm's possession custody or power.'*

11 September 2014

TW responded stating that *'we have carried out searches of the records held by us and our response to your request is as follows:*

> *Personal data records held by us are processed only in connection with our capacity as legal advisors. This data is exempt from the subject access provisions of the Act by virtue of Schedule 7 section 10 of the Act by reason that it consists of data in respect of which a claim to legal professional privilege applies.'*

3 October 2014

In a further letter, TW made the following point:

> *'Certain information held by our client is held in manual files with the majority loose leaf in boxes and so not in a relevant filing system for the purposes of [the 1998 Act] for the reason that the files contain multiple categories of information that are not structured by reference to individuals or criteria relating to individuals. Not all documents have been filed in chronological order and those that have are without any further structure that would enable specific information about a particular individual to be located without having to review the contents of the entire file.'*

This matter was then brought before the High Court and was then appealed to the Court of Appeal.

Submissions of the Parties

Taylor Wessing

- Grampian was entitled to rely on legal professional privilege in respect of the majority of the documents. This privilege attached to advice and requests for advice going back at least 30 years in addition to documents in relation to the Bahamian proceedings. The privilege had not been waived by Grampian.
- it would be disproportionate and/or unreasonable to expect TW to carry out a search to determine which of the documents were privileged and which were not. When TW carried out its review, TW would not have been focussing on the issue which of the documents in its files were within the scope of the Legal Professional Privilege Exception. Nevertheless, TW would have been able to form a reasonable judgment that a substantial part of them were within that exception and that it would be a time-consuming and expensive task to separate those documents out.

- in any event the Court should, as a matter of discretion under s7(9) of the DPA 1998, decline to make an order. The application had been brought for the purpose of obtaining documents for use in the Bahamian proceedings. The Court should permit the Bahamian Court to determine which documents (if any) were disclosable.

Dawson-Damer

- the DPA 1998 did contain an exemption in respect of data in respect of which a claim for legal professional privilege could be made in legal proceedings but this should be construed narrowly.
- The ICO's *Subject Access Code of Practice* issued in February 2014 showed that compliance with a SAR may involve significant effort and TW's cursory review of their files did not satisfy this requirement
- the motivation of the request was irrelevant

Having considered the evidence of the parties Lady Justice Arden made the following rulings:

- the narrow view as to the application of the legal professional privilege exemption was correct
- disproportionate effort must involve more than an assertion that it was too difficult to search through voluminous papers
- there was no "no other purpose" rule which was an automatic bar to the exercise of the section 7(9) discretion

In the light of this, the Court of Appeal referred this matter back to the High Court and asked them to consider three issues:

[2019] EWHC 1258 (Ch)

(i) **Were the paper files maintained by TW before it moved to electronic files in 2005-2008 a 'relevant filing system' for the purposes of s1(1) of the DPA 1998?**

The Deputy Judge concluded that TW's 35 paper files which were arranged in chronological order were a 'relevant filing system' for the purposes of the DPA 1998. This ruling was a departure from the Durant case referred to above and the Deputy Judge's reasoning was as follows:

- Durant was decided before the right to protection of personal data had been enshrined as a fundamental EU right
- the European Court of Justice case of Tietosuojavaltuutettu (*Case C-25/17*) was now the leading authority and, in the light of this, the approach taken in Durant was too restrictive
- the description of the files by reference to the client was a criterion that allowed access to personal data
- furthermore, personal data could be 'easily retrieved' as the files were arranged in chronological order and therefore this merely required a page turning exercise which was not unduly onerous

(ii) **Could TW rely on the legal professional privilege exemption contained in paragraph 10 of schedule 7 of the DPA 1998 in respect of any particular documents containing the claimants' personal data?**

The Deputy Judge ruled that TW were entitled to rely on the legal professional privilege exemption to withhold personal data.

(iii) Had TW breached its obligations under s7 of the DPA 1998 by failing or refusing to carry out reasonable and proportionate searches for the claimants' personal data?

The Deputy Judge ruled that TW were required to carry out further specific searches in order to comply with their obligations under s7 of the DPA 1998 which included:

- specific documents and categories of documents
- a search of the claimants' personal data on the Mimecast platform
- a search of the personal spaces in which TW employees (both past and present) could save documents and e-mails

Note that leave to appeal on this point has been granted.

In summary, the key points to note from these cases are as follows:

- paper files arranged in chronological order are likely to constitute a 'relevant filing system' under the DPA 1998 and by extension a 'filing system' under the GDPR
- not all information contained within electronic or paper-based information will be 'personal data'
- arguing disproportionate effort requires more than an assertion that it was too onerous to search through voluminous papers
- the motivation of the request is not a good reason for a court to decline to exercise its discretion to make an order for disclosure

8.8 Summary

The right of access will continue to be an area of disputes between controllers and data subjects for the foreseeable future. It will be interesting to see how this area of law develops as new cases are decided in respect of the new law. My instinct is that the courts will draw heavily on the cases decided under the old law and therefore any differences of approach may be fairly minimal in practice. Watch this space!

8.9 Practical steps

- familiarise yourself with the ICO's guidance on the right of access
- ensure that you have procedures in place to deal with such a request promptly
- train customer facing staff so that they can recognise such a request and know how to respond appropriately
- keep a log of all SARs received
- apply the rules on third party rights consistently
- familiarise yourself with the exemptions that are most relevant to your organisation

CHAPTER NINE
DIRECT MARKETING

9.1 Introduction

Immediately prior to the 25th May 2018, data subjects were seemingly deluged with communications from controllers urging them to 'opt-in' to receiving further marketing from them. Many of these communications were sent in the erroneous belief that consent was the only relevant lawful basis for processing personal data for direct marketing purposes. However, as has already been stated in chapter 5, there are scenarios where controllers can instead rely on their legitimate interests and therefore many of those communications were unnecessary.

In this chapter we will examine the requirements of the GDPR and the Privacy and Electronic Communications Regulations 2003 ('PECR') and consider what options are available to controllers in terms of direct marketing activity and also the usage of cookies.

We will also consider what the current position is in respect of the proposed ePrivacy Regulation which was intended to replace PECR in May 2018 but remains the subject of seemingly intractable arguments.

9.2 Guidance

Guidance on this topic can be obtained from the following places:

ICO's Direct Marketing Code of Practice

https://ico.org.uk/media/for-organisations/documents/1555/direct-marketing-guidance.pdf

At the time of writing the ICO is consulting on a new code of practice which can be accessed here:

https://ico.org.uk/media/about-the-ico/consultations/2616882/direct-marketing-code-draft-guidance.pdf

In this chapter, I will summarise the current state of the law as described in the new code of practice.

9.3 Meaning of 'direct marketing'

Direct marketing is defined in the DPA 2018 as:

> *'the communication (by whatever means) of advertising or marketing material which is directed to particular individuals'*[1]

The same definition also applies in respect of PECR which states that direct marketing will be defined in the same way as set out in the UK data protection regime.[2]

The ICO's Code of Practice states that there are four key elements to this definition and I will now consider each of them in turn:

9.3.1 Direct marketing purposes

This phrase is not defined either in the GDPR or in the DPA 2018 but according to the ICO the clear intention is that it is to be interpreted more broadly than merely sending direct marketing communications. In particular, the ICO states that if a controller has the ultimate intention of sending a direct marketing communication then all processing activities undertaken prior to this will also constitute processing for this purpose.

> *ICO Example*
>
> *A controller collects personal data from various sources in order to build up a profile on an individual – such as the products they buy,*

---

1 s122(5)

2 Regulation 2(2) PECR

the services they like to use, or the causes they are likely to support – with the intention that this is used to target advertising at them, whether by you or by a third party.

Other examples suggested by the ICO include:

- lead generation;
- list brokering;
- data enrichment;
- data cleansing,
- matching or screening;
- audience segmenting or other profiling; and
- contacting individuals to ask them for consent to direct marketing.

Finally, two other activities are said to be included:

- disclosing the data to third parties for them to use for their own direct marketing

- trying to generate leads by sending mass texts, emails or automated calls or cold-calling numbers registered with the Telephone Preference Service (TPS)

9.3.2 Advertising or marketing material

Again, this phrase is not defined in either the GDPR or the DPA 2018 but the ICO states that it is to be interpreted widely to cover *'any advertising or marketing material, not just commercial marketing.'*

Consequently, any material that promotes aims or ideals will fall within this definition such as:

- fundraising;

- political parties or candidates; or
- the use of public services.

If in any doubt, the ICO suggests that controllers should consider whether the communication is:

- promotional in nature – does it advertise goods or services or otherwise promote the organisation itself or its interests?; or
- more neutral and informative in nature – does it seek simply to provide information the individual needs in the context of the existing relationship?

In the former case the material would be advertising or marketing material but in the latter case it would not be.

9.3.3 Communication

The ICO states that any means of communication falls within the definition of 'direct marketing' including traditional methods such as mailshots and telemarketing as well as newer methods such as online marketing and social networking.

The GDPR applies to all forms of communication but it is important to note that PECR only applies to specific types of electronic communication which are:

- Telephone calls
- E-mails
- Text messages
- In-app messaging
- Push notifications

9.3.4 Directed to

This is the most important part of the definition and requires that the marketing material is directed to particular individuals. Examples given by the ICO are:

- personally addressed post;
- calls to a particular telephone number;
- emails sent to a particular email account;
- online advertising that is targeted to a particular individual; and
- advertising on social media that is targeted to a particular individual.

Consequently blanket marketing such as delivering leaflets to every house on a housing estate will not fall within this definition. Nevertheless, the ICO is of the view that the definition will include a scenario where a controller processes personal data behind the scenes and then remove the person's name from the actual material that is sent.

9.3.5 'Solicited' v 'unsolicited' marketing

Another point to note is that the legislation and the ICO draw a distinction between these two concepts. The general principles are as follows:

(i) Solicited direct marketing

This is defined as marketing material that a person has specifically requested. The ICO provides the following examples of solicited marketing:

ICO Example

An individual submits an online form to a double-glazing company requesting a quote. By sending this quote to the individual the company is responding to the individual's request, and so the marketing is solicited.

ICO Example

If someone specifically signs up to a service for the sole purpose of receiving marketing within certain defined parameters, we accept that messages sent within the parameters of that service are solicited. For example, some types of loyalty schemes or offer schemes.

In such cases there is no restriction on sending solicited direct marketing to an individual.

(ii) Unsolicited direct marketing

This is defined as direct marketing that has not been specifically requested.

The ICO suggests the following example:

ICO Example

When they requested the quote for double glazing, the individual (referred to above) also ticked a box opting in to receiving information about future home improvement offers from the company. A few months later, the company sends an email with details of a new offer.

This is unsolicited marketing, because the customer did not contact the company to specifically request information about that particular offer. However, this does not mean that the company should not have sent details of the new offer. They can do so because the individual has consented to receiving these offers.

In such cases, even though the individual has opted-in to receiving future marketing from the controller, the rules set out in the GDPR and PECR must be complied with.

9.3.6 Telephone Preference Service ('TPS')

A final point to note is that controllers engaging in telemarketing need to be aware of the existence of the TPS. The TPS is defined as being:

> *'a central opt out register whereby individuals can register their wish not to receive unsolicited sales and marketing telephone calls.'*[3]

PECR states that it is a legal requirement that companies do not make such calls to numbers registered on the TPS.[4] This topic will be discussed in more detail later in this chapter.

9.3.7 Examples of ICO enforcement action:

In recent years the ICO has engaged in enforcement action in a number of cases relating to direct marketing and I set out three examples below that illustrate how broadly the ICO will interpret the definition of 'direct marketing' referred to above.

(i) Charities

In April 2017 a number of high-profile charities received civil monetary penalties ranging from £6,000 to £18,000 for having engaged in promotional activities that contravened various aspects of the rules on direct marketing.

---

3 https://www.tpsonline.org.uk/tps/whatistps.html

4 Regulation 21(1)(b) PECR

(ii) Political campaigning

In February 2019, Leave.EU received a civil monetary penalty in the sum of £60,000 for sending one million unsolicited marketing e-mails prior to the Brexit referendum.

(iii) Marketing masquerading as customer service

Between 30th November 2016 and 10th December 2016 Moneysupermarket.com (MSC) sent 7,127,415 'Terms and Conditions Update' e-mails to unique e-mail addresses of which only 6,788,496 were successfully received.

The e-mails advised the recipients that MSC had updated their terms and conditions and highlighted their privacy policy which had been refreshed earlier in the year.

The e-mails also included a substantial section entitled 'Preference Centre Update' which read "We hold an e-mail address for you which means we could be sending your personalised news, products and promotions. You've told us in the past you prefer not to receive these. If you'd like to reconsider, simply click the following link to start receiving our e-mails". This was followed by a large 'click link' box entitled 'Go To Preferences'.

The ICO investigated following complaints and ruled that the e-mails constituted direct marketing. MSC received a civil monetary penalty in the sum of £80,000.

9.4 Direct Marketing - legal requirements

9.4.1 GDPR

The GDPR applies to all types of communications and sets out three specific requirements that must be satisfied by controllers wishing to process personal data for direct marketing purposes.

(i) Right to object

Article 21 of the GDPR states the following:

> 2. *Where personal data are processed for direct marketing purposes, the data subject shall have the right to object at any time to processing of personal data concerning him or her for such marketing, which includes profiling to the extent that it is related to such direct marketing.*
>
> 3. *Where the data subject objects to processing for direct marketing purposes, the personal data shall no longer be processed for such purposes.*

This right to object can be exercised using either of the following two approaches:

(a) Opt out

> *"We would like to send you information about our other products and services. If you do not wish to receive this then please tick here ..."*

In this case, if the box remains unticked then the controller can carry out direct marketing. However, if the box is ticked then the controller cannot carry out direct marketing.

(b) Opt-in

> *"We would like to send you information about our other products and services. If you do wish to receive this then please tick this box..."*

In this case, if the box remains unticked then the controller cannot carry out direct marketing. However, if the box is ticked then the controller can carry out direct marketing.

The opt-out approach was more widely used prior to the GDPR coming into force as less individuals would object to receiving direct marketing communications on that basis. At the time GDPR came into force many controllers decided to move to an opt-in statement mistakenly believing that this was now compulsory. However, as will be discussed further below, controllers still have a choice in most cases as to which of these two approaches they will adopt, albeit this will typically be determined by the lawful basis that they choose to rely upon.

(ii) Lawful basis

As has already been discussed in chapter 5, any processing of personal data requires a lawful basis. In terms of marketing, there are two well-established lawful bases and each of these will be discussed in turn.

(a) Consent

This is defined in article 4(11) as being:

> *'any freely given, specific, informed and unambiguous indication of the data subject's wishes by which he or she, by a statement or by a clear affirmative action, signifies agreement to the processing of personal data relating to him or her'*

This is a more onerous standard than that required under the DPA 1998. The result of this is that controllers wishing to rely on consent as their lawful basis need to ensure that they have an opt-in statement in place rather than an opt-out statement. Only the former can satisfy the requirements of 'unambiguous indication' and 'clear affirmative action'

The ICO also highlights two other points of note:

- controllers cannot make the provision of goods or services conditional upon the individual giving them consent to receive direct marketing as such consent would not be freely given

- controllers wishing to use special category data for direct marketing purposes can only do so if they have 'explicit consent' (ie obtained via a ticked opt-in statement)

(b) Legitimate Interests

Article 6(1)(f) states that processing can be carried out where it is:

> *'necessary for the purposes of the legitimate interests pursued by the controller or by a third party, except where such interests are overridden by the interests or fundamental rights and freedoms of the data subject which require protection of personal data, in particular where the data subject is a child'*

Recital 47 of the GDPR provides further guidance as to how this may apply to direct marketing:

> *The processing of personal data for direct marketing purposes may be regarded as carried out for a legitimate interest.*

As has been discussed in chapter 5, any controller wishing to rely on legitimate interests is strongly advised to carry out a legitimate interests assessment which contains the following elements:

- Purpose test – is there a legitimate interest behind the processing?
- Necessity test – is the processing necessary for that purpose?
- Balancing test – is the legitimate interest overridden by the individual's interests, rights or freedoms?

Assuming that a legitimate interests assessment can be satisfied, a controller can continue to use an opt-out statement as long as it complies with its obligations under articles 13-14 of the GDPR in terms of communicating this to the data subject via its privacy statement.

(c) Example

I set out a worked example of an LIA in respect of marketing in part B of this book.

(iii) Display of marketing information

Article 21(4) adds a new requirement to the way in which marketing information is to be displayed. It states that:

> *'At the latest at the time of the first communication with the data subject, the right referred to in paragraph … 2 shall be explicitly brought to the attention of the data subject and shall be presented clearly and separately from any other information.'*

Prior to the GDPR coming into force on 25th May 2018 it was not uncommon for controllers to provide information about marketing in a way that was difficult to access and understand. Article 21(4) makes it clear that the marketing information must be provided in a fashion so that it can be easily accessed and understood.

(iv) Retention period

Where a controller is relying on consent then this will not last indefinitely. Instead, the ICO notes that the length of time that it can be relied upon will depend on the following circumstances:

- the context in which it was given;
- the nature of the individual's relationship with the controller; and
- the individual's expectations.

In the light of this the ICO makes the following observations:

- consent for a one-off message, or consent that is clearly only intended to cover a short period of time or a particular context, does not count as ongoing consent for all future direct marketing.

- when sending direct marketing to new customers relying on consent collected by a third party, controllers should not rely on consent that was given more than six months ago

(v) **Summary**

The aforementioned rules apply equally to all types of direct marketing activity. However, as will be seen, there are additional requirements that apply solely in respect of telephone calls and electronic mail and we will now consider these in more detail.

9.4.2 PECR

PECR has been in force since 2003 and given the doubts about the ePrivacy Regulation it is likely that it will remain in force for the foreseeable future.

Additional guidance in respect of PECR is available here:

https://ico.org.uk/for-organisations/guide-to-pecr/

In terms of direct marketing the rules in PECR apply to the following types of marketing:

- Calls
- Electronic mail

Consequently, if a controller is seeking to engage in any of these activities they must comply with the requirements of the GDPR and also the requirements of PECR which will be discussed in more detail below.

(i) Calls

These are defined as:

> *'a connection established by means of a telephone service available to the public allowing two-way communication in real time'*

PECR draws a distinction between 'automated' and 'live' calls. The former being made electronically without the presence of a live operator and the latter being made by a live operator.

(a) Automated calls[5]

The rules are as follows:

- automated calls must not be made unless the recipient has specifically consented to receive them via an opt-in statement
- all such calls must display the sender's number and include the sender's name and contact details

(b) Live calls[6]

The basic rule is that controllers must not make unsolicited live calls to:

- anyone who has told the controller that they do not wish to receive such calls
- any number registered with the TPS unless the person has specifically consented to their calls – even if they are an existing customer

When making such a call, the controller must:

---

5 Regulation 19 PECR

6 Regulation 21 PECR

- say who is calling
- allow their number to be displayed to the person receiving the call, and
- provide a contact address or freephone number if asked.

In summary the ICO states that:

- controllers can call numbers that are not registered on the TPS without the individual's consent but only if there is no previous objection in line with the requirements of the GDPR.
- controllers can only call a number registered with the TPS if they have the individual's consent in order to override their general objection to direct marketing calls

(ii) **Electronic mail**

(a) **Definition**

> *means any text, voice, sound or image message sent over a public electronic communications network which can be stored in the network or in the recipient's terminal equipment until it is collected by the recipient and includes messages sent using a short message service'*[7]

The ICO suggests that it will include, but not be limited to, the following:

- E-mails
- Text messages
- In-app messaging
- Push notifications

7 Regulation 2 PECR

(b) General Rule

The general rule is found in regulation 22 which states that:

> *(2) Except in the circumstances referred to in paragraph (3), a person shall neither transmit, nor instigate the transmission of, unsolicited communications for the purposes of direct marketing by means of electronic mail unless the recipient of the electronic mail has previously notified the sender that he consents for the time being to such communications being sent by, or at the instigation of, the sender.*

In the light of the changes to the meaning of consent under the GDPR this would require a controller to use an opt-in statement which must be ticked in order to allow the controller to carry out such direct marketing activities.

(c) Exception

However, this requirement is qualified by paragraph 3 which states that:

> *(3) A person may send or instigate the sending of electronic mail for the purposes of direct marketing where—*
>
> *(a) that person has obtained the contact details of the recipient of that electronic mail in the course of the sale or negotiations for the sale of a product or service to that recipient;*
>
> *(b) the direct marketing is in respect of that person's similar products and services only; and*
>
> *(c) the recipient has been given a simple means of refusing (free of charge except for the costs of the transmission of the refusal) the use of his contact details for the purposes of such direct marketing, at the time that the details were initially collected, and, where he did not initially refuse the use of the details, at the time of each subsequent communication.*

This exception, known as the 'soft opt-in', effectively allows a controller to rely on an opt-out statement subject to the following criteria:

- the data subject's details must have been obtained in the course of a sale or negotiations for a sale
- the data subject must have been initially given an opt-out statement which they did not tick
- the controller who subsequently contacts the data subject must be the same as the controller who originally collected the data and must not conceal their identity
- the e-mail or SMS must be about that controller's similar products or services
- the e-mail or SMS must contain an opportunity to unsubscribe from receiving further communications

The effect of this 'soft opt-in' is to allow a significant number of controllers to contact their own customers and clients to tell them about their own products and services as long as those data subjects have not previously objected to receiving marketing messages.

9.4.3 Summary of GDPR and PECR Rules

I set out below some answers to questions that are commonly asked about this topic together with a table setting out the various possibilities in terms of compliance with the GDPR and the PECR.

(i) Do I have to rely on consent as my lawful basis post-GDPR?

As long as you are only processing personal data for direct marketing activity in respect of your own products and services you are not required to rely on consent and instead can rely on legitimate interests subject to carrying out a legitimate interests assessment. The position in respect of providing information to a third party will be discussed further below.

(ii) Do I have to use an opt-in statement post GDPR?

This will depend on the lawful basis that you are relying upon. If you rely on consent then you will need to use an opt-in statement. If you are relying on legitimate interests then you can rely on an opt-out statement subject to complying with other relevant requirements

(iii) How do I inform new customers / clients of the lawful basis?

This information can be provided to the customer / client as part of your privacy statement.

(iv) Does the soft opt-in continue to apply now that the GDPR is in force?

Yes, the soft opt-in continues to apply in the same way as before as long as the PECR remain in force.

This table summarises the relationship between the different aspects of the rules and also the options that are available.

Type of direct marketing	**GDPR**		**PECR**
	Right to object	**Lawful basis**	
Mail	Opt-out	Legitimate interests	N/A
	Opt-in	Consent	N/A
Live calls	Opt-out	Legitimate interests	Not override TPS
	Opt-in	Consent	Override TPS
Electronic mail	Opt-out	Legitimate interests	Soft opt-in
	Opt-in	Consent	Consent

9.4.4. Selling or sharing data with a third party

If a controller wishes to sell information about its customers to a third party so that they can be used for the third party's marketing purposes, the same considerations mentioned in respect of the GDPR and PECR also apply.

(i) Right to object

As has been discussed earlier in this chapter, this could be provided either on an opt-out or an opt-in basis. Any decision made will depend on the lawful basis selected but in this context the better course of action would normally be to rely upon an opt-in statement.

(ii) Lawful basis

As before, there are two lawful bases that potentially can be relied upon in respect of processing personal data for the purpose of direct marketing.

If a controller is seeking to rely upon consent the ICO makes the following comments:

- the consent must be valid (eg specific, unambiguous, informed, freely given)
- the controller must have a clear record of it
- the controller cannot infer that it has consent just because it is selling the list to organisations with similar aims or objectives

In conclusion, the ICO Guidance to the GDPR states that:

> *'any third-party controllers who will be relying on the consent must be named – precisely defined categories of third parties will not be acceptable under the GPDR definition.'*

If a controller is seeking to rely upon legitimate interests in order to disclose the information to a third party the ICO makes the following comments:

- it is possible to rely on the legitimate interests of the controller or those of the third party or a combination
- it is for each controller to justify its own actions
- legitimate interests cannot be relied upon to sell data for marketing purposes in respect of electronic mail
- legitimate interests cannot be relied upon to override the TPS

(iii) Display of marketing information

If a controller wishes to obtain personal data in order to sell this on to third parties for direct marketing purposes, this must be made clear to the individual at the outset, and the names of the proposed third parties must be provided to the individual at the same time.

(iv) TPS

If a controller is selling a marketing list containing telephone numbers it should make clear to buyers whether it has been pre-screened against the TPS register, and if so, on what date it was last screened.

(v) Records

Controllers need to maintain records of the following:

- how the details were collected
- when the details were collected; and
- what individuals were told

This needs to be done in order to comply with the controller's accountability requirements under the GDPR and also to be able to provide assurances to the buyer of the marketing list.

(vi) Summary

Selling marketing lists to third parties is more strictly regulated under the GDPR and PECR. In the light of the ICO's Guidance the strict position is as follows:

(a) Mailshots

The controller can sell a mailing list to a third party relying on an opt-out statement and legitimate interests as long as specific details of the third party were provided to the individual at the time of capture

(b) Calls

The controller can sell a mailing list to a third party relying on an opt-out statement and legitimate interests as long as:

- specific details of the third party were provided to the individual at the time of capture
- the controller has screened against the list against the TPS

The controller can sell a mailing list to a third party relying on an opt-in statement and consent as long as specific details of the third party were provided to the individual at the time of capture (there is no need to screen against the TPS)

(c) Electronic mail

The controller can sell a list to a third party relying on an opt-in statement and consent as long as specific details of the third party were provided to the individual at the time of capture.

The controller cannot sell a list to a third party relying on an opt-out statement and legitimate interest as the soft opt-in will not apply in these circumstances.

9.4.5 Using publicly available data

Controllers may sometimes wish to obtain data from sources other than the individual in order to carry out direct marketing and one of the ways in which this can happen is to use information available from publicly available sources.

The ICO defines the term 'publicly available' as referring to information available from the following places:

- the open version of the electoral register;
- Companies House;
- social media; and
- press articles or 'rich' lists

Information may be sought from such places in order to find new customers or to supplement the profile or data a controller already holds about that person. The ICO states that controllers wishing to engage in such activity need to comply with their obligations under the GDPR and PECR as appropriate and should not assume that such data is 'fair game'. In practice this requires controllers to comply with the following considerations:

(i) Transparency

Where information is collected from a publicly available source, controllers are required to provide privacy information to the individuals concerned no later than one month from obtaining the data.[8]

8 Articles 12, 14

(ii) Fairness

The ICO states that controllers must ensure that their processing of personal data is fair, taking into account the source of the data. In particular, controllers are required to consider whether the use of the data in this way would be unexpected by the individual. If it is unexpected then the data should not be used in this way.

ICO Examples

For example you cannot assume that simply because an individual has put their personal data into the public domain, they are agreeing to it being used for direct marketing purposes. An individual may want as many people as possible to read their social media post but that does not mean they are agreeing to have that data collected and analysed to profile them to target your direct marketing campaigns.

Likewise just because an individual's social media page has not been made private does not mean that you are free to use their personal data for direct marketing purposes.

(iii) PECR

Sending electronic marketing on the basis of information collected from publicly available sources is likely to breach PECR as it will not satisfy the soft opt-in.

9.4.6 Buying and renting lists

Many controllers will purchase or rent marketing lists but it is important to note that compliance with the GDPR and with PECR rests with the party using the list. It is not enough to rely on assurances given by the list provider.

The ICO suggests requesting the following information by way of due diligence prior to buying or renting such a list:

- *Who compiled the data – was it the organisation you are buying it from or was it someone else?*
- *Where was the data obtained from – did it come from the individuals directly or has it come from other sources?*
- *What privacy information was used when the data was collected – what were individuals told their data would be used for?*
- *When was the personal data compiled – what date was it collected and how old is it?*
- *How was the personal data collected – what was the context and method of the collection?*
- *Records of the consent (if it is 'consented' data) – what did individuals' consent to, what were they told, were you named, when and how did they consent?*
- *Evidence that the data has been checked against opt-out lists (if claimed) – can it be demonstrated that the TPS or CTPS has been screened against and how recently?*
- *How does the seller deal with individuals' rights – do they pass on objections?*

In addition, the ICO suggests that a contract should be put in place containing statements about the reliability of the personal data, as well as giving the purchaser reasonable control and audit powers.

Notwithstanding this, ultimate responsibility for compliance rests with the party using the list and they need to ensure that they do the following:

- screen the lists that they obtain against their own suppression lists to ensure they do not contact anyone who has previously objected to hearing from them

- provide individuals with the controller's own transparency information detailing anything they have not already been told.
- be prepared to deal with any inaccuracies or complaints arising from the use of the data

9.4.7 B2B marketing

One area that can lead to confusion is the extent to which there is a distinction between direct marketing targeted at individuals in their business capacity (B2B) and at individuals in their personal capacity (B2C). The GDPR does not contain such a distinction and therefore applies to both B2C and B2B marketing alike. However, PECR does refer to the concepts of 'corporate subscriber' and 'individual subscriber' and these issues will be discussed in more detail below.

(i) GDPR

The key principles are as follows:

- if a controller does not know the name of the person to whom direct marketing is being sent in a business then no personal data is being processed and the GDPR does not apply (for example, sending direct marketing by post addressed simply to 'the IT department' or email to 'info@company.com').
- if an individual is identified, either directly or indirectly, GDPR will apply even if they are acting in a business capacity (for example j.smith@company.com).
- if an individual's contact details are collected in a business capacity, then the controller must advise them of this and have a lawful basis in place (usually legitimate interests)
- such information can be provided on the first occasion that the controller contacts the individual

(ii) PECR

PECR draws a distinction between the following two concepts:

Corporate Subscriber	• a company within the meaning of Companies Act legislation; or • any other body corporate or entity which is a legal person distinct from its members; • who is a party to a contract with a provider of public electronic communications services for the supply of such services;
Individual Subscriber	• a living individual who is a party to a contract with a provider of public electronic communications services for the supply of such services;

The key principles are as follows:

- PECR rules on calls apply equally in respect of individual subscribers and corporate subscribers albeit the former may be registered with the TPS and the latter with the Corporate Telephone Preference Service ('CTPS')

- PECR rules on marketing by electronic mail do not apply to corporate subscribers. This means controllers can send B2B direct marketing emails or texts to any corporate body as long as they disclose who sent the e-mail and provide an unsubscribe link

- Sole traders and some types of partnership are not classed as corporate subscribers under PECR and should be treated as individual subscribers and should not be contacted by electronic mail unless they have consented or the soft opt-in applies

(iii) Summary

There has been much discussion in recent years about the comparable levels of risk associated with B2C and B2B marketing. A review of the civil monetary penalties levied by the ICO in the field of direct marketing clearly shows that the ICO has prioritised dealing with B2C infringements. Therefore, controllers may well be prepared to assume a greater degree of risk in respect of their B2B marketing arrangements but if in doubt should consider two suggestions from the ICO:

- if in any doubt, treat the details obtained as belonging to an individual subscriber and ensure compliance with the rules on electronic mail.

- keep a 'do not email or text' list of any businesses that object or opt out of direct marketing by electronic mail, and screen any new B2B direct marketing lists against it.

9.5 Cookies

The rules on cookies are currently found in PECR albeit they will be subject to change in the event that the ePrivacy Regulation is ever finalised.

9.5.1 Overview

Regulation 6 of PECR states that controllers must:

- tell people that the cookies are there;
- explain what the cookies are doing and why; and
- get the person's consent to store a cookie on their device (no other lawful bases are acceptable).

There are also a series of exemptions where consent is not required:

- the cookie is for the sole purpose of carrying out the transmission of a communication over an electronic communications network; or
- the cookie is strictly necessary to provide an 'information society service' (ie a service over the internet) requested by the subscriber or end user. Note that the cookie must be essential rather than convenient and must be essential for the purposes of the data subject and not of the controller

Cookies that are likely to be considered 'strictly necessary' are:

Load balancing cookies – these ensure the content of the page loads quickly and effectively by distributing the workload across several computers

Session cookies – these provide security in respect of the service provided to the customer – eg in respect of online banking

Cookies used to remember the goods that a customer wishes to buy (eg when they are added to a shopping basket and the customer then wishes to proceed to checkout)

9.5.2 Meaning of 'consent'

Consent in PECR is now defined as corresponding to the meaning set out on the GDPR and the DPA 2018.[9] Prior to the GDPR, consent was typically obtained by means of a message on the home page of a website stating that by continuing to use the website the individual gave their consent to various types of cookies being placed on their device. Clearly, the GDPR has introduced certain changes in terms of how consent can be obtained and the general consensus is that such messages are no longer valid.

---

9 Regulation 2(1) PECR

9.5.3 ICO's Guidance

The ICO has produced updated guidance that can be accessed here:

https://ico.org.uk/for-organisations/guide-to-pecr/guidance-on-the-use-of-cookies-and-similar-technologies/

However, the more accessible source of information on this topic is found in a 'myth-busting' blog produced by the ICO in July 2019 which can be accessed here:

https://ico.org.uk/about-the-ico/news-and-events/news-and-blogs/2019/07/blog-cookies-what-does-good-look-like/

The key points contained in this blog are as follows:

- controllers cannot rely on implied consent for cookies now that the GDPR is in force, instead the ICO says that:
    - *users must take a clear and positive action to consent to non-essential cookies;*
    - *websites and apps must tell users clearly what cookies will be set and what they do – including any third party cookies;*
    - *pre-ticked boxes or any equivalents, such as sliders defaulted to 'on', cannot be used for non-essential cookies;*
    - *users must have control over any non-essential cookies; and*
    - *non-essential cookies must not be set on landing pages before you the user's consent is gained*

- the strictly necessary exemption continues to apply to cookies that are essential to the provision of the service to the user and therefore consent is not required
- non-essential cookies, including third party cookies used for web analytics or online advertising, do still require consent
- analytics cookies are not strictly necessary because even though they can provide useful information they are not part of the functionality of the website
- statements such as 'by continuing to use this website you are agreeing to cookies' is not valid consent under the GDPR
- using a blanket approach like a cookie wall is unlikely to represent valid consent but the ICO is aware of differing opinions on this point and will be considering it further in due course
- controllers can only rely on consent as the lawful basis for setting cookies. Legitimate interests cannot be relied upon.

9.5.4 Future developments

The rules on cookies are probably the best example of the uneasy relationship between PECR and the GDPR, particularly in the context of the rules on consent. This was supposed to be resolved by the advent of the e-Privacy Regulation but, as will be discussed in more detail below, the timeframe for this remains uncertain.

In the meantime, the ICO suggests that controllers consider taking the following actions:

(i) Carry out a cookie audit

There are a number of cookie audit resources available online and this will enable a controller to at least assess the scale of their usage and what needs to be done about it. Examples of organisations that can provide such a service include:

- OneTrust
- Nymity
- Ghostery

The ICO's guidance suggests that a cookie audit should do the following:

- *for cookies that are already present, identify those that are operating on or through your website, using a combination of browser-based tools and server-side code review;*
- *confirm the purpose(s) of each of the cookies you use (or intend to use);*
- *confirm whether cookies are linked to other information held about users – such as usernames – and whether your use of cookies also involves (or will involve) processing personal data;*
- *identify what data each cookie holds or otherwise processes;*
- *confirm the type of cookie – session or persistent;*
- *distinguish between which cookies are strictly necessary and which ones aren't (and would therefore require clear and comprehensive information and consent);*
- *ensure that your consent mechanism enables users to control the setting of all non-essential cookies;*
- *determine the lifespans of any persistent cookies and whether these durations are justifiable for the stated purpose;*

- *determine whether each cookie is a first or third party cookie, and if it is a third party cookie who is setting it;*

- *double check that the privacy information provides accurate and clear information about each cookie;*

- *confirm what information you share with third parties, and what users are told about this; and*

- *document your findings and follow-up actions, and build in an appropriate review period.*

(ii) Improve how people are told about cookies

Another area of concern for the ICO is to ensure that information is provided about cookies in such a way so that the user will see it when they first visit a website. This should be done initially via the cookie consent mechanism and this should also be complemented with more information in the website's cookie / privacy policy

The ICO also suggests that the prominence of the cookie information could be improved as follows:

- *formatting – this might include changing the size of the link to the information or using a different font. The key is whether the link to this important information is distinguishable from "normal text" and other links;*

- *positioning – simply moving the link from the footer of the page to somewhere more likely to catch attention is an easy but effective thing to try; and*

- *wording – Making the hyperlink more than simply "privacy policy"; this could involve a link through some explanatory text ("Find out more about how our site works and how we put you in control.")*

Finally, the ICO stresses the need to ensure the information provided can be easily understood and suggests that controllers tailor their language to their audience and avoid using lengthy and overly complex terminology.

(iii) Obtain compliant consent

As has already been mentioned, there are a number of ways in which controllers have sought to obtain compliant consent. The ICO's guidance contains a series of comments on the different possible methods and I summarise her views below in a table:

Method	**Description**	**ICO Comments**
Settings led consent	Cookies are deployed when a user makes a choice over a site's settings. In these cases, consent could be sought as part of the process by which the user confirms what they want to do, or how they want the site to work.	*You must however take care that any processing of personal data related to the setting of preference cookies or other personalisation features is limited to what is necessary for this purpose.*
Feature-led consent	A website includes video clips or remembers what users have done on previous visits in order to personalise the content they are offered. Some cookies would then be stored if the user chose a particular feature of a website.	*However, you still need to provide clear and comprehensive information and obtain consent.* *Where the feature is provided by a third party, users will need to be made aware of this, and be given information on how the third*

		party uses cookies and similar technologies so that the user is able to make an informed choice.
Message boxes	Message boxes such as banners, pop-ups, message bars, header bars or similar techniques	*There are challenges with using these techniques. If users do not click on any the options available and go straight through to another part of your site, and you go ahead and set non-essential cookies on their devices, this would not be valid consent. This is because users who fail to engage with the consent box cannot be said to consent to the setting of these cookies.*
Browser settings	The user or subscriber sets up their browser so that only certain cookies are allowed.	*In future you may well be able to rely on the user's browser settings as part, or all, of the mechanism for satisfying yourself that you have consent to set cookies. For now, relying solely on browser settings will not be sufficient. Even when browser options are improved it is likely not all users will have the most up-to-date browser with the enhanced privacy settings needed for the settings to constitute an indication of consent.*

Terms and conditions	Statement in the website's terms and conditions explaining what cookies will be used.	*This will not be valid. Consent must be separate from other matters and cannot be bundled into terms and conditions or privacy notices. The key point is that you should be upfront with your users about your use of cookies. You should obtain consent by giving the user specific separate information about what they are being asked to agree to and providing them with a way to accept by means of a positive action to opt-in*
Cookie walls	A cookie wall – sometimes called a 'tracking wall' – requires users to 'agree' or 'accept' the setting of cookies before they can access an online service's content. This is also known as the 'take it or leave it approach'.	*If your use of a cookie wall is intended to require, or influence, users to agree to their personal data being used by you or any third parties as a condition of accessing your service, then it is unlikely that user consent will be considered valid.*
Pre-enablement	Non-essential cookies are set automatically on a landing page and the user's agreement is sought afterwards via a statement that says that *'by continuing to use this website you consent …'*	*This will not be valid. Just because users may be unlikely to select a particular non-essential cookie when given the choice, or because the cookie is not privacy intrusive, is not a valid reason to pre-enable it.*

		Enabling a non-essential cookie without the user taking a positive action before it is set on their device does not represent valid consent. By doing this, you are taking the choice away from the user.

(iv) Summary

Clearly there remains a degree of uncertainty about how to comply with these rules albeit some comfort can be derived from the fact that the ICO's website was technically in breach of these rules until recently when a helpful city solicitor pointed this out to them! Furthermore, enforcement action in this area has been very limited to date, although this is likely to change in the future.

9.6 ePrivacy Regulation

The first draft of the ePrivacy Regulation was published in January 2017 and the European Parliament approved the draft negotiation text in October 2017. It was scheduled to replace the PECR with effect from 25th May 2018 but over the course of three years and six presidencies the EU Council has failed to reach agreement on an approved text. The most recent attempt under the Finnish presidency saw the 'Finnish text' rejected by the European Parliament in late November 2019.

At the time of writing, the European Commission is due to present a further amended proposal sometime within the first half of 2020. In the meantime, the rules on e-mail and SMS marketing and the use of cookies continue to be found in PECR which sits increasingly uneasily alongside the GDPR.

9.7 Summary

The area of direct marketing remains one of the most complex that controllers have to deal with and this is only compounded by the ongoing uncertainty about the ePrivacy Regulation that shows no sign of being implemented anytime soon. It is also one of the areas where controllers are most likely to be in receipt of a civil monetary penalty albeit the focus is usually on B2C rather than B2B marketing.

9.8 Practical steps

GDPR

- consider what lawful basis is being relied upon
- if relying on legitimate interests, a legitimate interests assessment should be carried out
- if relying on consent ensure that the consent obtained is GDPR compliant

PECR

- ensure that you screen lists of telephone numbers against the TPS
- review the extent to which the soft opt-in can be relied upon
- carry out a cookie audit
- ensure that consent is being obtained in a GDPR compliant fashion
- consider how you can improve the way in which information about cookies is provided

CHAPTER TEN
SECURITY

10.1 Introduction

The issue of security has always represented the greatest area of risk for controllers and has led to significant fines being levied in certain cases. The basic requirements of the DPA 1998 are largely maintained in the GDPR as can be seen from the table below:

GDPR
Sixth Principle
data to be processed in a manner that ensures appropriate security of the personal data, including protection against unauthorised or unlawful processing and against accidental loss, destruction or damage, using appropriate technical or organisational measures ('integrity and confidentiality')
Article 32(1)
'Taking into account the state of the art, the costs of implementation and the nature, scope, context and purposes of processing as well as the risk of varying likelihood and severity for the rights and freedoms of natural persons, the controller and the processor shall implement appropriate technical and organisational measures to ensure a level of security appropriate to the risk'[1]

However, the GDPR does provide further guidance as to the type of appropriate measures to be taken, namely:[2]

(a) the pseudonymisation and encryption of personal data;

---

1 Article 32(1)

2 Article 32(1)

(b) the ability to ensure the ongoing confidentiality, integrity, availability and resilience of processing systems and services;

(c) the ability to restore the availability and access to personal data in a timely manner in the event of a physical or technical incident;

(d) a process for regularly testing, assessing and evaluating the effectiveness of technical and organisational measures for ensuring the security of the processing.

It is also important to note that the rules in the GDPR are stated specifically to apply to processors as well as to controllers.

However, the most significant change is in respect of personal data breaches. Under the DPA 1998 there was no requirement to inform either the ICO or the data subjects affected although the ICO always recommended voluntary reporting where the personal data breach was of a significant nature. Under the GDPR the rules have changed so that, in certain circumstances, a controller is required to inform the ICO, and in some cases the data subjects affected, when a personal data breach occurs.

Guidance on the issue of breach reporting was produced by what was then known as the A29WP[3] and is available on their website at https://ec.europa.eu/newsroom/article29/item-detail.cfm?item_id=612052

I summarise the key points of this guidance below, together with discussion of the relevant provisions of the GDPR.

3 Now known and referred to throughout this chapter as the European Data Protection Board ('EDPB')

10.2 Definition of 'personal data breach'

This is defined in the GDPR as:[4]

> *'a breach of security leading to the accidental or unlawful destruction, loss, alteration, unauthorised disclosure of, or access to, personal data transmitted, stored or otherwise processed'*

In addition to this, the GDPR states that:

> *'in assessing the appropriate level of security account shall be taken in particular of the risks that are presented by processing, in particular from accidental or unlawful destruction, loss, alteration, unauthorised disclosure of, or access to personal data transmitted, stored or otherwise processed.'*[5]

The EDPB further defines the key component parts of the definition of personal data breach as follows:

'destruction'	this is where the data no longer exists, or no longer exists in a form that is of any use to the controller.
'damage'	this is where personal data has been altered, corrupted, or is no longer complete.
'loss'	this should be interpreted as the data may still exist, but the controller has lost control or access to it, or no longer has it in its possession.
'unauthorised or unlawful processing'	may include disclosure of personal data to (or access by) recipients who are not authorised to receive (or access) the data, or any other form of processing which violates the GDPR

4 Article 4(12)

5 Article 32(2)

10.3 Types of personal data breaches

The EDPB, referring to previous guidance on the issue of personal data breaches, states that personal data breaches can be categorised as follows:

'Confidentiality breach'	where there is an unauthorised or accidental disclosure of, or access to, personal data.
'Availability breach'	where there is an accidental or unauthorised loss of access to, or destruction of, personal data.
'Integrity breach'	where there is an unauthorised or accidental alteration of personal data.

It is important for both controllers and processors to note that the concept of personal data breach goes beyond what is here defined as a confidentiality breach, albeit in practice this is the breach that is most likely to lead to enforcement action.

10.4 Consequences of a personal data breach

A personal data breach can lead to a variety of consequences for the data subjects affected and these can be categorised as physical, material and non-material. The EDPB suggests the following specific examples:

- loss of control over personal data
- financial loss
- identity fraud
- theft
- damage to reputation
- economic or social disadvantage
- discrimination

10.5 Notification of a personal data breach to the supervisory authority

In the light of the previous discussion the GDPR introduced a new obligation of notification which is as follows:[6]

> *'In the case of a personal data breach, the controller shall without undue delay and, where feasible, not later than 72 hours after having become aware of it, notify the personal data breach to the supervisory authority competent in accordance with Article 55, unless the personal data breach is unlikely to result in a risk to the rights and freedoms of natural persons. Where the notification to the supervisory authority is not made within 72 hours, it shall be accompanied by reasons for the delay.'*

The key points to note are:

10.5.1 Timing

The requirement to notify is stated to be without undue delay and not later than 72 hours from awareness

10.5.2 Awareness

The EDPB is of the view that a controller will have awareness when it has a:

> *'reasonable degree of certainty that a security incident has occurred that has led to personal data being compromised.'*

Clearly each case will be different in terms of when awareness may occur but the EDPB places emphasis on the need to respond promptly to any such incident by investigating it as a matter of urgency and taking any necessary remedial action as soon as possible

---

6 Article 33(1)

10.5.3 Delayed reporting

This is permitted where the delay is explained by reference to appropriate reasons. However, the GDPR also states that notification can take place in phases[7] and therefore it may be appropriate to make an initial notification and then provide more detailed information in due course.

10.5.4 Risk assessment

A key consideration, this will be discussed in more detail below in respect of this requirement and also the requirement of communication

10.5.5 Processors

Processors are required to notify the controller without undue delay after becoming aware of a personal data breach.[8]

10.5.6 Conditions where notification is not required

Where a personal data breach is '*unlikely to result in a risk to the rights and freedoms of natural persons*' then it will not require notification to the ICO.[9]

10.6 Content of the notification

The notification to the ICO must contain at least the following information:[10]

- description of the nature of the personal data breach including where possible, the categories and approximate number of data

7 Article 33(4)
8 Article 33(2)
9 Article 33(1)
10 Article 33(3)

subjects concerned and the categories and approximate number of personal data records concerned;

- the name and contact details of the data protection officer or other contact point where more information can be obtained;
- description of the likely consequences of the personal data breach;
- description of the measures taken or proposed to be taken by the controller to address the personal data breach, including, where appropriate, measures to mitigate its possible adverse effects.

The GDPR does not provide any further information on the level of detail required apart from the fact that approximate numbers will be sufficient. The EDPB gives the following examples of acceptable levels of detail:

Categories of data subjects	children and other vulnerable groups, people with disabilities, employees or customers
Categories of personal data records	health data, educational records, social care information, financial details, bank account numbers, passport numbers

10.7 Breach reporting form

It is important to note that the ICO has now produced a breach reporting form which can be accessed here:

https://ico.org.uk/for-organisations/report-a-breach/personal-data-breach/

By way of illustration I set out a sample scenario together with a completed form in Part B of this book.

10.8 Communication of a personal data breach to the data subject[11]

In addition to the requirement to notify the ICO, in certain circumstances the controller will also be required to notify the data subjects affected. The key obligation is that:

> *'When the personal data breach is likely to result in a high risk to the rights and freedoms of natural persons, the controller shall communicate the personal data breach to the data subject without undue delay.'*[12]

Furthermore the communication to the data subject referred to above shall describe in clear and plain language the nature of the personal data breach and contain the same information to be provided to the ICO, namely:[13]

- a description of the nature of the breach;
- the name and contact details of the data protection officer or other contact point;
- a description of the likely consequences of the breach; and
- a description of the measures taken or proposed to be taken by the controller to address the breach, including, where appropriate, measures to mitigate its possible adverse effects.

However, such communication shall not be required if any of the following conditions are met:[14]

- the controller has implemented appropriate technical and organisational protection measures, and that those measures

---

11 Article 34

12 Article 34(1)

13 Article 34(2)

14 Article 34(3)

were applied to the personal data affected by the personal data breach, in particular those that render the personal data unintelligible to any person who is not authorised to access it, such as encryption;

- the controller has taken subsequent measures which ensure that the high risk to the rights and freedoms of data subjects referred to in paragraph 1 is no longer likely to materialise (for example records that were lost are recovered almost immediately);
- it would involve disproportionate effort. In such a case, there shall instead be a public communication or similar measure whereby the data subjects are informed in an equally effective manner.

Finally, if the controller has not communicated the personal data breach to the data subject then the ICO may require it to do so.[15]

Examples of transparent communication methods suggested by the EDPB include:

- direct messaging (e.g. email, SMS, direct message),
- prominent website banners or notification,
- postal communications and prominent advertisements in print media

However, the EDPB suggest that a notification solely confined within a press release or corporate blog would not be an effective means of communicating a breach to an individual.

Other suggestions include using:

- several methods of communication, as opposed to using a single contact channel

15 Article 34(4)

- appropriate alternative formats
- communications in the recipient's native language

One final observation is that controllers need to demonstrate that they have complied with the necessary rules in accordance with the accountability principle and that although notification may not be required at the outset this needs to be kept under review.

10.9 Risk Assessment

The assessment of 'risk' and 'high risk' is of key importance to the requirements relating to notification and communication. The EDPB sets out a series of considerations to be borne in mind and I summarise these considerations below.

10.10 General Considerations

- Risk is to be assessed on the basis of an objective assessment with consideration given to both likelihood and severity.

- Risk will exist when a personal data breach leads to physical, material or non-material damage for the data subjects whose information is affected.

- When the breach involves information in the special categories then damage should be considered likely to occur.

- Where the consequences of a breach are more likely and/or more severe, the risk is higher and similarly where the likelihood of these occurring is greater, the risk is also heightened.

- Controllers should take a cautious approach and should notify even if they are in doubt as to whether this is necessary.

10.11 Specific Considerations

In addition to the general considerations the EDPB also outlines a series of specific considerations and I summarise these below:

10.11.1 The type of breach

Different types of breaches will have different consequences and this needs to be taken into consideration in assessing risk. For example, the disclosure of credit card details to a third party (confidentiality breach) will have different consequences to the loss of credit card details so that they are no longer available (availability breach)

10.11.2 The nature, sensitivity, and volume of personal data

The normal rule here is that the more sensitive the personal data the greater the risk of harm. However, it is important to note that controllers should also consider how the personal data that has been compromised might be used in conjunction with other personal data that may be available about the data subject. For example, the accidental disclosure of a client's e-mail address or telephone number will not usually lead to substantial damage, however disclosure of this personal data to the ex-husband of a client who is the subject of a restraining order, could have very severe consequences.

10.11.3 Ease of identification of individuals

Another consideration is the ease with which the personal data that has been compromised will allow a third party to identify the data subject affected. The greater the ease, the greater the risk. One way of reducing the likelihood of this happening is the use of pseudonymisation, wherever possible.

10.11.4 Severity of consequences for individuals.

Clearly, the greater the severity of the consequences, the greater the risk. Where the personal data that have been compromised contain information from the special categories then this is more likely to lead to consequences such as physical or psychological harm or identity fraud. Consideration should also be given to the vulnerability of the data subjects affected and also the permanence of the consequences.

10.11.5 Special characteristics of the individual

Where those affected are children or other vulnerable individuals then this is likely to lead to an assessment of greater risk.

10.11.6 The number of affected individuals

Normally, the greater the number of people affected the greater the level of risk. Nevertheless, depending on the circumstances, a breach affecting one data subject can have a severe impact.

10.11.7 Special characteristics of the controller

Some controllers will be at greater risk than others due to the information that they have in their possession. For example, an NHS Trust processing special categories of personal data on a daily basis will be at greater risk than a commercial organisation that only processes special categories of personal data on an occasional basis.

10.12 Documentation of personal data breaches

Regardless of whether or not a breach needs to be notified to the supervisory authority, or to the data subjects affected, the controller must document all breaches, as follows:[16]

> *'The controller shall document any personal data breaches, comprising the facts relating to the personal data breach, its effects and the remedial action taken. That documentation shall enable the supervisory authority to verify compliance with this Article.'*

16 Article 33(5)

The precise methodology and structure of the report is left to the controller to decide but this will need to include:

- the facts of the breach
- the effects of the breach
- the remedial action taken

The EDPB also recommends that the report should document the controller's reasoning in respect of its response to the personal data breach which would include the reasons why it thought the breach was unlikely to result in a risk to the rights and freedoms of individuals.

10.13 Summary

The GDPR does not introduce any radical changes in respect of security measures as can be seen by the continuing references to *'appropriate technical and organisational measures.'* However, controllers need to familiarise themselves with the personal data breach reporting requirements and ensure that their own employees and also any processors they use are aware of the timescales involved.

10.14 Practical steps

- review and update your existing security policies and procedures on a regular basis to ensure ongoing compliance.

- ensure that you have a documented notification procedure in place, setting out the process to be followed in the event of a breach and including how to:
    - contain, manage and recover the incident,
    - assess the risk, and
    - notify the breach.

- download and use the ICO's breach reporting form

- inform employees about the existence of such procedures and mechanisms and how they should react to breaches

- review your contractual arrangements with processors so as to ensure that processors are aware of their obligations to report breaches to the controller without undue delay

CHAPTER ELEVEN INTERNATIONAL TRANSFERS

11.1 Introduction

The GDPR largely maintains the regime set out in the DPA 1998 and therefore the basic rule is as follows:

> *'Any transfer of personal data which are undergoing processing or are intended for processing after transfer to a third country or to an international organisation shall take place only if, subject to the other provisions of this Regulation, the conditions laid down in this Chapter are complied with by the controller and processor, including for onward transfers of personal data from the third country or an international organisation to another third country or to another international organisation. All provisions in this Chapter shall be applied in order to ensure that the level of protection of natural persons guaranteed by this Regulation is not undermined.'*[1]

The ICO's guidance on this topic can be accessed here:

https://ico.org.uk/for-organisations/guide-to-data-protection/guide-to-the-general-data-protection-regulation-gdpr/international-transfers/

Clearly this is an area that remains uncertain due to Brexit and issues relating to post-Brexit data flows between the United Kingdom and the EEA will be discussed in more detail in chapter 15.

1 Article 44

11.2 Key questions

The ICO's guidance sets out five key questions that controllers need to consider before making such a transfer and I set out a summary of these questions below:

1. **Are we planning to make a restricted transfer of personal data outside of the EEA?**

- If no, you can make the transfer. If yes go to Q2

2. **Do we need to make a restricted transfer of personal data in order to meet our purposes?**

- If no, you can make the transfer without any personal data. If yes go to Q3

3. **Has the EU made an 'adequacy decision' in relation to the country or territory where the receiver is located or a sector which covers the receiver?**

- If yes, you can make the transfer. If no go to Q4

4. **Have we put in place one of the 'appropriate safeguards' referred to in the GDPR?**

- If yes, you can make the transfer. If no go to Q5

5. **Does an exception provided for in the GDPR apply?**

- If yes, you can make the transfer. If no you cannot make the transfer in accordance with the GDPR

- If you reach the end without finding a provision which permits the restricted transfer, you will be unable to make that restricted transfer in accordance with the GDPR

In this chapter we will consider each of these questions in turn.

11.2.1 Are we making a restricted transfer?

The ICO's Guidance states that a controller will be making a restricted transfer if:

- the GDPR applies to the processing of the personal data they are transferring
- they are sending personal data, or making it accessible, to a receiver to which the GDPR does not apply; and
- the receiver is a separate organisation or individual.

Note that this includes transfers to another company within the same corporate group. However, if they are sending personal data to someone employed by them or by their company, this is not a restricted transfer. The transfer restrictions only apply if they are sending personal data outside their organisation.

According to the ICO's Guidance, examples of restricted transfers would include:

> *A UK company uses a centralised human resources service in the United States provided by its parent company. The UK company passes information about its employees to its parent company in connection with the HR service.*

> *A UK company sells holidays in Australia. It sends the personal data of customers who have bought the holidays to the hotels they have chosen in Australia in order to secure their bookings.*

> *A UK insurance broker sends a set of notes about individual customers to a company in a non-EEA country. These notes are handwritten and are not stored on computer or in any particular*

order. The non-EEA company adds the notes to a computer customer management system.

A UK company loads personal data onto a UK server which is then available through a website, and you plan or anticipate that the website may be accessed from outside the EEA.

However, it is important to point out that transfer does not mean the same as transit. Transit describes a scenario where personal data is electronically routed from one EEA country to another EEA country via a non-EEA country. For example:

Personal data is transferred from a controller in France to a controller in Ireland (both countries in the EEA) via a server in Australia. There is no intention that the personal data will be accessed or manipulated while it is in Australia. Therefore the transfer is only to Ireland.

Assuming that a restricted transfer is being made the controller must then consider how such a restricted transfer might be justified.

11.2.2 Has the EU made an 'adequacy decision' in relation to the country or territory where the receiver is located or a sector which covers the receiver?

(i) Adequacy Decisions

The GDPR provides that:

'A transfer of personal data to a third country or an international organisation may take place where the Commission has decided that the third country, a territory or one or more specified sectors within that third country, or the international organisation in question ensures an adequate level of protection. Such a transfer shall not require any specific authorisation.'[2]

2 Article 45(1)

Guidance on these issues may be obtained from:

https://ec.europa.eu/info/law/law-topic/data-protection/international-dimension-data-protection/adequacy-decisions_en

In deciding whether a country should be the beneficiary of an adequacy decision the European Commission will take into consideration the following factors:

- Legal framework
- Presence of an effective and functioning supervisory authority
- Participation in international agreements

At the time of writing, the following countries have benefitted from an adequacy decision:

- Andorra
- Argentina
- Canada
- Guernsey, Jersey, Isle of Man
- Switzerland
- Israel
- Faroe Islands
- New Zealand
- Uruguay
- Japan

Consequently a controller to whom the GDPR applies may transfer personal data to a controller or a processor in any of these countries without requiring any further safeguards.

(ii) EU – US Privacy Shield

In respect of the United States of America the European Commission has created the EU-US Privacy Shield which has been in operation since August 2016. Essentially, it only allows transfers to specific US based entities who have registered voluntarily with this scheme and by doing so have agreed to comply with data protection rules of a similar nature to those found in the GDPR.

Before relying on this scheme to justify a transfer it is advisable to consult the most recent list of US based entities who are registered and this can be done at:

https://www.privacyshield.gov/list

Also worthy of note is that the validity of these arrangements has been challenged by an Austrian privacy activist, Max Schrems. Schrems successful in obtaining a declaration from the European Court of Justice that the previous 'Safe Harbor' regime did not provide adequate safeguards and he has raised a similar challenge to the EU-US Privacy Shield.

At the time of writing, the Advocate General has delivered an opinion largely focussing on the issue of standard contractual clauses (see below for more information) which suggests that the EU-US Privacy Shield can continue.[3]

11.2.3 Can the parties put in place one of the 'appropriate safeguards' referred to in the GDPR?[4]

> *'In the absence of a decision pursuant to Article 45(3), a controller or processor may transfer personal data to a third country or an international organisation only if the controller or processor has provided appropriate safeguards, and on condition that enforceable data*

3 http://curia.europa.eu/juris/documents.jsf?num=C-311/18

4 Article 46

subject rights and effective legal remedies for data subjects are available.[5]

The following safeguards may be relied upon to transfer personal data to a third country without the need for specific authorisation by a supervisory authority:

(a) a legally binding and enforceable instrument between public authorities or bodies;

(b) binding corporate rules in accordance with Article 47;

(c) standard data protection clauses adopted by the Commission in accordance with the examination procedure referred to in Article 93(2);

(d) standard data protection clauses adopted by a supervisory authority and approved by the Commission pursuant to the examination procedure referred to in Article 93(2);

(e) an approved code of conduct pursuant to Article 40 together with binding and enforceable commitments of the controller or processor in the third country to apply the appropriate safeguards, including as regards data subjects' rights; or

(f) an approved certification mechanism pursuant to Article 42 together with binding and enforceable commitments of the controller or processor in the third country to apply the appropriate safeguards, including as regards data subjects' rights.

In addition to this, subject to authorisation from an appropriate supervisory authority the following safeguards may be appropriate:[6]

5 Article 46(1)

6 Article 46(3)

(a) contractual clauses between the controller or processor and the controller, processor or the recipient of the personal data in the third country or international organisation; or

(b) provisions to be inserted into administrative arrangements between public authorities or bodies which include enforceable and effective data subject rights.

(i) Standard Contractual Clauses

A restricted transfer can be made where the parties have entered into a contract containing standard data protection clauses as adopted by the European Commission.

These 'standard contractual clauses' are also known as 'model clauses' and they must be entered into by the EEA based data exporter and the non-EEA based data importer.

The clauses contain obligations on the part of the data exporter and the data importer as well as rights for the data subjects affected which can be enforced directly against either of the parties. They must be used in their entirety without amendment albeit additional clauses can be added in respect of other matters provided that they do not contradict the standard contractual clauses. Additional data importers or exporters can also be added provided they are also bound by the standard contractual clauses.

There are currently two sets of clauses:

- 2004 – Controller – Controller
- 2010 – Controller – Processor

(a) EEA Controller – Non-EEA Controller

These can be accessed here:

https://eur-lex.europa.eu/legal-content/EN/TXT/?uri=CELEX%3A32004D0915

(b) EEA Controller – Non-EEA Processor

These can be accessed here:

https://eur-lex.europa.eu/legal-content/en/TXT/?uri=CELEX%3A32010D0087

The European Commission is planning to update these clauses so as to comply with the GDPR but has not done this at the time of writing. In the meantime, the existing clauses remain valid and contracts entered into using these clauses will continue to be valid even once the European Commission has adopted new clauses.

The ICO has produced template contracts containing explanatory notes and guidance. These can be accessed at the following location:

https://ico.org.uk/for-organisations/guide-to-data-protection/guide-to-the-general-data-protection-regulation-gdpr/international-transfers/

One final point to note is that if the restricted transfer is being made from a controller to a processor it also needs to comply with the GDPR rules about using processors.

(c) Schrems II

As has already been noted above, the validity of these standard contractual clauses has been challenged before the European Court of Justice by the privacy activist, Max Schrems. On the 19th December 2019 the Advocate General handed down his opinion[7] and noted that the clauses remain valid. Of course, the full decision of the court is awaited in due course.

7 http://curia.europa.eu/juris/documents.jsf?num=C-311/18

(ii) Binding Corporate Rules

Binding corporate rules have been in existence for some time and only apply in respect of internal transfers between companies in the same group. The GDPR provides more information and greater clarity about the usage of these:

Each supervisory authority is permitted to approve binding corporate rules as long as they[8]:

(a) are legally binding and apply to and are enforced by every member concerned of the group of undertakings, or group of enterprises engaged in a joint economic activity, including their employees;

(b) expressly confer enforceable rights on data subjects with regard to the processing of their personal data; and

(c) fulfil the requirements laid down in paragraph 2.

The binding corporate rules must specify at least:[9]

(a) the structure and contact details of the group of undertakings, or group of enterprises engaged in a joint economic activity and of each of its members;

(b) the data transfers or set of transfers, including the categories of personal data, the type of processing and its purposes, the type of data subjects affected and the identification of the third country or countries in question;

(c) their legally binding nature, both internally and externally;

(d) the application of the general data protection principles, in particular purpose limitation, data minimisation, limited

---

8 Article 47(1)

9 Article 47(2)

storage periods, data quality, data protection by design and by default, legal basis for processing, processing of special categories of personal data, measures to ensure data security, and the requirements in respect of onward transfers to bodies not bound by the binding corporate rules;

(e) the rights of data subjects in regard to processing and the means to exercise those rights, including the right not to be subject to decisions based solely on automated processing, including profiling in accordance with Article 22, the right to lodge a complaint with the competent supervisory authority and before the competent courts of the Member States in accordance with Article 79, and to obtain redress and, where appropriate, compensation for a breach of the binding corporate rules;

(f) the acceptance by the controller or processor established on the territory of a Member State of liability for any breaches of the binding corporate rules by any member concerned not established in the Union; the controller or the processor shall be exempt from that liability, in whole or in part, only if it proves that that member is not responsible for the event giving rise to the damage;

(g) how the information on the binding corporate rules, in particular on the provisions referred to in points (d), (e) and (f) of this paragraph is provided to the data subjects in addition to Articles 13 and 14;

(h) the tasks of any data protection officer designated in accordance with Article 37 or any other person or entity in charge of the monitoring compliance with the binding corporate rules within the group of undertakings, or group of enterprises engaged in a joint economic activity, as well as monitoring training and complaint-handling;

(i) the complaint procedures;

(j) the mechanisms within the group of undertakings, or group of enterprises engaged in a joint economic activity for ensuring the verification of compliance with the binding corporate rules. Such mechanisms shall include data protection audits and methods for ensuring corrective actions to protect the rights of the data subject. Results of such verification should be communicated to the person or entity referred under point (h) and to the board of the controlling undertaking of a group of undertakings, or of the group of enterprises engaged in a joint economic activity, and should be available upon request to the competent supervisory authority;

(k) the mechanisms for reporting and recording changes to the rules and reporting those changes to the supervisory authority;

(l) the cooperation mechanism with the supervisory authority to ensure compliance by any member of the group of undertakings, or group of enterprises engaged in a joint economic activity, in particular by making available to the supervisory authority the results of verifications of the measures referred to in point (j);

(m) the mechanisms for reporting to the competent supervisory authority any legal requirements to which a member of the group of undertakings, or group of enterprises engaged in a joint economic activity is subject in a third country which are likely to have a substantial adverse effect on the guarantees provided by the binding corporate rules; and

(n) the appropriate data protection training to personnel having permanent or regular access to personal data.

(iii) Comparison

In the circumstances, controllers may be faced with a choice between standard contractual clauses ('SCC') and binding corporate rules ('BCR'). However, my recommendation would be that SCCs would normally be the better option for the following reasons:

(a) Complexity

Although the GDPR does contain further guidance in respect of BCRs the reality is that their creation and approval is still relatively complex. In contrast, the SCCs are well established and the format does not require any further elaboration.

(b) Timing

The approval process for BCRs can be lengthy whereas SCCs can be put in place very quickly indeed as they do not need approval from a regulator.

(c) Cost

Clearly the time and complexity mean that BCRs will lead to a considerable cost being incurred whereas this will not be the case for the SCCs.

(d) Scope

As has been noted, the BCRs only apply to internal transfers within a group of companies whereas the SCCs will cover both internal and external transfers where needed.

11.2.4 Does one of the exceptions found in the GDPR apply?[10]

The list of additional derogations under DPA 1998 is largely maintained in the GDPR. Overseas transfers are therefore permitted in the following additional instances:

(a) the data subject has explicitly consented to the proposed transfer, after having been informed of the possible risks of such transfers for the data subject due to the absence of an adequacy decision and appropriate safeguards;

(b) the transfer is necessary for the performance of a contract between the data subject and the controller or the implementation of pre-contractual measures taken at the data subject's request;

(c) the transfer is necessary for the conclusion or performance of a contract concluded in the interest of the data subject between the controller and another natural or legal person;

(d) the transfer is necessary for important reasons of public interest;

(e) the transfer is necessary for the establishment, exercise or defence of legal claims;

(f) the transfer is necessary in order to protect the vital interests of the data subject or of other persons, where the data subject is physically or legally incapable of giving consent;

(g) the transfer is made from a register which according to Union or Member State law is intended to provide information to the public and which is open to consultation either by the public in general or by any person who can demonstrate a legitimate interest, but only to the extent that the conditions laid down in Union or Member State law for consultation are fulfilled in the particular case.

10 Article 49

I set out below a series of extracts from the ICO's guidance dealing with each of the key exceptions in turn:

Exception 1. Has the individual given his or her explicit consent to the restricted transfer?

As a valid consent must be both specific and informed, you must provide the individual with precise details about the restricted transfer. You cannot obtain a valid consent for restricted transfers in general.

You should tell the individual:

- *the identity of the receiver, or the categories of receiver;*
- *the country or countries to which the data is to be transferred;*
- *why you need to make a restricted transfer;*
- *the type of data;*
- *the individual's right to withdraw consent; and*
- *the possible risks involved in making a transfer to a country which does not provide adequate protection for personal data and without any other appropriate safeguards in place.*

Given the high threshold for a valid consent, and that the consent must be capable of being withdrawn, this may mean that using consent is not a feasible solution.

Exception 2. Do you have a contract with the individual? Is the restricted transfer necessary for you to perform that contract?

Are you about to enter into a contract with the individual? Is the restricted transfer necessary for you to take steps requested by the individual in order to enter into that contract?

This exception explicitly states that it can only be used for occasional restricted transfers. This means that the restricted transfer may happen more than once but not regularly. If you are regularly making restricted transfers, you should be putting in place an appropriate safeguard.

The transfer must also be necessary, which means that you cannot perform the core purpose of the contract or the core purpose of the steps needed to enter into the contract, without making the restricted transfer. It does not cover a transfer for you to use a cloud based IT system.

Public authorities cannot rely on this exception when exercising their public powers.

Exception 3. Do you have (or are you entering into) a contract with an individual which benefits another individual whose data is being transferred? Is that transfer necessary for you to either enter into that contract or perform that contract?

As set out in Exception 2, you may only use this exception for occasional transfers, and the transfer must be necessary for you to perform the core purposes of the contract or to enter into that contract.

You may rely on both Exceptions 2 and 3: Exception 2 for the individual entering into the contract and Exception 3 for other people benefiting from that contract, often family members.

Exceptions 2 and 3 are not identical. You cannot rely on Exception 3 for any restricted transfers needed for steps taken prior to entering in to the contract.

Public authorities cannot rely on this exception when exercising their public powers.

Exception 4: You need to make the restricted transfer for important reasons of public interest.

There must be an EU or UK law which states or implies that this type of transfer is allowed for important reasons of public interest, which may be in the spirit of reciprocity for international co-operation. For example an international agreement or convention (which the UK or EU has signed) that recognises certain objectives and provides for international co-operation. This can be relied upon by both public and private entities.

If a request is made by a non-EEA authority, requesting a restrictive transfer under this exception, and there is an international agreement such as a mutual assistance treaty (MLAT), you should consider referring the request to the existing MLAT or agreement.

You should not rely on this exception for systematic transfers. Instead, you should consider one of the appropriate safeguards. You should only use it in specific situations, and each time you should satisfy yourself that the transfer is necessary for an important reason of public interest.

Exception 5: You need to make the restricted transfer to establish if you have a legal claim, to make a legal claim or to defend a legal claim.

This exception explicitly states that you can only use it for occasional transfers. This means that the transfer may happen more than once but not regularly. If you are regularly transferring personal data, you should put in place an appropriate safeguard.

The transfer must be necessary, so there must be a close connection between the need for the transfer and the relevant legal claim.

The claim must have a basis in law, and a formal legally defined process, but it is not just judicial or administrative procedures. This means that you can interpret what is a legal claim quite widely, to cover, for example:

- *all judicial legal claims, in civil law (including contract law) and criminal law. The court procedure does not need to have been started, and it covers out-of-court procedures. It covers formal pre-trial discovery procedures.*
- *administrative or regulatory procedures, such as to defend an investigation (or potential investigation) in anti-trust law or financial services regulation, or to seek approval for a merger.*

You cannot rely on this exception if there is only the mere possibility that a legal claim or other formal proceedings may be brought in the future.

Public authorities can rely on this exception, in relation to the exercise of their powers.

Exception 6: You need to make the restricted transfer to protect the vital interests of an individual. He or she must be physically or legally incapable of giving consent.

This applies in a medical emergency where the transfer is needed in order to give the medical care required. The imminent risk of serious harm to the individual must outweigh any data protection concerns.

You cannot rely on this exception to carry out general medical research. If the individual is physically and legally capable of giving consent, then you cannot rely on this exception.

11.3 Summary

In summary, the existing regime is largely maintained and therefore there are a number of possible ways in which a controller can transfer personal data outside of the EEA in a compliant fashion, albeit note that the exceptions should only be applied on an occasional basis. Of course, Brexit will have an impact on these rules and this is discussed in more detail in chapter 15.

11.4 Practical steps

- review existing procedures for the transfer of personal data outside of the EEA
- verify whether you can rely on the EU-US Privacy Shield to cover transfers to the USA
- consider whether BCR would be appropriate in respect of intra-group transfers
- review existing contractual arrangements with third parties and consider inserting standard contractual clauses if this has not been done already
- if relying on explicit consent then ensure that this complies with the GDPR's requirements

CHAPTER TWELVE
DATA PROTECTION OFFICERS[1]

12.1 Introduction

Under the DPA 1998 there was no requirement to appoint a data protection officer ('DPO'), however, the GDPR requires controllers and processors to appoint a DPO in the following circumstances:[2]

- the processing is carried out by a public authority or body, except for courts acting in their judicial capacity;
- the core activities of the controller or the processor consist of processing operations which, by virtue of their nature, their scope and/or their purposes, require regular and systematic monitoring of data subjects on a large scale; or
- the core activities of the controller or the processor consist of processing on a large scale of special categories of data pursuant to Article 9 and personal data relating to criminal convictions and offences referred to in Article 10.

Further guidance on the meaning of these definitions can be found in the guidance note prepared on this topic by the European Data Protection Board ('EDPB') that can be accessed at:

http://ec.europa.eu/information_society/newsroom/image/document/2016-51/wp243_en_40855.pdf

In summary, their comments are as follows:

1 Articles 37-39

2 Article 35(1)

12.2 Definitions

12.2.1 Core activities

> *'the key operations to achieve the controller's or processor's objectives. These also include all activities where the processing of data forms as inextricable part of the controller's or processor's activity.'*

They stress the importance of contrasting core activities such as the processing of a patient's medical records by a hospital with ancillary activities such as a hospital paying employees or having standard IT support activities. A hospital would carry out both but would need to designate a DPO because of the core activities rather than because of the ancillary activities.

12.2.2 Large Scale

The GDPR does not define this but the EDPB suggest the following factors should be considered:

- the number of data subjects concerned – either as a specific number or as a proportion of the relevant population
- the volume of data and/or the range of different data items being processed
- the duration, or permanence, of the data processing activity
- the geographical extent of the processing activity

Examples of large-scale processing include:

- processing of patient data in the regular course of business by a hospital
- processing of customer data in the regular course of business by an insurance company or a bank

- processing of personal data for behavioural advertising by a search engine

Examples that do not constitute large-scale processing include:

- processing of patient data by an individual physician
- processing of personal data relating to criminal convictions and offences by an individual lawyer

12.2.3 Regular and systematic

The notion of regular and systematic monitoring of data subjects is not defined in the GDPR, but the EDPB provide further insight as follows:

'regular' is defined as meaning one or more of the following:

- ongoing or occurring at particular intervals for a particular period
- recurring or repeated at fixed times
- constantly or periodically taking place

'systematic' as meaning one or more of the following:

- occurring according to a system
- pre-arranged, organised or methodical
- taking place as part of a general plan for data collection
- carried out as part of a strategy

Specific examples would include:

- operating a telecommunications network;
- providing telecommunications services;

- profiling and scoring for purposes of risk assessment (e.g. for purposes of credit scoring,
- establishment of insurance premiums, fraud prevention, detection of money-laundering); location tracking, for example, by mobile apps;
- loyalty programs;
- behavioural advertising;
- monitoring of wellness, fitness and health data via wearable devices;
- closed circuit television;
- connected devices e.g. smart meters, smart cars, home automation, etc.

In summary, controllers and processors that regularly process personal data in respect of employees, customers or clients on a large scale will be required to appoint a DPO.

Having decided that it is necessary to appoint a DPO then there are certain further considerations to be borne in mind and I set out a summary of the key points below.

12.3 Designation of the Data Protection Officer[3]

There are two important points to note:

- a group of companies may appoint a single DPO provided that the DPO is easily accessible from each establishment.[4]
- DPOs are to be designated on the basis of professional qualities and, in particular, expert knowledge of data protection law and

3 Article 37

4 Article 37(2)

practices and the ability to fulfil the tasks referred to in Article 39.[5]

This latter point is the subject of some debate at present in terms of what is meant by 'professional qualities' and also 'expert knowledge'. There is no further guidance available but my view is that anyone with a professional qualification who has received some basic data protection training, with particular emphasis on the GDPR, is likely to satisfy this requirement.

12.4 Position of the Data Protection Officer[6]

The key characteristics of this position as set out in the GDPR are as follows:

Requirement	Description
Involvement	The controller and the processor shall ensure that the data protection officer is involved, properly and in a timely manner, in all issues which relate to the protection of personal data.
Support	The controller and processor shall support the data protection officer in performing the tasks referred to in Article 39 by providing resources necessary to carry out those tasks and access to personal data and processing operations, and to maintain his or her expert knowledge.
Relationship with senior man-agement	The controller and processor shall ensure that the data protection officer does not receive any instructions regarding the exercise of those tasks. He or she shall not be dismissed or penalised by

5 Article 37(5)

6 Article 38

	the controller or the processor for performing his tasks. The data protection officer shall directly report to the highest management level of the controller or the processor.
Point of contact	Data subjects may contact the data protection officer with regard to all issues related to processing of their personal data and to the exercise of their rights under this Regulation.
Secrecy and confidentiality	The data protection officer shall be bound by secrecy or confidentiality concerning the performance of his or her tasks, in accordance with Union or Member State law
Other duties	The data protection officer may fulfil other tasks and duties. The controller or processor shall ensure that any such tasks and duties do not result in a conflict of interests.

Most of these requirements can be fulfilled easily enough by controllers and processors, as appropriate, and it is helpful to note that the DPO is not limited to advising solely on the GDPR. Some concerns may be raised about the level of support and resource to be provided but the extent of this will clearly depend on the sensitivity of the personal data and the scope and sophistication of the processing being carried out.

12.5 Tasks of the Data Protection Officer[7]

The DPO is required to carry out the following basic tasks:[8]

- to inform and advise their employer and their fellow employees of their obligations under the GDPR

7 Article 39

8 Article 39(1)

- to monitor compliance with the GDPR and other related legislation including but not limited to:
    - reviewing policies and procedures
    - assigning responsibilities,
    - awareness-raising
    - training staff involved in processing operations
    - carrying out audits
- to advise on and monitor the performance of data protection impact assessments
- to cooperate and consult with the ICO as necessary
- to act as the contact point for the ICO

All of these tasks are to be carried out taking into consideration the level of risk and the nature, scope, context and purposes of processing.[9]

12.6 Notification of a DPO

Assuming that a controller decides to appoint a DPO then this appointment needs to be notified to the ICO. More information about how to do this is available here:

https://ico.org.uk/for-organisations/data-protection-fee/your-data-protection-officer-is/

In essence, an e-mail needs to be sent to dataprotectionfee@ico.org.uk with the subject line 'Add a DPO'. The e-mail must include the following information:

9 Article 39(2)

- the registration number of the organisation;
- whether the controller is required to provide the details of the DPO, or whether it is doing so voluntarily; and
- the name, address, phone number and/or email address of the DPO if they are an individual (eg a member of staff or a member of your organisation); or
- the name, address, phone number and/or email address of the external organisation that will be carrying out the DPO's duties on the controller's behalf.

The e-mail should also clearly state whether the controller wishes the ICO to publish the name of the DPO if they are an individual.

12.7 Summary

Although many small to medium enterprises may not be required by law to appoint a DPO my view is that it is still advisable to make such an appointment where possible. Putting to one side the difficulty of finding a willing candidate, the bigger issues are then about ensuring that person has adequate training and resources to fulfil their role successfully and that they have sufficient visibility at board level.

12.8 Practical steps

- consider whether the appointment of a DPO is necessary
- if not, consider whether it is a good idea anyway in practice
- select an appropriately qualified employee and ensure they are given adequate training
- review how the DPO will report to senior management

- ensure the DPO has sufficient time and resources to carry out their duties appropriately
- ensure the DPO's details are available to data subjects and to the ICO

CHAPTER THIRTEEN ENFORCEMENT

13.1 Introduction

The rules on enforcement are found in both the GDPR and the DPA 2018. The GDPR focusses on the increased administrative fines that can now be levied while the DPA 2018 focusses on the various enforcement options that are available to the ICO which are largely the same as in the DPA 1998.

13.2 GDPR

The GDPR allows supervisory authorities to levy administrative fines applying the following principles:[1]

> *'Each supervisory authority shall ensure that the imposition of administrative fines pursuant to this Article in respect of infringements of this Regulation … shall in each individual case be effective, proportionate and dissuasive.'*

In deciding on the level of such a fine the supervisory authority shall have regard to the following factors:[2]

(a) the nature, gravity and duration of the infringement taking into account the nature scope or purpose of the processing concerned as well as the number of data subjects affected and the level of damage suffered by them;

(b) the intentional or negligent character of the infringement;

(c) any action taken by the controller or processor to mitigate the damage suffered by data subjects;

---

1 Article 83(1)

2 Article 83(2)

(d) the degree of responsibility of the controller or processor taking into account technical and organisational measures implemented by them pursuant to Articles 25 and 32;

(e) any relevant previous infringements by the controller or processor;

(f) the degree of cooperation with the supervisory authority, in order to remedy the infringement and mitigate the possible adverse effects of the infringement;

(g) the categories of personal data affected by the infringement;

(h) the manner in which the infringement became known to the supervisory authority, in particular whether, and if so to what extent, the controller or processor notified the infringement;

(i) in case measures referred to in Article 58(2) have previously been ordered against the controller or processor concerned with regard to the same subject-matter, compliance with those measures;

(j) adherence to approved codes of conduct pursuant to Article 40 or approved certification mechanisms pursuant to Article 42; and

(k) any other aggravating or mitigating factor applicable to the circumstances of the case, such as financial benefits gained, or losses avoided, directly or indirectly, from the infringement.

Where a controller or processor infringes several provisions then the fine shall not exceed the amount specified for the gravest infringement.[3]

The GDPR then sets out a two-tiered system of administrative fines with significantly increased maximum amounts:

---

3 Article 83(3)

Tier 1:[4]

Administrative fines up to 10,000,000 EUR, or in the case of an undertaking, up to 2% of the total worldwide annual turnover of the preceding financial year, whichever is higher:

(a) the obligations of the controller and the processor pursuant to Articles 8, 11, 25, 26, 27, 28, 29, 30, 31, 32, 33, 34, 35, 36, 37, 38, 39, 42 and 43;

(b) the obligations of the certification body pursuant to Articles 42 and 43;

(c) the obligations of the monitoring body pursuant to Article 41(4).

The breaches covered by (a) relate to:

- Controller – processor agreements
- Security breaches
- Data protection impact assessments
- Data protection officers

Tier 2:[5]

Administrative fines up to 20 000 000 EUR, or in the case of an undertaking, up to 4 % of the total worldwide annual turnover of the preceding financial year, whichever is higher:

(a) the basic principles for processing, including conditions for consent, pursuant to Articles 5, 6, 7 and 9;

(b) the data subjects' rights pursuant to Articles 12 to 22;

---

4 Article 83(4)

5 Article 83(5)

(c) the transfers of personal data to a recipient in a third country or an international organisation pursuant to Articles 44 to 49;

(d) any obligations pursuant to Member State law adopted unter Chapter IX;

(e) non-compliance with an order or a temporary or definitive limitation on processing or the suspension of data flows by the supervisory authority pursuant to Article 58(2) or failure to provide access in violation of Article 58(1).

This also applies to failure to comply with an order by a supervisory authority under Article 58(2).[6]

13.3 DPA 2018

The DPA 2018 carries over many of the provisions of the DPA 1998 in terms of enforcement and I set out a brief summary of these below

13.3.1 Information Notices ss142-145

The key provisions are as follows:

- the ICO can send an information notice to a controller, processor or other person requesting information that it reasonably requires[7]
- the information notice must state the grounds on which it is given and an explanation as to why the information is required by the ICO[8]

6 Article 83(6)

7 s142(1)

8 s142(2)

- the information notice may specify details of the information; the form in which it is to be provided; the time and place at which it is to be provided[9]
- an information notice must provide information about the consequences of failing to comply and the right of appeal[10]
- there are certain restrictions on the ICO's right to send an information notice[11]
- knowingly or recklessly providing a false statement in respect of an information notice is an offence[12]
- if a party fails to provide information in response to an information notice the ICO can obtain an information order from the courts[13]

13.3.2 Assessment Notices ss146-147

Under these sections, the ICO may require a controller or processor to permit the ICO to carry out an assessment as to whether they are compliant with data protection legislation.[14]

An assessment notice may require the controller or processor to:[15]

- allow the ICO to enter premises;
- direct the ICO to specific documents, equipment or material
- assist the ICO in viewing information

9 s142(3)
10 s142(4)
11 s143
12 s144
13 s145
14 s146(1)
15 s146(2)

- provide copies of information requested by the ICO
- permit the ICO to examine all of the above
- provide an explanation to the ICO in respect of all of the above
- permit the ICO to observe the processing of personal data
- make available for interview a specified number of people

An assessment notice must also:

- specify the time or times at which, or period or periods within which, the above requirements must be complied with[16]
- explain the consequences of failure to comply and the right to appeal[17]

There are certain restrictions placed on the ICO's right to send an assessment notices.[18]

13.3.3 Enforcement Notices ss149-153

Enforcement notices can be served by the ICO where a person has failed or is failing in one of four ways. In such a case, the enforcement notice will require the person to:[19]

- take steps specified in the enforcement notice; or
- refrain from taking steps specified in the enforcement notice

The four types of failure are as follows:

16 s146(4)
17 s146(5)
18 s147
19 s149(1)

(1) **Controller or processor has failed or is failing to comply with any of the following:**[20]

(a) a provision of Chapter II of the GDPR or Chapter 2 of Part 3 or Chapter 2 of Part 4 of this Act (principles of processing);

(b) a provision of Articles 12 to 22 of the GDPR or Part 3 or 4 of this Act conferring rights on a data subject;

(c) a provision of Articles 25 to 39 of the GDPR or section 64 or 65 of this Act (obligations of controllers and processors);

(d) a requirement to communicate a personal data breach to the Commissioner or a data subject under section 67, 68 or 108 of this Act;

(e) the principles for transfers of personal data to third countries, non-Convention countries and international organisations in Articles 44 to 49 of the GDPR or in sections 73 to 78 or 109 of this Act.

(2) **A monitoring body has failed, or is failing, to comply with an obligation under Article 41 of the GDPR (monitoring of approved codes of conduct).**[21]

(3) **A certification provider:**[22]

(a) does not meet the requirements for accreditation,

(b) has failed, or is failing, to comply with an obligation under Article 42 or 43 of the GDPR (certification of controllers and processors), or

20 s149(2)

21 s149(3)

22 s149(4)

(c) has failed, or is failing, to comply with any other provision of the GDPR (whether in the person's capacity as a certification provider or otherwise).

(4) A controller has failed, or is failing, to comply with regulations under section 137[23]

Requirements imposed in respect of each of the four failures must be appropriate for the purpose of remedying the failure[24]
The following additional considerations are also of relevance:

- In deciding whether to give an enforcement notice under s149(2) the ICO must consider whether the failure has caused or is likely to cause any person damage or distress.[25]
- Enforcement notices must state what the person has failed or is failing to do and provide the ICO's reasons for this[26]
- The ICO's powers under s149(1)(b) can be exercised in respect of all processing of personal data by that person or in respect of specific personal being processed[27]
- Enforcement notices may specify the time or times at which, or period or periods within which, a requirement imposed by the notice must be complied with[28]
- Enforcement notices must provide information about the consequences of failure to comply and the right to appeal[29]

---

23 s149(5)
24 s149(6)-(7)
25 s150(2)
26 s150(1)
27 s150(3)
28 s150(4)
29 s150(5)

Example

A good example of an enforcement notice under the DPA 2018 is in respect of AIQ, a Canadian based controller specialising in data analytics in respect of political campaigning. The ICO ruled that they were caught by the application of the GDPR[30] and the DPA 2018[31] and were in breach of Articles 5, 6 and 14 of the GDPR.

The ICO's enforcement notice required them within 30 days of the date of the notice to:

> *'cease processing any personal data of UK or EU citizens obtained from UK political organisations or otherwise for the purposes of data analytics, political campaigning or any other advertising purposes'*

An appeal is ongoing. More information can be found here:

https://ico.org.uk/media/action-weve-taken/enforcement-notices/2259362/r-letter-ico-to-aiq-060718.pdf

13.3.4 Powers of entry and inspection s154, sch 15

Schedule 15 permits the issuing of a warrant where the ICO has reasonable grounds for suspecting that:[32]

- a controller or processor has failed or is failing as described in section 149(2), or
- an offence under this Act has been or is being committed, and
- there are reasonable grounds for suspecting that evidence of the failure or of the commission of the offence is to be found on

30 Article 3(2)

31 s207

32 Sch 15 para 1(1)

premises specified in the information or is capable of being viewed using equipment on such premises.

Furthermore, a warrant may be issued in connection with an assessment notice where the ICO can satisfy the court that a controller or processor has failed to comply with a requirement imposed by an assessment notice[33]

13.3.5 Civil Monetary Penalties ss155-59 and sch16

Civil monetary penalties may be issued by the ICO where:

(a) a person has failed or is failing as described in section 149(2), (3), (4) or (5), or

(b) a person has failed to comply with an information notice, an assessment notice or an enforcement notice[34]

When deciding whether to give a penalty notice and in determining the size of the penalty the ICO is required to take into consideration the factors outlined in article 83(1)-(2) of the GDPR.[35]

Details of the maximum amounts that can be awarded are set out in s157. The term 'Standard Maximum Amount'[36] is used to describe amounts up to 10 million euros / 2% global turnover and the term 'Higher Maximum Amount'[37] is used to describe amounts up to 20 million euros / 4% global turnover.

---

33 Sch 15 Para 2(1)

34 s155(1)

35 s155(2)-(3)

36 s157(6)

37 s157(5)

The maximum amount of a penalty in pounds sterling is to be determined by applying the spot rate of exchange set by the Bank of England on the day on which the penalty notice is given.[38]

13.3.6 Fixed penalties for non-compliance with charges regulations[39]

Controllers are required to comply with the registration fees set out in the Data Protection (Charges and Information) Regulations 2018. Failure to do so is a breach of s137 DPA 2018 and can lead to a civil monetary penalty under s158 DPA 2018.

The maximum amount that may be specified is 150% of the highest charge payable by a controller in respect of a financial year in accordance with the regulations, disregarding any discount available under the regulations.[40]

13.3.7 Schedule 16 Penalties

This schedule sets out a series of formalities that must be observed by the ICO and I summarise these below.

(i) Notice of Intent

This preliminary document must be served before giving a person a penalty notice[41] and must contain the following information:[42]

- the name and address of the person to whom the ICO proposes to give a penalty notice;

38 s157(7)

39 s158

40 s158(3)

41 Sch 16 para 2(1)

42 Sch 16 para 3(1)-(2)

- the reasons why the ICO proposes to give a penalty notice (including details of the circumstances of failure and the nature of the personal data involved in the failure)
- an indication of the amount of the penalty the ICO proposes to impose, including any aggravating or mitigating factors that the ICO proposes to take into account.

It must also state:[43]

- that the person may make written representations about the ICO's intention to give a penalty notice, and
- the period within which such representations may be made (not less than 21 days from the date of the notice)

The ICO has a period of six months from the date of the notice of intent within which to issue a Penalty Notice save that this period can be extended for a further period of time by mutual agreement.[44]

(ii) Penalty Notice

Penalty notices cannot be given before the period for making representations stated in the notice of intent has elapsed.[45]

Any oral or written representations must be considered by the ICO when deciding whether to give a penalty notice. [46]

Penalty notices must contain:[47]

---

43 Sch 16 para 3(3)
44 Sch 16 para 2(2)-(3)
45 Sch 16 para 4(1)
46 Sch 16 para 4(2)
47 Sch 16 para 5(1)-(2)

- the name and address of the person to whom it is addressed;
- details of the notice of intent given to the person;
- whether the ICO received oral or written representations in accordance with the notice of intent;
- the reasons why the ICO proposes to impose the penalty including a description of the circumstances of the failure, and where the notice is given in respect of a failure described in section 149(2), the nature of the personal data involved in the failure.
- the reasons for the amount of the penalty, including any aggravating or mitigating factors that the ICO has taken into account;
- details of how the penalty is to be paid;
- details of the rights of appeal under section 162;
- details of the ICO's enforcement powers under this Schedule.

Penalties must be paid to the ICO within the period set out in the penalty notice which must be not less than 28 days beginning when the penalty notice is given.[48]

(iii) Right of Appeal

Note that controllers or processors who have received a penalty notice have a right of appeal to the First Tier Tribunal and from there to the Upper Tribunal.[49]

48 Sch 16 para 6(1)-(2)

49 s162 DPA 2018

13.4 Regulatory Action Policy ('RAP')

The ICO is required to publish details of its regulatory action policy[50] and following a consultation in 2018 this is now available here:

https://ico.org.uk/media/about-the-ico/documents/2259467/regulatory-action-policy.pdf

This document is 29 pages in length but is fairly accessible in terms of structure and layout. I summarise its key content below:

13.4.1 Preliminary comments

The ICO's begins by highlighting the approach that she wishes to take:

> *'This Policy sets out a risk-based approach to taking regulatory action against organisations and individuals that have breached the provisions of the data protection, freedom of information and other legislation, set out in our Aims below. As with earlier versions of the policy it focusses on areas of highest risk and most harm and the principles we apply in exercising our powers.'*

She then highlights several ways in which she intends to do this in practice:

- *'we will take action proportionately, we will exercise discretion as to when, in what manner, and to what extent enforcement is required;*
- *we will be selective when exercising this discretion, looking at the features and context of each case, as well as applying our resources more broadly to the areas of greatest risk and potential or actual harm to the community;*
- *we will apply our fining and other enforcement powers where they are effective, proportionate and dissuasive (to both the indi-*

50 ss168-169

vidual or organisation receiving the fine and more generally to those processing personal data'

13.4.2 Aggravating factors

Drawing heavily on the content of the GDPR and DPA 2018 she sets out the following aggravating factors:

- whether the attitude and conduct of the individual or organisation concerned suggests an intentional, wilful or negligent approach to compliance or unlawful business or operating model;
- whether relevant advice, warnings, consultation feedback, conditions or guidance from the ICO and/or the Data Protection Officer (for data protection cases) has not been followed;
- in data protection cases, whether the relevant individual or organisation is certified by a body that has been accredited under Article 43 of the GDPR or has failed to follow an approved or statutory code of conduct;
- the relevant individual or organisation's prior regulatory history, including pattern, number and type of complaints about the issue;
- the vulnerability, if any, of the individuals affected, in particular by virtue of their age or other protected characteristic under the Equality Act 2010;
- the state and nature of any protective or preventative measures and technology available, including by design;
- the manner in which the breach or issue became known to the ICO and, if relevant, failure or delay by the relevant individual or organisation to notify the ICO of the breach or issue; and

- any financial (including budgetary) benefits gained or financial losses avoided by the relevant individual or organisation, directly or indirectly.

13.4.3 Mitigating factors

Also drawing heavily on the GDPR and the DPA 2018 she sets out the following mitigating factors:

- any action taken by a relevant individual or organisation to mitigate or minimise any damage (including delay) suffered by individuals;
- in data protection cases, whether the relevant individual or organisation has followed an approved or statutory code of conduct
- the state and nature of any protective or preventative measures and technology available; and
- early notification by the relevant individual or organisation to the ICO of the breach or issue.

13.4.4 Statutory Guidance

The next section of the RAP sets out a detailed summary of the procedures to be followed in respect of the various enforcement options available under the DPA 2018 which were discussed earlier in this chapter.

13.4.5 Penalty Notices

Having listed out the factors to be considered under the GDPR when deciding whether a penalty is appropriate, the ICO makes the following comment:

'In the majority of cases we will reserve our powers for the most serious cases, representing the most severe breaches of information rights obligations. These will typically involve wilful, deliberate or negligent acts, or repeated breaches of information rights obligations, causing harm or damage to individuals. In considering the degree of harm or damage we may consider that, where there is a lower level of impact across a large number of individuals, the totality of that damage or harm may be substantial, and may require a sanction.'

The ICO then provides a list of scenarios that are more likely to lead to the imposition of a penalty:

- a number of individuals have been affected;
- there has been a degree of damage or harm (which may include distress and/or embarrassment);
- sensitive personal data has been involved;
- there has been a failure to comply with an information notice, an assessment notice or an enforcement notice
- there has been a repeated breach of obligations or a failure to rectify a previously identified problem or follow previous recommendations.;
- wilful action (including inaction) is a feature of the case;
- there has been a failure to apply reasonable measures (including relating to privacy by design) to mitigate any breach (or the possibility of it); and
- there has been a failure to implement the accountability provisions of the GDPR.

Finally the ICO highlights the approach to be taken when determining the amount of any penalty:

Step 1. An 'initial element' removing any financial gain from the breach.

Step 2. Adding in an element to censure the breach based on its scale and severity, taking into account the considerations identified at section 155(2)-(4) of the DPA.

Step 3. Adding in an element to reflect any aggravating factors.

Step 4. Adding in an amount for deterrent effect to others.

Step 5. Reducing the amount (save that in the initial element) to reflect any mitigating factors, including ability to pay (financial hardship).

The ICO concludes that the amount will generally be higher in the following cases:

- vulnerable individuals or critical national infrastructure are affected;
- there has been deliberate action for financial or personal gain;
- advice, guidance, recommendations or warnings (including those from a data protection officer or the ICO) have been ignored or not acted upon;
- there has been a high degree of intrusion into the privacy of a data subject;
- there has been a failure to cooperate with an ICO investigation or enforcement notice; and
- there is a pattern of poor regulatory history by the target of the investigation.

13.5 European Enforcement Regime

Finally, the GDPR sets out various provisions relating to enforcement at a European level and I briefly summarise these below

13.5.1 European Data Protection Board (EDPB)[51]

The EDPB is comprised of the heads of each of the national supervisory authorities as well as the European Data Protection Supervisor. Day to day enforcement action remains the responsibility of each national supervisory authority but the EDPB does a have a role to play in ensuring consistency of approach across member states by monitoring compliance with the GDPR.[52]

13.5.2 Cross Border Processing

This is defined in the GDPR as:[53]

- processing of personal data which takes place in the context of the activities of establishments in more than one Member State of a controller or processor in the Union where the controller or processor is established in more than one Member State; or
- processing of personal data which takes place in the context of the activities of a single establishment of a controller or processor in the Union but which substantially affects or is likely to substantially affect data subjects in more than one Member State.

Where an infringement arises from cross border processing the GDPR sets out a procedure for identifying a lead supervisory authority which

51 Article 68

52 Article 70

53 Article 4(23)

shall direct enforcement action as appropriate in cooperation with other interested supervisory authorities.[54]

The ICO gives the following example:[55]

A fashion retailer:

- *has a single office in London which handles all its customer data; and*
- *it sells via its website to the UK, France and Italy.*

The fashion retailer is cross-border processing in the UK, France and Italy, to the extent the London office's processing of the customer data substantially affects data subjects in France and Italy.

13.5.3 Lead supervisory authority

This is defined as:

'the supervisory authority of the main establishment or of the single establishment of the controller or processor shall be competent to act as lead supervisory authority for the cross-border processing carried out by that controller or processor in accordance with the procedure provided in Article 60.'[56]

The ICO gives the following examples:

Examples

If there is a data security breach of the fashion retailer relating to UK, French and Italian customers, the ICO would investigate and bring enforcement action, such as a fine.

---

54 Article 60

55 https://ico.org.uk/media/for-organisations/data-protection-and-brexit/data-protection-if-theres-no-brexit-deal-1-0.pdf

56 Article 56(1)

The French and Italian supervisory authorities would provide input to the ICO investigation and enforcement action, but ***they would not be able to carry out their own investigation or take independent enforcement action.*** *This means the fashion retailer would receive only a single fine but it would reflect the impact of the breach on individuals in the UK, France and Italy. This is a key benefit of the One-Stop-Shop.*

If a French citizen wants to complain about the fashion retailer regarding a failure to respond to a subject access request, the French citizen may put their complaint to the French supervisory authority. The French authority will contact the ICO, and the ICO may choose to investigate the complaint itself or agree to the French authority investigating.

13.5.4 Impact of Brexit

The impact of a no deal Brexit on these procedures and processes in discussed in more detail in chapter 15.

13.6 Enforcement Examples

At the time of writing there are relatively few examples of enforcement action having been taken for breaches of the GDPR. I set out below a summary of some of the action taken to date.

13.6.1 EEA Countries

Country	Infringement	Amount
Greece	Consent wrongly obtained as a lawful basis for processing employee personal data. Regulator ruled that consent was inappropriate given the imbalance in the relationship between the employer and the employees.	150,000 €

Romania	Video surveillance system had been in operation since 2016 without any information being provided to the data subjects affected.	2,500 €
Sweden	Facial recognition cameras used in a school classroom to record attendance. Consent relied on as lawful basis. Regulator ruled that consent was inappropriate given the imbalance in the relationship between the school and parents. Furthermore, less intrusive alternatives could have been used.	19,000 €
Poland	Personal data was obtained indirectly by the controller in respect of 6 million people. The controller only provided privacy information to 90,000 people in respect of whom it held e-mail addresses. It failed to provide information to the rest on the basis the cost would be disproportionate. The regulator disagreed. https://edpb.europa.eu/news/national-news/2019/first-fine-imposed-president-personal-data-protection-office_et	220,000 €
France	A car insurance company held information insecurely on its website so that unauthorised access was possible without authentication	180,000 €

	The French regulator received 10,000 complaints about Google's usage of personal data. After investigation they ruled that Google were in breach of their obligations under the GDPR in the following ways: • Lack of transparency • Inadequate information • Lack of valid consent re ad personalization https://www.cnil.fr/en/cnils-restricted-committee-imposes-financial-penalty-50-million-euros-against-google-llc	50,000,000 €

13.6.2 UK Enforcement

At the time of writing, enforcement within the UK has been limited.

(i) Notices of Intent

These have been issued to two organisations and I summarise each case in turn below:

(a) British Airways

The incident began in June 2018 and was notified to the ICO by British Airways in September 2018. Hackers diverted user traffic from BA's main website to a false website and harvested information relating to approximately 500,000 customers (including log in, payment card, and travel booking details as well name and address information).

The ICO's investigation found that poor security arrangements were to blame for the breach and a notice of intent was served on BA on 8th July

2019 stating that the ICO proposed to issue a monetary penalty in the sum of £183.39 million (approximately 1.5% of BA's global turnover).

More information is available here:

https://ico.org.uk/about-the-ico/news-and-events/news-and-blogs/2019/07/statement-ico-announces-intention-to-fine-british-airways/

(b) Marriott Hotels

In this case a total of 339 million guest records relating to 30 million people resident in 31 EEA were exposed via a cyber incident. Of those affected approximately seven million lived in the UK. The vulnerability began when the systems of Starwood Hotels were compromised in 2014. Starwood were then acquired by Marriott in 2016 and the exposure was not discovered until 2018.

The ICO's investigation found that Marriott had failed to undertake sufficient due diligence when it bought Starwood and also should have taken further steps to secure its systems. The ICO issued a notice of intent on 8th July 2019 stating that it proposed to issue a monetary penalty in the sum of £99,200,396 (approximately 1% of Marriott's global turnover).

More information is available here:

https://ico.org.uk/about-the-ico/news-and-events/news-and-blogs/2019/07/intention-to-fine-marriott-international-inc-more-than-99-million-under-gdpr-for-data-breach/

In both of these case the ICO agreed in January 2020 to extend the statutory six month period for consideration by a further three months until the 31st March 2020. Watch this space!

(ii) Monetary Penalties

At the time of writing the ICO has only issued one monetary penalty to Doorstep Dispensaree Limited (DDL), a London-based pharmacy, in the sum of £275,000. DDL had failed to ensure security of special category data. In particular, approximately 500,000 documents were left in unlocked containers at the rear of its premises in Edgware which included the following information:

- names and addresses,
- dates of birth
- NHS numbers
- medical information
- prescriptions

More information is available here:

https://ico.org.uk/action-weve-taken/enforcement/doorstep-dispensaree-ltd-mpn/

13.7 Summary:

The framework for enforcement under the GDPR and the DPA 2018 is now well-established and the RAP is also a useful resource. However, what is now needed to complete the picture are a series of monetary penalty notices so that controllers and processors are better able to analyse what this means for them in practice.

13.8 Practical steps

- familiarise yourself with the enforcement regime in the GDPR and the DPA 2018
- obtain a copy of the RAP

- respond promptly to any communications received from the ICO
- seek to mitigate the effect of any breach as a matter of urgency and explain how you have done this

CHAPTER FOURTEEN
COMPENSATION

14.1 Introduction

Data subjects have always had a right to claim compensation for breaches of data protection legislation and this right is maintained and arguably enhanced by the provisions of the GDPR and the DPA 2018.

14.2 GDPR

Article 82 of the GDPR sets out the key principles as follows:

- data subjects can receive compensation from either the controller or processor when they have suffered material or non-material damage due to an infringement of the GDPR[1]

- processors will only be liable for damage where they have not complied with the rules contained in the GDPR that specifically relate to processors or where they have acted outside of, or contrary to, lawful instructions from the controller[2]

- controllers and processors will be exempt from liability if they can show that they were not in any way responsible for the event giving rise to the damage[3]

- where more than one party is responsible then they shall each be held fully responsible to compensate the data subject but shall then be able to claim back from the other party an amount corresponding to their fault[4]

---

1 Article 82(1)

2 Article 82(2)

3 Article 82(3)

4 Article 82(3)-(4)

14.3 DPA 2018

The principles set out in the GDPR are repeated to a large extent in ss168-169 of the DPA 2018. However, some clarification is provided as to the meaning of 'damage'

- in respect of compensation for contravention of the GDPR 'non-material damage' includes distress[5]
- in respect of compensation for contravention of other data protection legislation 'damage' is defined as including financial loss and damage not involving financial loss, such as distress[6]

14.4 Recent Case Law

There are two recent cases that provide some further insight into these matters. It is important to note that both of them apply to the law as set out in the DPA 1998 (principally s13) but they still provide useful guidance as to the approach that the court is likely to take in future when considering claims for compensation arising from breaches of the provisions of either the GDPR or the DPA 2018.

Various Claimants v Wm Morrisons Supermarkets PLC

Facts:

In this case a claim was brought by 5,518 employees of Morrisons' supermarkets alleging that their employer was either directly or vicariously liable for infringements of the DPA 1998 arising out of the criminal actions of Andrew Skelton, a Senior IT Auditor employed by Morrisons.

In the course of his employment Mr. Skelton had obtained the personal data of more than 100,000 employees and had uploaded this infor-

5 s168(1)

6 s169(5)

mation onto a file sharing website. He was promptly caught and the information was removed but the employees alleged that by allowing this to happen Morrisons were in breach of their statutory duty under s4(4) of the DPA 1998, namely:

> *'... it shall be the duty of a data controller to comply with the data protection principles in relation to all personal data with respect to which he is the data controller'*

High Court Decision [2017] EWHC 3113 (QB) Langstaff J

(i) Primary Liability

The principal allegation was that Morrisons were in breach of their security obligations under principle 7 of the DPA 1998. The court carried out a detailed review of Morrisons' actions in this regards and made the following findings:

- it was reasonable to allow Mr Skelton access and to trust him with the data despite his previous (minor) disciplinary warning on an unrelated matter

- the use of the USB by Mr Skelton was necessary for his required role as the email server limit meant he could not pass the data to the external auditor by email

- Morrisons' monitoring of Mr Skelton's (and all employees) internet activities was adequate

- Morrisons had, however, failed in one respect. It should have ensured Mr Skelton had deleted the employee data after a reasonable period after his purpose for having access to it had passed. The court found however, that this failing was not causative of the data breach or any connected third-party loss in any event as it would not have prevented the criminal misuse of the data by Mr Skelton.

In summary, the court held that Morrisons was not primarily liable under the DPA 1998, for breach of confidence or misuse of private information.

(ii) Vicarious Liability

Morrisons argued that they were not vicariously liable because:

- the act of posting the data to the web was temporally and physically disengaged from the time when the data was copied by Skelton, and was placed on the web at a time when Skelton was not at work.
- at the time he did so, Morrisons were not data controllers within the meaning of the DPA 1998 in respect of the payroll data disclosed. They were not "on the field".
- all the aspects of the tort had to be within the course of employment and here they were not.
- the act was motivated by a grudge, and previous case law showed that this was a significant factor to take into account.
- vicarious liability should be applied strictly and should not easily be extendable: to hold Morrisons liable here would be such an extension and was impermissible.
- finding in favour of Morrisons would amount to the court facilitating a criminal's objective in harming his employer, which the court should set its face against.

These arguments were rejected by the court and Langstaff J ruled that Morrisons were vicariously liable for the following reasons:

- the principle of vicarious liability was potentially applicable where an employee committed a breach of statutory duty, even where such duty rested on the employee alone, unless the specific statute expressly or impliedly indicated otherwise.

- the criminal behaviour was at the outer reaches of vicarious liability and each case would turn on its facts and required a detailed review of the employee's specific acts.

- in reaching its conclusion the court needed to consider the key factual issues carefully and grapple with the policy issue of who should ultimately bear related losses the (likely insured) employer who put the employee in the relevant position or the innocent claimant who would often otherwise need to recover from an impecunious employee defendant.

- Mr Skelton had acted in the course of his employment as there was an unbroken thread between his employment and the data breach and (importantly) Morrisons had specifically entrusted him with the data in issue for the purpose of disclosure to an external auditor.

- although some of Mr Skelton's nefarious activities had been conducted at home on his own computer, this did not sufficiently disconnect them from his employment.

However, the judge did make the following observation in respect of his decision:

> *'The point which most troubled me in reaching these conclusions was the submission that the wrongful acts of Skelton were deliberately aimed at the party whom the claimants seek to hold responsible, such that to reach the conclusion I may have seem to render the court an accessory in furthering his criminal aims' para 198*

Court of Appeal Decision [2018] EWCA Civ 2339 Sir Terence Etherton MR

The Court of Appeal upheld the decision of the High Court and made the following points:

- drawing on the case of Mohamud v Wm Morrisons Supermarkets plc [2016] AC 667 the Master of the Rolls noted that Lord Toulson in that case had stated that *'the risk of an employee misusing his position is one of life's unavoidable facts' Para 40*

- in terms of the 'field of activities' the breach arose during the operation of tasks that had been entrusted to the employee

- therefore there was a 'sufficient connection' between the position in which Mr. Skelton was employed and his wrongful conduct and this meant that the employer should be held vicariously liable

- the criminal motivation behind Mr. Skelton's behaviour was irrelevant

- the ability of Morrisons to insure against any loss was relevant as they were better placed to bear the loss than the uninsured employees

Summary:

At the time of writing, this case has now been heard by the Supreme Court and a decision is awaited. Of course the other interesting issue that has not yet been considered by any court is the appropriate amount of compensation to be awarded in such cases. It remains to be seen what, if anything, will be awarded in respect of this.

If the previous case did not address the issue of amount of compensation some guidance is available from the case of:

Lloyd v Google

Facts:

Richard Lloyd, a former executive director of Which?, sought to instigate a claim on behalf of 4.4 million Apple i-phone users. He alleged that Google secretly tracked some of their internet activity and obtained browser generated information ('BGI'), for commercial purposes, between 9th August 2011 and 15th February 2012, without their consent.

In particular, he alleged that Google were in breach of their statutory duty under section 4(4) of the DPA 1998 and had failed to comply with the first, second and seventh data protection principles set out in Part I of Schedule 1 to the DPA 1998. Consequently, Mr. Lloyd sought, on behalf of the represented class, damages under section 13 of the DPA 1998 for infringement of their data protection rights, commission of the wrong, and loss of control over their data protection rights and suggested that each person should be compensated in the sum of £750.00. The claim was backed by a litigation funder to the tune of 15 million pounds.

The Court of Appeal had previously ruled in the case of Vidal-Hall v Google [2015] EWCA Civ 311 on the basis of analogous underlying facts, but with one crucial difference. In that case, the individual claimants claimed damages for distress as a result of Google's breaches of the DPA. In this case, Mr Lloyd claimed a uniform amount by way of damages on behalf of each person within the defined class without seeking to allege or prove any distinctive facts affecting any of them, save that they did not consent to the abstraction of their data.

In order to bring such a class action it was necessary for the English courts to grant permission to serve the proceedings outside the jurisdiction on Google in the USA. This request was contested and in reaching his decision it was necessary for Warby J to review the following legislation.

Relevant Legislation

Article 23 of the Data Protection Directive 1995

1. Member States shall provide that any person who has suffered damage as a result of an unlawful processing operation or of any act incompatible with the national provisions adopted pursuant to this Directive is entitled to receive compensation from the controller for the damage suffered.

Section 13 of the Data Protection Act 1998

(1) An individual who suffers damage by reason of any contravention by a data controller of any of the requirements of this Act is entitled to compensation from the data controller for that damage.

(2) An individual who suffers distress by reason of any contravention by a data controller of any of the requirements of this Act is entitled to compensation from the data controller for that distress if—

(a) the individual also suffers damage by reason of the contravention, or

(b) the contravention relates to the processing of personal data for the special purposes.

CPR Part 19.6

(1) Where more than one person has the same interest in a claim –

(a) the claim may be begun; or

(b) the court may order that the claim be continued,

by or against one or more of the persons who have the same interest as representatives of any other persons who have that interest.

(2) The court may direct that a person may not act as a representative.

(3) Any party may apply to the court for an order under paragraph (2).

(4) Unless the court otherwise directs any judgment or order given in a claim in which a party is acting as a representative under this rule –

(a) is binding on all persons represented in the claim; but

(b) may only be enforced by or against a person who is not a party to the claim with the permission of the court

High Court Decision [2018] EWHC 2599 (QB) Warby J

Warby J began by noting that England was clearly the most appropriate place for the claim to be tried as the representative class was restricted to those resident in England and Wales.

Of greater importance, however, was the open question of whether the represented class in this case could show a good arguable case that the conduct complained of did cause or involve anything that was properly characterised as "damage", for which compensation was recoverable under the DPA 1998.

This led him to consider two key questions:

(i) Did the claim disclose any reasonable basis for seeking compensation under the DPA 1998?

He ruled that there was no reasonable basis for the following reasons:

- as a matter of statutory construction, the wording of both section 13(1) and article 23 required a causal link between the infringement and the damage claimed

- this was a logical conclusion given that some contraventions of the DPA 1998 would not result in damage and other available remedies included rectification, blocking, and erasure of inaccurate data were available

- therefore, the conclusion in *Vidal-Hall* did not apply where "the breach of duty had caused neither material loss nor emotional harm, and had had no other consequences for the data subject"

(ii) **Was there was a real prospect that the court would permit the claim to continue as a representative action under CPR Part 19.6?**

- he ruled that the fundamental "non-bendable" threshold point was that the class must all have the same interest in the claim, on the basis of facts ascertained or assumed at the relevant time. On these facts this was not the case.

- the representative claim brought by Mr. Lloyd would only succeed if

  - "every member of the class [had] suffered the *same* damage (or their share of a readily ascertainable aggregate amount [was] clear)", and

  - different potential defences were not available in respect of claims by different members of the class.

- the amount of compensation to be awarded to each claimant would depend on the facts and neither the breach of duty nor the impact of it was uniform across the entire class membership.

- consequently, the tariff strategy adopted by Mr Lloyd reflected neither the law nor the factual reality.

(iii) **Discretion**

Notwithstanding his decision in respect of the previous two questions, Warby J also considered the provisions of CPR Part 19.6(2) under which a judge has a general discretion as to whether or not to allow a claimant to act as a representative. He made the following key observations:

- it was possible for a person to sue in a representative capacity without the authority of those they represented, provided the conditions in CPR 19.6 were met and the overriding objective was borne in mind.

However, he noted that:

- the costs, and court time required would be considerable, and the compensation that each represented individual was likely to recover would be "modest at best".

- the main beneficiaries of any award at the end of the litigation would be the funders and the lawyers by a considerable margin

- *'it was a striking feature of the case that in the five or six years since the Safari Workaround was identified and publicised none of the millions of such individuals in this jurisdiction had demonstrated any interest ... by coming forward to claim ... other than Ms Vidal-Hall, her co-claimants and Mr. Lloyd'*

Therefore, he concluded that:

- Mr. Lloyd should not *"be permitted to consume substantial resources in the pursuit of litigation on behalf of others who have little to gain from it, and have not authorised the pursuit of the claim, nor indicated any concern about the matters to be litigated".*

Summary

Warby J dismissed Mr Lloyd's application for permission to serve Google outside the jurisdiction on the basis that:

(i) none of the represented class had suffered "damage" under section 13 of the Data Protection Act 1998

(ii) the members of the class did not anyway have the "same interest" within CPR Part 19.6(1) so as to justify allowing the claim to proceed as a representative action, and

(iii) of his own initiative he would exercise his discretion under CPR Part 19.6(2) against allowing the claim to proceed.

Permission to appeal was granted by Lewison LJ on 21st January 2019, on the grounds of the novelty of the claim and the procedure for dealing with it, together with the public interest in data breaches, the potential number of persons affected and the potential sums of money involved

Court of Appeal Decision [2019] EWCA Civ 1599

The leading judgment was given by Sir Geoffrey Vos who considered the following three questions:

Issue 1: Was the judge right to hold that a claimant could not recover uniform per capita damages for infringement of their data protection rights under section 13 without proving pecuniary loss or distress?

The judge began by noting that the parties agreed that if it was decided that the infringement of the Directive and the DPA 1998 was considered trivial or de minimis then the court should refuse to award 'loss of control' damages.

He then proceeded to consider the correct approach to interpretation of the relevant provisions of article 23 of the Directive and s13(2) of the DPA 1998 and made the following observations:

- the Court of Appeal said in *Vidal-Hall* at [72]: "[i]t is a well-established principle of EU law that legal terms have an autonomous meaning which will not necessarily accord with their interpretation in domestic law"

- the phrase "[a]n individual who suffers damage by reason of any contravention" was entitled to compensation, found in section 13 was implementing the provision of article 23 to the effect that "any person who has suffered damage as a result of an unlawful processing operation ... is entitled to receive compensation".

- accordingly, the language of both provisions was to be construed as a matter of EU law.

Against this background, he noted that these claims should be characterised as the class members' loss of control or loss of autonomy over their personal data and proceeded to consider whether control over data was an asset that had value. His key findings were as follows:

- English law did not technically regard data as property but it was clearly protected under EU law

- it was clear that a person's BGI had economic value as it could be sold.

- for example, EU citizens typically obtained free wi-fi at an airport in exchange for providing their personal data, otherwise they would have to pay for it

- in this case Google was able to sell BGI collected from numerous individuals to advertisers who wished to target them with their advertising.

- consequently such data, and consent to its use, had an economic value

- a person's control over data or BGI did have a value and therefore loss of that control also had a value

He concluded that, to an extent, these points were sufficient to answer the question of whether, in theory, a person could recover compensation under section 13 and article 23. However, he felt it was also necessary to consider whether this kind of loss of control over data could properly be considered damage in the legal sense in which the term "damage" was used in article 23 and section 13.

He considered several previous cases and then examined the provisions of the GDPR and the DPA 2018 noting that:

- he could not interpret a Directive by reference to the Regulation that had replaced it but it was helpful to consider how the GDPR dealt with damage.

- recital 85 to the GDPR stated that:

  "A personal data breach may, if not addressed in an appropriate and timely manner, result in physical, material or non-material damage to natural persons such as ***loss of control over their personal data*** *or limitation of their rights, discrimination, identity theft or fraud, financial loss, unauthorised reversal of pseudonymisation, damage to reputation, loss of confidentiality of personal data protected by professional secrecy or any other significant economic or social disadvantage to the natural person concerned".*

- recital 85 was noteworthy because "loss of control" over personal data was given as an example of the kind of "physical, material or non-material damage" that might be caused to natural persons as a result of a data breach.

- such a conclusion was in accordance with his earlier conclusion on the EU law position on the availability of damages for non-trivial data processing breaches in respect of loss of control.

- finally, s169(5) of the Data Protection Act 2018 provided a non-exclusive definition of "damage" that included financial loss and damage not involving financial loss, such as distress.

His conclusion was that:

> *'For the reasons, I have given, I would conclude that damages are in principle capable of being awarded for loss of control of data under article 23 and section 13, even if there is no pecuniary loss and no distress. The words in section 13 "[an] individual who suffers damage by reason of [a breach] is entitled to compensation" justify such an interpretation, when read in the context of the Directive... Only by construing the legislation in this way can individuals be provided with an effective remedy for the infringement of such rights.' Para 70*

Issue 2: Was the judge right to hold that the members of the class did not have the same interest under CPR Part 19.6(1) and were not identifiable?

(i) Same Interest

It is a well-established principle that the persons represented in a claim brought under CPR Part 19.6 must have the "same interest" in the claim. When considering the High Court's ruling in respect of this matter the judge took the view that Warby J had applied too stringent a test of "same interest", largely because of his views on the meaning of 'damage'.

The Court of Appeal took a different view for the following reasons:

- the claimants that Mr Lloyd sought to represent all had their BGI – something of value - taken by Google without their consent in the same circumstances during the same period, and were not seeking to rely on any personal circumstances affecting any individual claimant

- furthermore, the represented class were all victims of the same alleged wrong, and had all sustained the same loss, namely loss of control over their BGI.

- once the claim was understood in this way it was impossible to imagine that Google could raise any defence to one represented claimant that did not apply to all others.

- the wrong was the same, and the loss claimed was the same

- the represented parties did have the same interest

(ii) Identifiable Class

Warby J rejected the class definition suggested by Mr. Lloyd and the two suggested methods by which the class could be made certain before the trial:

(a) by disclosure from Google, and

(b) by self-certification of class members

The first of these approaches was rejected by Warby J as being "Micawberite", and the latter as being open both to honest error and abuse. He concluded that the class was not identifiable.

The Court of Appeal was of the view that the only applicable test was that

> *'it must be possible to say of any particular person whether or not they qualify for membership of the represented class of persons by virtue of having" the same interest as Mr Lloyd "[a]t all stages of the proceedings, and not just at the date of judgment.'*

On the facts of this case the judge could not see how this test was not satisfied because:

- in theory every affected person, would know whether he satisfied the conditions specified by Mr. Lloyd
- Google's data would be able to identify who was, and who was not, in the class.
- both of these exercises could be undertaken at any time and any abuse would be very limited
- the ability to use the representative procedure was not dependent on the number of claimants

and therefore concluded that Warby J ought to have held that the members of the represented class had the same interest under CPR Part 19.6(1) and that they were identifiable.

Issue 3: Could the judge's exercise of discretion be vitiated?

In the High Court, Warby J stated that whatever he decided on the first two issues he would have exercised his discretion in not allowing the claim to proceed. The Court of Appeal noted that a detached observer may have felt that Warby J was heavily influenced by his conclusions on the first two issues.

Furthermore Mr. Lloyd contended before the Court of Appeal that Warby J had considered several matters that he should not have done, namely:

(a) his view that the main beneficiaries of the claim would be the funders and the lawyers

(b) the fact that the litigation would generate significant costs and that the amount recovered by each class member would be modest

(c) that none of the millions of affected individuals had come forward to complain

(d) the inability to identify the members of the class, and

(e) that the members of the class had not authorised the claim.

The Court of Appeal accepted that Warby J was justified in considering the first three factors but not the latter two factors. These factors were irrelevant to his discretion as the class was identifiable and it was well established that the members of a represented class did not have to have authorised the claim.

Consequently, the Court of Appeal was able to exercise its discretion afresh and the judge concluded that the claim should proceed for the following reasons:

- a representative action was the only way that these claims could be pursued

- the claim could not be characterised as 'officious litigation' because the claim sought to call Google to account for its allegedly wholesale and deliberate misuse of personal data without consent, undertaken with a view to commercial profit.

- it was not disproportionate to pursue such litigation in circumstances where, as was common ground, there was no other remedy.

- the case might be costly and might use valuable court resources, but it would ensure that there was a civil compensatory remedy for what appeared, at first sight, to be clear, repeated and widespread breaches of Google's data processing obligations

Conclusion – paras 88-90

Sir Geoffrey Vos concluded that:

> *'For the reasons I have tried to give as shortly as possible, I take the view that the judge ought to have held: (a) that a claimant can recover damages for loss of control of their data under section 13 of DPA, without proving pecuniary loss or distress, and (b) that the members of the class that Mr Lloyd seeks to represent did have the same interest under CPR Part 19.6(1) and were identifiable.*
>
> *The judge exercised his discretion as to whether the action should proceed as a representative action on the wrong basis and this court can exercise it afresh. If the other members of the court agree, I would exercise our discretion so as to allow the action to proceed.*
>
> *I would, therefore, allow the appeal, and make an order granting Mr Lloyd permission to serve the proceedings on Google outside the jurisdiction of the court.'*

This case is highly likely to be the subject of an appeal. Given the jurisdictional complexities that first need to be resolved it is likely to be sometime before we have a definitive answer from the courts in terms of the meaning of 'damage' and also the amount to be awarded.

14.5 Other cases

At the time of writing there are a number of other class actions that are in the process of coming before the courts.

14.5.1 British Airways

This case relates to the BA security breach referred to earlier and further information about this can be obtained by visiting the website set up by the solicitors pursuing this action:

https://www.badatabreach.com/

14.5.2 Equifax

Another topical case which has now made its first appearance before the courts relates to a security breach by Equifax which led to them receiving a monetary penalty in the sum of £500,000 in September 2018. The security breach affected approximately 15 million UK residents

Proceedings were commenced in October 2019 by Richard Atkinson as a representative claimant. Atkinson has argued that Equifax should pay up to £100 million in compensation. Equifax are currently seeking to dispute this claim using similar arguments raised in the Lloyd v Google case.

14.6 Summary

There is no doubt that the number of compensation claims arising out of breaches of the GDPR and DPA 2018 will continue to increase over the next few years. However, the precise impact of this remains unknown and we await further decisions from the courts as to the full extent of the meaning of 'damage' and also the level of compensation that will be awarded.

14.7 Practical steps

- carry out regular training on the obligations of employees under the GDPR and the DPA 2018
- establish clear guidance for all employees in terms of their handling of personal data
- put in place effective mechanisms for supervising employee usage of personal data
- use risk assessments to identify particular areas of vulnerability
- investigate the possibility of insurance

CHAPTER FIFTEEN
BREXIT

15.1 Introduction

The United Kingdom left the European Union on 31st January 2020. At the time of writing, the UK is now in an 11-month transition period until 31st December 2020 (unless extended) during which the trading relationship will remain the same and the UK will continue to follow EU rules. However, there remains a great deal of uncertainty about what will happen at the end of this period with three possibilities being discussed:

- a detailed agreement will be concluded by this date
- the transition period will be extended
- a no-deal Brexit will occur

The working assumption of this chapter is that there remains a significant risk of a no-deal Brexit on 31st December 2020 and therefore I will draw on the available guidance and summarise what the effect of such an outcome will be and how to prepare for it.

15.2 Sources of information

There are two main sources of information that are worth considering:

15.2.1 ICO's Guidance

The ICO has a number of resources which can be accessed at the following place:

https://ico.org.uk/for-organisations/data-protection-and-brexit/

There are three documents which are of particular interest to controllers and processors

(i) ICO's main guide to a no-deal Brexit

This is the most detailed document and covers all of the key issues in depth. Last updated in September 2019, it can be accessed directly here:

https://ico.org.uk/media/for-organisations/data-protection-and-brexit/data-protection-if-theres-no-brexit-deal-1-0.pdf

(ii) ICO's guide for small businesses

As the name suggests this is a much more succinct document which sets out a series of practical steps that should be taken depending on the precise circumstances of the small business. It can be accessed here:

https://ico.org.uk/for-organisations/data-protection-and-brexit/data-protection-and-brexit-for-small-organisations/

(iii) ICO's interactive tool re data flows

This document is an interactive tool that allows organisations to consider the best way to facilitate data flows in the event of a no-deal Brexit and also contains a tool for constructing an agreement based on the standard contractual clauses. It is available here

https://ico.org.uk/for-organisations/data-protection-and-brexit/keep-data-flowing-from-the-eea-to-the-uk-interactive-tool/

15.2.2 EDPB's Guidance

The EDPB has produced a document relating to data flows in the event of a no-deal Brexit which was last updated on the 4th October 2019. It can be accessed here:

https://edpb.europa.eu/sites/edpb/files/files/file1/edpb-2019-02-12-infonote-nodeal-brexit-october_en.pdf

15.3 Ongoing application of the GDPR

The GDPR is an EU Regulation that also applies to the EEA states. On leaving the EU the UK will no longer be an EU member state and therefore the GDPR will no longer be law within the UK. The UK government intends to write the GDPR into UK law with some minor amendments and this will be known as the UK GDPR which will apply alongside an amended DPA 2018. The GDPR will continue to apply to all EEA states and will be referred to in UK law as the EU GDPR.

The net effect of this is that the main principles, obligations and rights will continue as before but there will be an impact in three key areas which are discussed below

15.4 Key changes

There are three main issues that UK based controllers and processors need to be aware of:

- international data transfers
- appointment of EU representatives
- EU regulatory oversight of cross border processing

15.4.1 International data transfers

Please note that this section should be read in conjunction with the existing rules described in more detail in chapter 11 which will not be repeated in detail here.

In the event of a no-deal Brexit, the ICO states that UK-based organisations that are subject to the GDPR and transfer personal data to or from other countries (including European countries) will need to comply with two sets of rules:

- UK rules governing transfers of data outside of the UK
- EU rules on transfers from countries outside the UK (including the EU) into the UK

(i) UK rules governing transfers of data outside of the UK

The ICO states that organisations will be making a restricted transfer outwards from the UK if:

- the UK GDPR applies to the processing of the personal data that are being transferred;
- the UK GDPR does not apply to the importer of the data, usually because they are located in a country outside the UK (which may be in the EU, the EEA or elsewhere); and
- the sender of the personal data, and the receiver of the data are separate organisations (even if they are both companies in the same group).

For example:

> *A UK company passes employee information to a centralised group human resources service provided by its parent company in Germany. After the UK exits the EU, this will be a restricted transfer under the UK GDPR.*

(a) Transfers to the EEA

The UK government has stated that such restricted transfers to the EEA can continue in the same way as present.

(b) Transfers to countries benefitting from an adequacy decision

The UK government intends to recognize all adequacy decisions of the European Commission that have been made prior to exit date and therefore these transfers will continue as before

(c) Transfers to the USA under EU-US Privacy Shield

The UK government's intention is that this will continue to apply in a modified format. In the event of a no-deal Brexit, UK organisations will be able to transfer data to US based organisations that are registered with the EU-US Privacy Shield as long as the US entity updates its public commitment statement so as to state expressly that it applies to transfers from the UK.

(d) Standard Contractual Clauses

The UK government intends to recognize the European Commission's standard contractual clauses as providing an appropriate safeguard and the ICO has created template contracts that can be used.

(e) Binding Corporate Rules (BCRs)

The UK government has agreed to recognize BCRs authorised under EU procedures prior to the exit date.

(f) Exceptions

The list of exceptions set out in the GDPR will continue to apply post exit date and therefore these can be relied upon as appropriate

In summary, restricted transfers outwards from the UK will continue to operate in almost exactly the same away as at present even in the event of a no-deal Brexit.

(ii) EU rules on transfers from countries outside the UK (including the EU) into the UK

This section applies to all UK organisations receiving personal data from the EEA.

On the exit date, EEA based senders of personal data to a UK based organisation will have to continue to comply with the EU GDPR and the UK will be treated as a third state at that point. Furthermore, in the event of a no-deal Brexit the UK will not be the beneficiary of an adequacy decision.

Consequently, under the EU GDPR an EEA controller or processor will only be able to make a restricted transfer to a UK based organization if any of the following apply:

(a) Standard contractual clauses

If the parties enter into an agreement containing the standard contractual clauses then a restricted transfer to the UK can be made.

(b) Binding corporate rules

If the parties have put in place BCRS covering a UK based entity, and this has been approved under EU procedures before exit date, then restricted transfers to the UK will be permitted to continue

(c) Exceptions

The list of exceptions set out in the EU GDPR will continue to apply post exit date and therefore these can be relied upon as appropriate

(d) EDPB Guidance

As mentioned above the EDPB has produced an information note and this suggests the following five steps to be taken by organisations transferring data to the UK in the event of a no-deal Brexit:

Step 1 Identify what processing activities will imply a personal data transfer to the UK

Step 2 Determine the appropriate data transfer instrument for your situation

Step 3 Implement the chosen data transfer instrument to be ready for the exit date

Step 4 Indicate in your internal documentation that transfers will be made to the UK

Step 5 Update your privacy notice accordingly to inform individuals

In summary, restricted transfers from the EEA to the UK will operate in a more limited fashion until such time as the UK is the beneficiary of an adequacy decision. In the meantime. EEA based controllers and processors making regular restricted transfers to UK based organisations should look to put in place agreements containing the standard contractual clauses.

15.4.2 Appointment of Representatives

(i) UK based controllers or processors

UK based controllers or processors that do not have a branch, office or other establishment in any other EU or EEA state but either:

- offer goods or services to individuals in the EEA; or
- monitor the behaviour of individuals in the EEA.

will be required to continue to comply with the EU GDPR post Brexit.

Furthermore, the EU GDPR requires such UK based entities carrying out such activities to appoint a representative in the EEA based in one of the member states where some of the individuals whose data are being processed are located.

The key features of this appointment are as follows:

- the representative needs to be authorised in writing to act on the UK based entity's behalf in respect of EU GDPR compliance and to deal with regulators and data subjects as appropriate

- the representative may be an individual, company or other organization based within the EEA that is capable of representing the UK based entity's interests

- details of the representative must be given to all EEA based individuals whose personal data are being processed by the UK based entity – for example in a privacy statement

- this information must be easily accessible to supervisory authorities – for example on a website

- the appointment of the representative needs to be in writing and set out the terms of the relationship

- appointment of a representative does not affect the responsibility or liability of the UK based entity under the EU GDPR

(ii) **EEA based controllers or processors**

Post Brexit, the UK government intends to place a similar requirement to appoint a UK based representative on EU based controllers or processors that do not have a branch, office or other establishment in any other EU or EEA state but either:

- offer goods or services to individuals in the UK; or
- monitor the behaviour of individuals in the EEA.

15.4.3 EU regulatory oversight of cross border processing

UK based controllers and processors who are carrying out cross border processing will experience changes in respect of which data protection authorities they will be dealing with.

The ICO highlights four possible scenarios:

(a) **Scenario 1**

Before exit date:

You are cross-border processing in relation to two establishments: one in the UK and one in another EU or EEA state.

Your processing is not likely to substantially affect individuals in any other EU or EEA state.

After exit date:

You will no longer be cross-border processing. You will no longer be processing personal data in the context of the activities of establishments in two or more EU or EEA states.

The One-Stop-Shop and lead authority arrangements will no longer apply to your processing. You will have to deal with both the ICO and the supervisory authority in the other EU or EEA state where you are established

(b) **Scenario 2**

Before exit date:

You are cross-border processing for two establishments: one in the UK and one in another EU or EEA state.

Your processing in the context of the activities of both the UK and EEA establishment **is likely** to substantially affect individuals in other EU or EEA states.

After exit date:

Processing in the context of your UK establishment is no longer cross-border processing.

Processing in the context of your EEA establishment, which substantially affects data subjects in other EU or EEA states, will continue to be cross-border processing. Its local supervisory authority will be the lead supervisory authority in the EEA in respect of that cross-border processing.

You will have to deal with both the ICO and the EEA lead supervisory authority

(c) **Scenario 3**

Before exit date:

You are cross-border processing in relation to three or more establishments: one in the UK and two or more in other EU or EEA states.

Your processing may or may not substantially affect individuals in any other EU or EEA state.

After exit date:

The UK establishment is no longer cross-border processing.

Your EU or EEA establishments will still be cross-border processing. You will have to deal with both the ICO and your EEA lead supervisory authority. You should review the EDPB's Guidance to work out which is your lead authority.

(d) Scenario 4

Before exit date:

You are cross-border processing with an establishment only in the UK, and no establishment in any other EU or EEA state.

Your processing **is likely** to substantially affect individuals in one or more other EU or EEA state.

After exit date:

You will not be carrying out cross-border processing under the EU GDPR as you have no office, branch or other establishment in the EEA.

You may still need to comply with the EU GDPR to the extent that your processing relates to the offering of goods or services to, or the monitoring of the behaviour of, individuals in the EEA.

You may have to deal with the ICO and the supervisory authorities in all EU and EEA states where individuals are located if you process their personal data in connection with those activities.

In summary, there are a number of possible permutations that may arise depending on the nature of the processing being carried out. What is certain is that the current simplicity of the one stop shop will no longer apply to UK based controllers and processors in the event of a no deal Brexit.

15.5 Summary

The impact of a no deal Brexit in the field of data protection is rather mixed. On the one hand the basic principles, obligations and rights will continue under the UK GDPR with minimal change. On the other hand, a no deal Brexit will lead to added bureaucracy, changes to arrangements for international transfers and a more complex enforcement regime. Controllers and processors need to take steps now to ensure as smooth a transition as possible to whatever the new arrangements turn out to be.

15.6 Practical steps

International transfers

- analyse existing data flows between the UK and the EEA and vice versa
- consider how you will ensure that transfers from the EEA to the UK can continue in the event of a no deal Brexit
- use the ICO's interactive tool to prepare an agreement using standard contractual clauses
- if sending data outwards from the UK you should update your documentation to reflect this
- if relying on the EU-US Privacy Shield then ensure that the US based entity has updated their commitment to privacy statement

Appointment of representatives

- consider whether you need to appoint an EEA based representative
- if necessary, decide the location of your EEA based representative
- enter into a contract setting out your respective responsibilities

- consider how you will provide information about your representative to the data subjects and make it available to supervisory authorities

Cross border processing

- review whether you are carrying out any cross border processing
- if you are, consider who your lead supervisory authority is
- if you intend to continue cross border processing post exit date, and the ICO is your lead supervisory authority, consider who will become your lead supervisory authority post exit

PART B

PRACTICAL EXAMPLES

General Overview

Having considered the content of the previous chapters, controllers and processors may be forgiven for feeling a little overwhelmed. The aim of this part of the book is to set out a series of practical examples that will assist organisations seeking to implement some of the more complicated aspects of the GDPR. The examples given are illustrative only and set out a high-level response to the scenarios discussed in each case. In practice, more detail would usually be required.

The topics that will be covered are as follows:

1. Data protection impact assessment
2. Legitimate interests assessment
3. Privacy statement
4. Security breach reporting

In each case I will begin by outlining a particular scenario and will then suggest an appropriate response.

EXAMPLE ONE
DATA PROTECTION IMPACT ASSESSMENT

In order to illustrate this concept, I set out below a worked example of a data protection impact assessment carried out in respect of a proposed use of employee data. The assessment is divided into the relevant sections and in each part I set out the key requirements and questions together with my suggested high level responses. Please note that this issue is discussed in more detail in chapter 3 of this book and that there is a sample DPIA template produced by the ICO which is available at appendix 4.

A large corporation decides that it wishes to require all warehouse operatives (2,500 in total located at 10 different warehouses in the UK and overseas) to wear a 'smart bracelet' in order to monitor their behaviour during the time that they are in the warehouse.

The device can be used to monitor an employee's presence during work hours, when they visit the toilet or take a break, the distance that they travel and the speed at which they travel within the warehouse.

Employees who do not meet certain targets, based on the information gathered by the smart bracelet, will be subject to disciplinary action

Step 1 – Identify the need

This first stage requires a controller to analyse whether the proposed processing is caught by any of the following:

- EDPB's 'high risk' list
- Three specific scenarios from GDPR Article 35(3)
- ICO's list

In our example I would suggest that the following matters would be relevant:

EDPB's high risk list

The most relevant factors would be:

- Evaluation or scoring.
- Automated decision-making with legal or similar significant effect.
- Systematic monitoring.
- Sensitive data or data of a highly personal nature.
- Data processed on a large scale.
- Innovative use or applying new technological or organisational solutions.

35(3) Scenarios

The most relevant of these would be:

> *a systematic and extensive evaluation of personal aspects relating to natural persons which is based on automated processing, including profiling, and on which decisions are based that produce legal effects concerning the natural person or similarly significantly affect the natural person;*

ICO List (bearing in mind the comments of the EDPB)

- New technologies
- Large-scale profiling
- Biometrics
- Tracking

In summary there is no doubt that a DPIA needs to be carried out in our example.

Step 2 – Describe the processing

The second stage requires the controller to set out four types of information as described below, with my suggested high-level responses alongside.

(i) The **nature** of the processing (what you plan to do with the data)

DPIA Requirement	**High-level response**
How you collect the data;	Data will be collected from the employee's smart bracelet
How you store the data;	Data will be stored on the device and also remotely
How you use the data;	Data collected will be used to assess the performance of individual employees
Who has access to the data;	Employees in the IT and HR departments as well as line managers will be allowed access
Who you share the data with;	Data will be shared with employees in other group companies
Whether you use any processors;	Processors will be used in terms of the collection and storage of the data

Retention periods;	Six years following termination of employment
Security measures;	Data will be encrypted and employees will only be granted limited access via password
Whether you are using any new technologies;	It is likely that the collection of data in this way will constitute a new technology, not least because an existing technology is being used for a novel purpose
Whether you are using any novel types of processing; and	As above
Which screening criteria you flagged as likely high risk.	See above at step 1

(ii) The **scope** of the processing (what the processing covers)

DPIA Requirement	**High-level response**
The nature of the personal data;	Employee movements around the warehouse during the working day
The volume and variety of the personal data;	Considerable. Each employee will be monitored throughout each working day.
The sensitivity of the personal data;	Depending on the settings the device may collect health related data

The extent and frequency of the processing;	All day, every day while the employee is at work
The duration of the processing;	Throughout the employee's employment in roles affected
The number of data subjects involved;	2,500
The geographical area covered.	UK and other locations overseas

(iii) The **context** of the processing (the wider picture, including internal and external factors which might affect expectations or impact)

DPIA Requirement	High-level response
The source of the data;	The device worn by employees
The nature of your relationship with the individuals;	Employer / employee
The extent to which individuals have control over their data;	They would be able to request a printout of their data
The extent to which individuals are likely to expect the processing;	They will be informed of the processing before it begins
Whether they include children or other vulnerable people;	Not included
Any previous experience of this type of processing;	None

Any relevant advances in technology or security;	Increased accuracy of these devices means that they are now suitable for use in this way.
Any current issues of public concern;	Increasing use of automated decision making and profiling
In due course, whether you comply with any GDPR codes of conduct (once any have been approved under Article 40) or GDPR certification schemes.	N/A
Whether you have considered and complied with relevant codes of practice.	N/A

(iv) The **purpose** of the processing (the reason why you want to process the personal data)

DPIA Requirement	**High-level response**
Your legitimate interests, where relevant;	Management of employees
The intended outcome for individuals;	Better performance management
The expected benefits for you or for society as a whole.	More efficient workplace

Step 3 – Consider consultation

Having completed step 2, the next step requires controllers to consider consulting interested parties. In this example the following parties would, potentially, need to be consulted:

- Data processors (organisations providing the technology)
- Internal stakeholders (IT and HR)
- Existing contacts (employees – preferably involving trade unions as appropriate)

The employees in particular may raise a series of concerns and therefore if the controller wishes to disregard these it will need to set out its reasons and also consider carefully how any risks can be reduced.

Step 4 – Necessity and proportionality

Post consultation, the controller needs to consider whether the proposed processing is necessary and proportionate. I set out the relevant factors below together with my high-level responses.

DPIA Requirement	High-level response
Your lawful basis for the processing;	Legitimate interests of the controller
How you will prevent function creep;	Clearly define what data will be collected; disable certain functionality on the device to limit what will actually be collected
How you intend to ensure data quality;	Carry out a series of tests before the technology is implemented

How you intend to ensure data minimisation;	See above re function creep Ensure that the device can be de-activated during rest breaks
How you intend to provide privacy information to individuals;	In the employee handbook; specific communication made to all employees by e-mail; notices throughout the premises
How you implement and support individuals rights;	Advice re their ability to access and review their data collected by the device
Measures to ensure your processors comply;	Data processing agreement will be put in place
Safeguards for international transfers.	A combination of standard contractual clauses and EU/US Privacy Shield will be relied upon

In the circumstances, I think it is arguable that the proposed processing is necessary and proportionate but this then requires the controller to identify and assess the risks associated with the proposed processing.

Step 5 – Identification and assessment of risk

The ICO's Guidance sets out a series of risk factors to be considered and I will now apply each of them to our example and assess the likely risk using the ICO's suggested matrix:

Describe the source of risk and nature of potential impact on individuals. Include associated compliance and corporate risks as necessary	**Likelihood of harm**	**Severity of impact**	**Overall risk**
	Remote, possible or probable	**Minimal, significant or severe**	**Low, medium or high**
Inability to exercise rights (including but not limited to privacy rights);	Probable	Significant	High
Inability to access services or opportunities;	Possible	Significant	Medium
Loss of control over the use of personal data;	Probable	Severe	High
Discrimination;	Possible	Significant	Medium
Identity theft or fraud;	Possible	Significant	Medium
Financial loss;	Probable	Severe	High
Reputational damage;	Possible	Minimal	Low
Physical harm;	Possible	Minimal	Low
Loss of confidentiality;	Probable	Significant	Medium

Re-identification of pseudonymised data	Possible	Minimal	Low
Any other significant economic or social disadvantage	Probable	Significant	Medium

Note that the decision re level of risk is made by reference to the following grid:

Severity of impact	Serious Harm	Low Risk	High Risk	High Risk
	Some Impact	Low Risk	Medium Risk	High Risk
	Minimal Impact	Low Risk	Low Risk	Low Risk
		Remote	Reasonable Possibility	More likely than not
		Likelihood of harm		

As can be seen from our example there are a number of areas where there may be a medium or high risk to the rights and freedoms of individual data subjects and therefore it is necessary to consider step 6.

Step 6 – Risk reduction measures

The ICO's Guidance sets out a series of options that controllers can consider applying in order to reduce the risks identified above and suggests that the following table can be used to record the information and the controller's assessment. I will now proceed to apply this methodology in respect of **one** of the areas of high risk that I have identified.

Risk	**Options to reduce or limit risk**	**Effect on risk**	**Residual risk**	**Measure approved**
		Elimi-nated, reduce or accepted	**Low, medium or high**	**Yes/no**
Loss of control over personal data	• deciding not to collect certain types of data; • reducing the scope of the processing; • reducing retention periods; • taking additional tech-nological security measures; • training staff to ensure risks are anticipated and managed; • anonymising or pseudonymising data where possible; • writing internal guidance or processes to avoid risks; • adding a human element to review automated decisions; • using a different tech-nology; • making changes to privacy notices; • implementing new systems to help indi-viduals to exercise their rights.	Reduced	Medium	Yes

Of course, it would also be necessary to carry out the same exercise in respect of the remaining high and medium risks, but I have not done this for the sake of space and time.

Step 7 – Sign-off and record outcomes

Having completed step 6 the controller would need to record their conclusions using the following table.

Item	Name/date	Notes
Measures approved by		Integrate actions back into project plan, with date and responsibility for completion
Residual risks involved		If accepting any residual high risk, consult the ICO before going ahead
DPO advice provided		DPO should advise on compliance, step 6 measures and whether processing can proceed
Summary of DPO advice		
DPO advice accepted or overruled by:		If overruled you must explain your reasons
Comments		
Consultation response overruled by:		If your decision departs from individuals' views, you must explain your reasons

<table>
<tr><td colspan="3">Comments</td></tr>
<tr><td>This DPIA will be kept under review by:</td><td></td><td>The DPO should also review ongoing compliance with DPIA</td></tr>
</table>

Steps 8-9 – Integration and review

Having completed the DPIA the ICO's Guidance suggests a series of actions that should be carried out and I summarise these below together with my high-level responses.

DPIA Requirement	**High-level response**
Integrate the outcomes of your DPIA back into your project plans.	In this case it would be necessary to liaise with those responsible for the implementation of this project.
Identify any action points and who is responsible for implementing them	We would need to allocate these to the appropriate people.
Monitor the ongoing performance of the DPIA and, if necessary, repeat the process before your plans are finalised.	We would need to decide who was responsible for this.
Where a controller has decided to accept a high risk, either because it was not possible to mitigate or because the costs of mitigation were too high, it needs to consult the ICO before it can go ahead with the processing	This would not be necessary in the light of the mitigating factors referred to above

Keep the DPIA under review, and repeat it if there is a substantial change to the nature, scope, context or purposes of the processing.	We would need to establish how often a review would take place and who would be responsible
Consider whether publication of the DPIA is appropriate (sensitive data can be redacted)	Strictly speaking there is no requirement to publish but it may be sensible to do so albeit having redacted any particularly sensitive data.

Summary

Having carried out the DPIA, and assuming that it is practicable to implement the proposed risk reduction measures, my conclusion would be that the controller could proceed with the proposed processing without the need to contact the ICO. However, they would need to keep the DPIA under careful review and update it as appropriate.

EXAMPLE TWO LEGITIMATE INTERESTS ASSESSMENT

In order to illustrate this concept, I set out below a worked example of a legitimate interests assessment ('LIA') carried out in respect of direct marketing. The assessment is divided into three sections and in each section I set out the questions asked in the LIA together with my high level answers. Please note that the issues of legitimate interests and direct marketing are discussed in more detail in chapters 5 and 9 respectively.

A controller providing products and services to its customers via an e-commerce website wants to contact its customers in order to advise them of its own similar products and services that may be of interest to them. Previously they have relied upon the individuals' consent but now wish to consider whether they can rely on legitimate interests as their lawful basis. In order to do this they carry out the following legitimate interests assessment

Purpose test – are you pursuing a legitimate interest?	
Questions	**High-level responses**
Why do you want to process the data – what are you trying to achieve?	Direct marketing purposes – in order to advise customers of products and services that may be of interest to them
Who benefits from the processing? In what way?	The controller benefits from the processing in terms of increased sales but the data subject also benefits in terms of being made aware of products and services that they may wish to purchase

Are there any wider public benefits to the processing?	N/A
How important are those benefits?	N/A
What would the impact be if you couldn't go ahead?	The controller would not be able to promote its own products and services to its existing customers
Would your use of the data be unethical or unlawful in any way?	No, as long as the other requirements of the GDPR and related legislation are complied with

Necessity test: is the processing necessary for that purpose?	
Questions	**High-level responses**
Does this processing actually help to further that interest?	Yes it does. Processing data in the proposed manner will allow the controller to provide information to data subjects about its products and services
Is it a reasonable way to go about it?	Yes, as long as the requirements of the GDPR and related legislation are complied with
Is there another less intrusive way to achieve the same result?	This is highly unlikely. Any other ways would be likely to be more intrusive.

Balancing test: do the individual's interests override the legitimate interest?	
Questions	**High-level responses**
What is the nature of your relationship with the individual?	The controller is a business retailing products and services and the data subject is someone who has previously purchased those products and/or services.
Is any of the data particularly sensitive or private?	The data to be processed for marketing purposes will be the data subjects' contact details and previous purchase history. Special categories data will not be used.
Would people expect you to use their data in this way?	Yes, data subjects are well used to controllers seeking to sell additional products and services to existing customers.
Are you happy to explain it to them?	Yes, this will be made clear in the ways set out below.
Are some people likely to object or find it intrusive?	Yes, and the controller will ensure that such objections are accurately documented so as to ensure that no further contact is made
What is the possible impact on the individual?	The data subject may become irritated on receipt of a marketing communication
How big an impact might it have on them?	The impact is likely to be low

Are you processing children's data?	No
Are any of the individuals vulnerable in any other way?	No
Can you adopt any safeguards to minimise the impact?	Yes, a series of safeguards can be adopted. (i) Information provided in our privacy statement (ii) Information at the point of capture of the data (iii) Institution of clear procedures to ensure that any objections are processed in a timely fashion (iv) All marketing communications will contain information as to how the data subject can object to receiving any further marketing information from us
Can you offer an opt-out?	Yes, and this will be offered as part of the data capture process and on subsequent communications

Summary

Having carried out these three tests my view would be that, subject to complying with the other relevant requirements of the GDPR and related legislation, the direct marketing envisaged in this scenario could proceed, on the basis of the legitimate interests of the controller. However, as mentioned above, care would need to be taken to review and revise the LIA if additional marketing activities were proposed in the future.

EXAMPLE THREE
PRIVACY STATEMENT

In order to illustrate this concept, I set out below a worked example of a simple privacy statement for a small to medium size law firm which typically collects information directly from its clients but may sometimes receive information from a third-party source. The aim of this statement is to comply with the controller's obligations to provide information to the data subject under articles 13 and 14 of the GDPR and this issue is discussed in more detail in chapter 7.

In each case, the suggested text appears in the left-hand column and the right-hand column then refers to the relevant provisions of the GDPR (in italics) and this is then followed by further commentary.

Privacy Statement	**Articles and commentary**
Who are we? *MJK LLP is a limited liability partnership incorporated in England and Wales and is a 'controller' under the General Data Protection Regulation and the Data Protection Act 2018.*	***Articles 13(1)(a) and 14(1)(a)*** *the identity and the contact details of the controller and, where applicable, of the controller's representative* It is assumed that the controller's contact details will be stated in other accompanying documentation.
What data will we collect? *We will only collect information from you that is relevant to the matter that we are dealing with. In particular, we may collect the following information*	***Article 14(1)(d)*** *the categories of personal data concerned;*

from you which is defined as 'personal data': • *Personal details* • *Family, lifestyle and social circumstances* • *Financial details* • *Business activities of the person whose details we are processing*	Note that these categories are deliberately broad. There is no need to list out every precise type of personal data that may be collected.
Special Categories *We may also collect information that is referred to as being in a 'special category'. This could include:* • *Physical or mental health details* • *Racial or ethnic origin* • *Religious beliefs or other beliefs of a similar nature* • *Criminal convictions* • *Sexual orientation*	***Article 14(1)(d)*** *the categories of personal data concerned;* Note that these categories are stated as found in the GDPR. There are other examples of special categories data but these have been omitted as being less likely to be collected.
Basis for processing personal data *The basis on which we process your personal data is one or more of the following:* • *It is necessary for the performance of our contract with you*	***Articles 13(1)(c) and 14(1)(c)*** *the legal basis for the processing;* ***Articles 13(1)(d) and 14(2)(b)*** *where the processing is based on point (f) of Article 6(1), the legitimate interests pursued by the controller or by a third party;*

<table>
<tr>
<td>

- *It is necessary for us to comply with a legal obligation*
- *It is in our legitimate interests to do so*
- *You have given us your consent (this can be withdrawn at any time by advising our data protection officer)*

Legitimate interests

In specific situations, we require your data to pursue our legitimate interests in a way which might reasonably be expected as part of running our business and which does not materially impact your rights, freedom or interests

For example:

- *we may contact you to tell about other services we provide that we think may be of interest to you*
- *we may invite you to participate in webinars about topics that may be of interest or to networking events that we organise from time to time*

You will always have a right to object to receiving further communications

</td>
<td>

Articles 13(2)(c) and 14(2)(d)

where the processing is based on point (a) of Article 6(1) or point (a) of Article 9(2), the existence of the right to withdraw consent at any time, without affecting the lawfulness of processing based on consent before its withdrawal;

Note that the lawful bases are stated here in outline form so that they are easier for the data subject to understand.

Other lawful bases are available but the most relevant to this scenario have been selected.

Specific legitimate interests have been stated as required.

The right to withdraw consent at any time is also referred to on two occasions.

</td>
</tr>
</table>

Basis for processing special categories data The basis on which we process your special categories data is one or more of the following: • *you have given us your consent (this can be withdrawn at any time by advising our data protection officer)* • *it is necessary to protect your vital interests* • *you have chosen to make the data public* • *it is necessary for the establishment, exercise or defence of legal claims on your behalf* • *it is necessary for reasons of substantial public interest*	
How will we use your data? *We may use your information for the following purposes:* • *Provision of legal services including advising and acting on behalf of clients* • *Promotion of our goods and services* • *Provision of education and training to customers and clients*	***Articles 13(1)(c) and 14(1)(c)*** *the purposes of the processing for which the personal data are intended* Note that the categories are deliberately broad in their nature and are based upon categories previously suggested by the ICO. They would, of course, need to be amended depending on the nature of the controller's activities.

• *Maintaining accounts and records* • *Supporting and managing staff*	
Who will we share your information with? *Under our Code of Conduct there are very strict rules about who we can share your information with and this will normally be limited to other people who will assist with your matter. This may include:* • *Barristers* • *Medical Experts* • *Private investigators* • *Healthcare professionals, social and welfare organisations* • *Courts and tribunals* *Where you authorise us, we may also disclose your information to your family, associates or representatives and we may also disclose your information to debt collection agencies if you do not pay our bills.*	***Articles 13(1)(e) and 14(1)(e)*** *the recipients or categories of recipients of the personal data, if any;* This list is very legal centric and would clearly need to be amended depending on the nature of the controller's activities.
Who do we receive information from? *While acting for you we may receive information about you from the following sources:*	***Article 14(2)(f)*** *from which source the personal data originate, and if applicable, whether it came from publicly accessible sources;*

• *Estate agents* • *Claims management companies* • *Accountants and other professionals* • *Central and local government* *Please be assured that this information will be treated confidentially at all times and will only be used where necessary.*	This requirement is often overlooked by controllers who may forget that they will be receiving information about data subjects from third party sources. As before, the list of sources would need to be amended depending on the nature of the controller's activities.
How long will we keep your information for? • *We will normally keep your information throughout the period of time that we do work for you and afterwards for a period of six years as we are required to do by law and also by the regulations that apply to us.* • *In some cases (for example where we have prepared a will for you) we may retain your information for a longer period and we will advise you of this at the time* • *More information is set out in our data retention policy which is available on request from the data protection officer*	***Articles 13(2)(a) and 14(2)(a)*** *the period for which the personal data will be stored, or if that is not possible, the criteria used to determine that period;* Most controllers will have a detailed data retention policy in order to comply with their obligations under the fifth principle. However, it is not necessary to provide that document here. Instead the better approach is to provide some basic information and advise the data subject that further information is available from the DPO if required.

Transfers to third countries	*Articles 13(1)(f) and 14(1)(f)*
• *We may from time to time transfer your personal data to a country outside of the EEA.* • *Normally this will be necessary for the performance of your contract with us or for the exercise or defence of legal claims on your behalf* • *Sometimes we may transfer for other reasons and we will ensure that appropriate safeguards are in place at all times*	*where applicable, the fact that the controller intends to transfer personal data to a third country or international organisation and the existence or absence of an adequacy decision by the Commission, or in the case of transfers referred to in Article 46 or 47, or the second subparagraph of Article 49(1), reference to the appropriate or suitable safeguards and the means by which to obtain a copy of them or where they have been made available.* Almost all controllers will make such transfers at some stage and therefore a brief comment about safeguards should be included. Obviously, this is an area that needs to be kept under review in the light of Brexit and further information is contained in chapters 11 and 15 of this book.
What rights do you have?	***Articles 13(2)(b) and 14(2)(c)***
You have the following rights under the GDPR: • *Right to be informed* • *Right of access*	*the existence of the right to request from the controller access to and rectification or erasure of personal data or restriction of processing concerning the data subject or to object to processing*

• *Right to rectification* • *Right to erasure* • *Right to restriction of processing* • *Right to data portability* • *Right to object* • *Rights concerning automated decision-making and profiling* *Further information about your rights is available on request from our data protection officer at [insert details]*	*as well as the right to data portability;* Articles 12-23 of the GDPR set out detailed rules in respect of these rights. However, in a privacy statement it would normally be sufficient to provide a list of the rights together with a contact point if an individual wished to enquire further.
Right of access • *You have a right to see the information we hold about you* • *To access this you need to provide a request in writing to our data protection officer, together with proof of identity* • *We will usually process your request free of charge and within 30 days however we reserve the right to charge a reasonable administration fee and to extend the period of time by a further two months if the request is manifestly unfounded or vexatious and/or is very complex* • *We will disclose to you all the personal data that we hold about you but be aware that sometimes exemptions may apply*	This section is not strictly necessary but some controllers may deem it a good idea to include some basic information as this is a right commonly used by data subjects.

• *Full details are available in our data subject access policy which is available on request from the data protection officer*	
Right to erasure • *You have a right to ask us to erase your personal data in certain cases (details may be found in Article 17 of the GDPR)* • *We will deal with your request free of charge and within 30 days but reserve the right to refuse to erase information that we are required to retain by law or regulation, or that is required to exercise or defend legal claims* • *To exercise your right to erasure please contact our data protection officer*	This section is not strictly necessary but some controllers may deem it a good idea to include some basic information as this is a right commonly used by data subjects.
Who can you complain to? • *If you are unhappy about how we are using your information or how we have responded to your request then initially you should contact the data protection officer [insert details]* • *If your complaint remains unresolved then you can contact the Information Commissioner's Office, details available at www.ico.org.uk*	***Articles 13(1)(b) and 14(1)(b)*** *the contact details of the data protection officer, where applicable;* ***Articles 13(2)(d) and 14(2)(e)*** *the right to lodge a complaint with a supervisory authority;*

	Note that a general reference to the DPO and a general reference to the ICO's website will suffice to comply with these obligations

Additional obligations

There are two other obligations that I have deliberately omitted from the privacy statement for lack of relevance in this scenario. They are as follows:

Article 13(2)(e)

- *whether the provision of personal data is a statutory or contractual requirement, or a requirement necessary to enter into a contract, as well as whether the data subject is obliged to provide the personal data and of the possible consequences of failure to provide such data;*

Articles 13(2)(f) and 14(2)(g)

- *the existence of automated decision-making, including profiling, referred to in Article 22(1) and (4) and, at least in those cases, meaningful information about the logic involved, as well as the significance and the envisaged consequences of such processing for the data subject.*

Summary

The precise lay-out and content of a privacy statement is discussed in more detail in chapter 7 of this book but suffice to say that most small to medium enterprises should use a document of the sort set out above as the starting point for compliance with their obligations under articles 13 and 14.

EXAMPLE FOUR SECURITY BREACH REPORTING

In order to illustrate this concept, I set out below a security incident scenario together with a completed version of the ICO's security breach reporting form. Please note that the issue of security and breach reporting is discussed in more detail in chapter 10 of this book.

A large UK university maintains a spreadsheet in respect of its students (10,000 in total). Normally it is only available to members of the Student Relations Department and other University departments as and when necessary. It is not password protected.

At 9.30am on 10th February, a new employee in the Student Relations Department is instructed by his line manager to send a copy of this spreadsheet by e-mail to the team responsible for first year students at the Vice-Chancellor's Office (e-mail address firstyearstudentsteam@uni.ac.uk). He carries out this instruction but, relying on predictive text, accidentally sends the e-mail to all first year students at the university using the e-mail address firstyearstudents@uni.ac.uk (3,000 recipients in total).

The new employee had not yet received any data protection training as he only started ten days ago and the relevant trainer was absent on that day. Training is scheduled to take place the following week.

At 11am on 10th February, a first-year student e-mails the employee to say that she has received the spreadsheet which contains the following information:

- *Name*
- *Course details*
- *Dietary requirements*
- *Membership of student societies*

- *Details of arrears in respect of fees*

She asks why this information has been made available and is very unhappy about it.

The employee apologies and explains that there has been an error. He tries to contact his line manager for advice on what to do, but she is in a meeting all day and cannot be disturbed.

The employee then receives a second call from another student who points out that the spreadsheet contains hidden columns, and that one of these columns contains the next of kin and associated contact details for all students detailed in the document. The caller asks to speak to the employee's line manager.

At 2.30pm on 10th February, and as a result of further calls now alerting senior staff members of the issue, a further e-mail is sent out, by the new employee, asking all recipients to delete the previous e-mail and stating that anyone accessing the spreadsheet will be in breach of University regulations.

Subsequently, approximately 48 hours later, the Student Relations Director decides to add an apology to the intranet that can be seen by all students and employees. At this point the Student Relations Director decides to inform the University's DPO of the breach and at 2:30pm on 12th February, the DPO looks at the spreadsheet. She discovers it contains additional information relating to 500 current and previous students. The following categories of personal data are identified as being present:

- *Medical conditions*
- *Dates of consultations with student counsellors*
- *Race*
- *Ethnicity*
- *Sexual orientation*

At this stage, the DPO sets out to fully investigate the matter by speaking to their IT department and the Student Relations Director.

The DPO then proceeds to complete the ICO's breach reporting form.

ico.
Information Commissioner's Office

Report a personal data breach

This form is for organisations that have experienced a personal data breach and need to report it to the ICO. Please do not include any of the personal data involved in the breach when completing this form. For example, do not provide the names of data subjects affected by the breach. If we need this information, we will ask for it later.

You should ensure the information provided is as accurate as possible and supply as much detail as possible.

If you have already spoken to a member of ICO staff about this breach, please give their name:

Report type

◉ Initial report

○ Follow-up report

(Follow-up reports only) ICO case reference: →

Reason for report – after consulting the guidance

◉ I consider the incident meets the threshold to report

○ I do not consider the incident meets the threshold to report, however I want you to be aware

○ I am unclear whether the incident meets the threshold to report

About the breach

What has happened?

Tell us as much as you can about what happened, what went wrong and how it happened.

[insert here a brief summary of events as set out in the scenario]

Was the breach caused by a cyber incident?

○ Yes

◉ No

○ Don't know

How did you find out about the breach?

I was informed by the university's Student Relations Director.

When did you discover the breach?

Date: 12th February

Time: 2.30pm

When did the breach happen?

Date: 10th February

Time: 9.30am

Categories of personal data included in the breach (tick all that apply)

☒ Data revealing racial or ethnic origin

☒ Political opinions

☒ Religious or philosophical beliefs

☐ Trade union membership

☐ Sex life data

☒ Sexual orientation data

☐ Gender reassignment data

☒ Health data

☒ Basic personal identifiers, eg name, contact details

☐ Identification data, eg usernames, passwords

☒ Economic and financial data, eg credit card numbers, bank details

☐ Official documents, eg driving licences

☐ Location data

☐ Genetic or biometric data

☐ Criminal convictions, offences

☐ Not yet known

☐ Other (please give details below)

Number of personal data records concerned?

One spreadsheet was sent to 3,000 e-mail addresses in error

How many data subjects could be affected?

Approximately 10,000

Categories of data subjects affected (tick all that apply)

☐ Employees

☐ Users

☐ Subscribers

☒ Students

☐ Customers or prospective customers

☐ Patients

☐ Children

☐ Vulnerable adults

☐ Not yet known

☒ Other (please give details below)

Former students

Potential consequences of the breach

Please describe the possible impact on data subjects, as a result of the breach. Please state if there has been any actual harm to data subjects

As of yet, we are not aware of any actual harm caused to data subjects. The possible impact could include:

loss of control over personal data
financial loss
identity fraud
discrimination

What is the likelihood that data subjects will experience significant consequences as a result of the breach?

- ○ Very likely
- ○ Likely
- ● Neutral - neither likely nor unlikely
- ○ Unlikely
- ○ Very unlikely
- ○ Not yet known

Please give details

(Cyber incidents only) Has the confidentiality, integrity and/or availability of your information systems been affected?

- ○ Yes
- ○ No
- ○ Don't know

(Cyber incidents only) If you answered yes, please specify (tick all that apply)

- ☐ Confidentiality
- ☐ Integrity
- ☐ Availability

(Cyber incidents only) Impact on your organisation

- ○ High - you have lost the ability to provide all critical services to all users
- ○ Medium - you have lost the ability to provide a critical service to some users
- ○ Low - there is no loss of efficiency, or a low loss of efficiency, and you can still provide all critical services to all users
- ○ Not yet known

(Cyber incidents only) Recovery time

- Regular - you can predict your recovery time, with existing resources
- Supplemented - you can predict your recovery time with additional resources
- Extended - you cannot predict your recovery time, and need extra resources
- Not recoverable - recovery from the incident is not possible, eg backups can't be restored
- Complete - recovery is complete
- Not yet known

Had the staff member involved in this breach received data protection training in the last two years?

- Yes
- (•) No
- Don't know

(Initial reports only) If there has been a delay in reporting this breach, please explain why

The breach has been reported within less than 72 hours of our becoming aware

(Follow-up reports only) Describe any measures you had in place before the breach with the aim of preventing a breach of this nature*

Taking action

Describe the actions you have taken, or propose to take, as a result of the breach

Include, where appropriate, actions you have taken to fix the problem, and to mitigate any adverse effects, eg confirmed data sent in error has been destroyed, updated passwords, planning information security training.

A further e-mail has been sent asking recipients to delete the e-mail containing the spreadsheet
We have changed the relevant first year student e-mail addresses so that they are more distinct in future.

This spreadsheet has been divided into separate spreadsheets for each year group
All spreadsheets are now password protected
The employee in question together with all employees in that department will be receiving GDPR training as soon as possible
We have advised all those affected (both present and former students) of the breach

(Follow-up reports only) Outline any steps you are taking to prevent a recurrence, and when you expect they will be completed*

Have you told data subjects about the breach?

- (•) Yes, we've told affected data subjects
- ( ) We're about to, or are in the process of telling data subjects
- ( ) No, they're already aware
- ( ) No, but we're planning to
- ( ) No, we've decided not to
- ( ) We haven't decided yet if we will tell them or not
- ( ) Something else (please give details below)

Have you told, or are you planning to tell any other organisations about the breach?

eg the police, other regulators or supervisory authorities. In case we need to make contact with other agencies

- ( ) Yes
- (•) No
- ( ) Don't know

If you answered yes, please specify

About you

Organisation (data controller) name

University of XXXX

Registered organisation address

XXXX

Person making this report

In case we need to contact you about this report

Name: → John Smith

Email: → XXXX

Phone: → XXXX

Data protection officer

Or the senior person responsible for data protection in your organisation

☒ Same details as above

Name: →

Email: →

Phone: →

Sending this form

Initial report

If this is your initial report, please send your completed form to casework@ico.org.uk, with 'Personal data breach notification' in the subject field.

Follow up report

If this is a follow up report, please *reply to the email we sent you*, attaching this completed form to it. (Make sure you leave the subject line as it is – this will ensure your follow-up gets added to your case).

OR, send by post to:

The Information Commissioner's Office
Wycliffe House
Water Lane
Wilmslow
Cheshire
SK9 5AF

Please note that we cannot guarantee security of forms or any attachments sent by email.

What happens next?

You should read our guidance to determine what steps you should take.

Based on the information you have provided, we will contact you within seven calendar days to provide information about our next steps. If this is your initial report, we'll give you a case reference number. If we consider the incident is minor or you have indicated that you do not consider it meets the threshold for reporting, you may not receive a response from us.

If your correspondence relates to an existing case, we'll add it to your case for your case officer to consider.

If you need any help in completing this form, please contact our helpline on 0303 123 1113 (operates 9am to 5pm Monday to Friday).

For information about what we do with personal data see our privacy notice.

Practical steps:

Having completed the form, the controller needs to decide what steps to take next. I would suggest the following:

(i) Report the breach to the ICO using the completed form

(ii) Report the breach formally to the individuals affected

This communication would set out similar information to that provided to the ICO and should advise all those with concerns to contact the controller's data protection officer.

(iii) Implement immediate remedial actions

This would include:

- sending a further e-mail asking all recipient s of the original e-mail to delete it together with its contents
- speaking directly to anyone who had contacted the controller directly to express concerns

(iv) Establish a working party

This would include the DPO, members of the legal and compliance departments, and a member of the senior management team to deal with the effects of the breach and to investigate its causes

(v) Carry out a further, more detailed investigation into the circumstances surrounding the breach.

This would include the following specific steps:

- interviewing all those concerned
- reviewing all existing policies and procedures and analysing what went wrong

- preparing a detailed report for senior management summarising the key events and suggesting appropriate remedial action

(vi) Liaise with insurers and external legal advisors about the possibility of compensation claims and how to deal with them

(vii) Deliver the report to senior management together with recommendations for preventing a recurrence and setting out a series of practical steps to be implemented

(viii) Implement further remedial actions

These would include:

- changing the relevant e-mails addresses so that they are more distinct
- dividing the spreadsheet into a series of spreadsheets
- all spreadsheets to be password protected
- the employee in question to receive data protection training
- all other employees to receive data protection refresher training

(ix) Liaise with the ICO as to the further steps taken and implement any additional actions they suggest.

(x) Record all these steps in the controller's security incident log.

Summary

This scenario highlights the importance of having clear data security procedures in place and ensuring that all employees receive regular training in this area. It also highlights the need for employees to report such incidents as soon as possible to the DPO so that the DPO can review what has happened and decide whether the ICO needs to be informed within the statutory reporting period of 72 hours from awareness.

PART C

APPENDICES

This section contains certain additional information that readers may find useful, namely:

1. General Data Protection Regulation Overview
2. Data Protection Act 2018 Overview
3. Definitions – comparison of the key definitions of the DPA 1998 and the GDPR
4. Data Protection Impact Assessment Template
5. Resources

APPENDIX ONE
GENERAL DATA PROTECTION REGULATION OVERVIEW

Chapter	Term	Article
I – General Provisions	Subject Matter and Objectives	1
	Material Scope	2
	Territorial Scope	3
	Definitions	4
II – Principles	Principles relating to processing of personal data	5
	Lawfulness of processing	6
	Conditions for consent	7
	Processing of personal data of a child re information society services	8
	Processing of special categories of personal data	9
	Processing of personal data relating to criminal convictions and offences	10
	Processing not allowing identification	11
III – Rights of Data Subjects	**Section 1 – Transparency and Modalities**	
	Transparent information, communication and modalities	12
	Section 2 – Information and access to data	
	Information to be provided where personal data collected	13
	Information to be provided where personal data have not been obtained	14
	Right of access by the data subject	15

	Section 3 – Rectification and Erasure	
	Right to rectification	16
	Right to erasure ('right to be forgotten')	17
	Right to restriction of processing	18
	Notification obligation regarding rectification, erasure or restriction	19
	Right to data portability	20
	Section 4 – Right to object and automated individual decision-making	
	Right to object	21
	Automated individual decision-making, including profiling	22
	Section 5 – Restrictions	
	Restrictions	23
IV – Controller and Processor	**Section 1 – General Obligations**	
	Responsibility of the controller	24
	Data protection by design and by default	25
	Joint Controllers	26
	Representatives of controllers or processors not established in the Union	27
	Processor	28
	Processing under the authority of the controller and processor	29
	Records of processing activities	30
	Cooperation with the supervisory authority	31
	Section 2 – Security of Personal Data	
	Security of processing	32
	Notification of a personal data breach to the supervisory authority	33
	Communication of a personal data breach to the data subject	34

	Section 3 – Data Protection Impact Assessment and Prior Consultation	
	Data protection impact assessment	35
	Prior consultation	36
	Section 4 – Data Protection Officer	
	Designation of the data protection officer	37
	Position of the data protection officer	38
	Tasks of the data protection officer	39
	Section 5 – Codes of Conduct and Certification	
	Codes of conduct	40
	Monitoring of approved codes of conduct	41
	Certification	42
	Certification Bodies	43
V – Transfer of personal data to third countries and international organisations	General principle for transfers	44
	Transfers on the basis of an adequacy decision	45
	Transfers subject to appropriate safeguards	46
	Binding corporate rules	47
	Transfers or disclosures not authorised by Union law	48
	Derogations for specific situations	49
	International cooperation for the protection of personal data	50
VI – Independent Supervisory Authorities	**Section 1 – Independent Status**	
	Supervisory Authority	51
	Independence	52
	General conditions for the members of the supervisory authority	53
	Rules on the establishment of the supervisory authority	54
	Professional Secrecy	50

	Section 2 – Competence, Tasks and Powers	
	Competence	55
	Competence of the lead supervisory authority	56
	Tasks	57
	Powers	58
	Activity Reports	59
VII – Cooperation and consistency	**Section 1 – Cooperation**	
	Cooperation between lead supervisory authority and others concerned	60
	Mutual assistance	61
	Joint operations of supervisory authorities	62
	Section 2 – Consistency	
	Consistency mechanism	63
	Opinion of the Board	64
	Dispute Resolution by the Board	65
	Urgency procedure	66
	Exchange of information	67
	Section 3 – European Data Protection Board	
	European Data Protection Board	68
	Independence	69
	Tasks of the Board	70
	Reports	71
	Procedure	72
	Chair	73
	Tasks of the Chair	74
	Secretariat	75
	Confidentiality	76

VIII – Remedies Liability and Sanctions	Right to lodge a complaint with a supervisory authority	77
	Right to an effective judicial remedy against a supervisory authority	78
	Right to an effective judicial remedy against a controller or processor	79
	Representation of data subjects	80
	Suspension of Proceedings	81
	Right to compensation and liability	82
	General conditions for imposing administrative fines	83
	Penalties	84
IX. Provisions relating to specific processing situations	Processing and freedom of expression and information	85
	Processing and public access to official documents	86
	Processing of the national identification number	87
	Processing in the context of employment	88
	Safeguards and derogations relating to processing for archiving purposes in the public interest, scientific or historical research purposes or statistical purposes	89
	Obligations of secrecy	90
	Existing data protection rules of churches and religious associations	91
X. Delegated Acts andImplementing Acts	Exercise of the Delegation	92
	Committee Procedure	93
XI. Final Provisions	Repeal of Directive 95/46/EC	94
	Relationship with Directive 2002/58/EC	95
	Relationship with previously concluded agreements	96
	Commission Reports	97

APPENDIX TWO DATA PROTECTION ACT 2018 OVERVIEW

CONTENTS

13 Obligations of credit reference agencies
14 Automated decision-making authorised by law: safeguards

Restrictions on data subject's rights

15 Exemptions etc
16 Power to make further exemptions etc by regulations

Accreditation of certification providers

17 Accreditation of certification providers

Transfers of personal data to third countries etc

18 Transfers of personal data to third countries etc

Specific processing situations

19 Processing for archiving, research and statistical purposes: safeguards

Minor definition

20 Meaning of "court"

CHAPTER 3 OTHER GENERAL PROCESSING

Scope

21 Processing to which this Chapter applies

Application of the GDPR

22 Application of the GDPR to processing to which this Chapter applies
23 Power to make provision in consequence of regulations related to the GDPR

Exemptions etc

24 Manual unstructured data held by FOI public authorities
25 Manual unstructured data used in longstanding historical research

26 National security and defence exemption
27 National security: certificate
28 National security and defence: modifications to Articles 9 and 32 of the applied GDPR

PART 3 LAW ENFORCEMENT PROCESSING

CHAPTER 1 SCOPE AND DEFINITIONS

Scope

29 Processing to which this Part applies

Definitions

30 Meaning of "competent authority"
31 "The law enforcement purposes"
32 Meaning of "controller" and "processor"
33 Other definitions

CHAPTER 2 PRINCIPLES

34 Overview and general duty of controller
35 The first data protection principle
36 The second data protection principle
37 The third data protection principle
38 The fourth data protection principle
39 The fifth data protection principle
40 The sixth data protection principle
41 Safeguards: archiving
42 Safeguards: sensitive processing

CHAPTER 3 RIGHTS OF THE DATA SUBJECT

Overview and scope

43 Overview and scope

Information: controller's general duties

44 Information: controller's general duties

Data subject's right of access

45 Right of access by the data subject

Data subject's rights to rectification or erasure etc

46 Right to rectification
47 Right to erasure or restriction of processing
48 Rights under section 46 or 47: supplementary

Automated individual decision-making

49 Right not to be subject to automated decision-making
50 Automated decision-making authorised by law: safeguards

Supplementary

51 Exercise of rights through the Commissioner
52 Form of provision of information etc
53 Manifestly unfounded or excessive requests by the data subject
54 Meaning of "applicable time period"

CHAPTER 4 CONTROLLER AND PROCESSOR

Overview and scope

55 Overview and scope

General obligations

56 General obligations of the controller
57 Data protection by design and default
58 Joint controllers
59 Processors
60 Processing under the authority of the controller or processor
61 Records of processing activities
62 Logging
63 Co-operation with the Commissioner

64 Data protection impact assessment
65 Prior consultation with the Commissioner

Obligations relating to security

66 Security of processing

Obligations relating to personal data breaches

67 Notification of a personal data breach to the Commissioner
68 Communication of a personal data breach to the data subject

Data protection officers

69 Designation of a data protection officer
70 Position of data protection officer
71 Tasks of data protection officer

CHAPTER 5 TRANSFERS OF PERSONAL DATA TO THIRD COUNTRIES ETC

Overview and interpretation

72 Overview and interpretation

General principles for transfers

73 General principles for transfers of personal data
74 Transfers on the basis of an adequacy decision
75 Transfers on the basis of appropriate safeguards
76 Transfers on the basis of special circumstances

Transfers to particular recipients

77 Transfers of personal data to persons other than relevant authorities

Subsequent transfers

78 Subsequent transfers

CHAPTER 6 SUPPLEMENTARY

79 National security: certificate
80 Special processing restrictions
81 Reporting of infringements

PART 4 INTELLIGENCE SERVICES PROCESSING CHAPTER 1 SCOPE AND DEFINITIONS

Scope

82 Processing to which this Part applies

Definitions

83 Meaning of "controller" and "processor"
84 Other definitions

CHAPTER 2 PRINCIPLES

Overview

85 Overview

The data protection principles

86 The first data protection principle
87 The second data protection principle
88 The third data protection principle
89 The fourth data protection principle
90 The fifth data protection principle
91 The sixth data protection principle

CHAPTER 3 RIGHTS OF THE DATA SUBJECT

Overview

92 Overview

Rights

93 Right to information
94 Right of access
95 Right of access: supplementary
96 Right not to be subject to automated decision-making
97 Right to intervene in automated decision-making
98 Right to information about decision-making
99 Right to object to processing
100 Rights to rectification and erasure

CHAPTER 4 CONTROLLER AND PROCESSOR

Overview

101 Overview

General obligations

102 General obligations of the controller
103 Data protection by design
104 Joint controllers
105 Processors
106 Processing under the authority of the controller or processor

Obligations relating to security

107 Security of processing

Obligations relating to personal data breaches

108 Communication of a personal data breach

CHAPTER 5 TRANSFERS OF PERSONAL DATA OUTSIDE THE UNITED KINGDOM

109 Transfers of personal data outside the United Kingdom

CHAPTER 6 EXEMPTIONS

110 National security
111 National security: certificate

112 Other exemptions
113 Power to make further exemptions

PART 5 THE INFORMATION COMMISSIONER

The Commissioner

114 The Information Commissioner

General functions

115 General functions under the GDPR and safeguards
116 Other general functions
117 Competence in relation to courts etc

International role

118 Co-operation and mutual assistance
119 Inspection of personal data in accordance with international obligations
120 Further international role

Codes of practice

121 Data-sharing code
122 Direct marketing code
123 Age-appropriate design code
124 Data protection and journalism code
125 Approval of codes prepared under sections 121 to 124
126 Publication and review of codes issued under section 125(4)
127 Effect of codes issued under section 125(4)
128 Other codes of practice

Consensual audits

129 Consensual audits

Records of national security certificates

130 Records of national security certificates

Information provided to the Commissioner

131 Disclosure of information to the Commissioner
132 Confidentiality of information
133 Guidance about privileged communications

Fees

134 Fees for services
135 Manifestly unfounded or excessive requests by data subjects etc
136 Guidance about fees
Charges

137 Charges payable to the Commissioner by controllers
138 Regulations under section 137: supplementary

Reports etc

139 Reporting to Parliament
140 Publication by the Commissioner
141 Notices from the Commissioner

PART 6 ENFORCEMENT

Information notices

142 Information notices
143 Information notices: restrictions
144 False statements made in response to information notices
145 Information orders

Assessment notices

146 Assessment notices
147 Assessment notices: restrictions

Information notices and assessment notices: destruction of documents etc

148 Destroying or falsifying information and documents etc

Enforcement notices

149 Enforcement notices
150 Enforcement notices: supplementary
151 Enforcement notices: rectification and erasure of personal data etc
152 Enforcement notices: restrictions
153 Enforcement notices: cancellation and variation
Powers of entry and inspection
154 Powers of entry and inspection

Penalties

155 Penalty notices
156 Penalty notices: restrictions
157 Maximum amount of penalty
158 Fixed penalties for non-compliance with charges regulations
159 Amount of penalties: supplementary

Guidance

160 Guidance about regulatory action
161 Approval of first guidance about regulatory action

Appeals etc

162 Rights of appeal
163 Determination of appeals
164 Applications in respect of urgent notices

Complaints

165 Complaints by data subjects
166 Orders to progress complaints

Remedies in the court

167 Compliance orders
168 Compensation for contravention of the GDPR
169 Compensation for contravention of other data protection legislation

Offences relating to personal data

170 Unlawful obtaining etc of personal data
171 Re-identification of de-identified personal data
172 Re-identification: effectiveness testing conditions
173 Alteration etc of personal data to prevent disclosure to data subject

The special purposes

174 The special purposes
175 Provision of assistance in special purposes proceedings
176 Staying special purposes proceedings
177 Guidance about how to seek redress against media organisations
178 Review of processing of personal data for the purposes of journalism
179 Effectiveness of the media's dispute resolution procedures

Jurisdiction of courts

180 Jurisdiction

Definitions

181 Interpretation of Part 6

PART 7 SUPPLEMENTARY AND FINAL PROVISION

Regulations under this Act 182 Regulations and consultation

Changes to the Data Protection Convention

183 Power to reflect changes to the Data Protection Convention

Rights of the data subject

184 Prohibition of requirement to produce relevant records
185 Avoidance of certain contractual terms relating to health records
186 Data subject's rights and other prohibitions and restrictions

Representation of data subjects

187 Representation of data subjects with their authority
188 Representation of data subjects with their authority: collective proceedings
189 Duty to review provision for representation of data subjects
190 Post-review powers to make provision about representation of data subjects

Framework for Data Processing by Government

191 Framework for Data Processing by Government
192 Approval of the Framework
193 Publication and review of the Framework
194 Effect of the Framework

Data-sharing: HMRC and reserve forces

195 Reserve forces: data-sharing by HMRC

Offences

196 Penalties for offences
197 Prosecution
198 Liability of directors etc
199 Recordable offences
200 Guidance about PACE codes of practice

The Tribunal

201 Disclosure of information to the Tribunal
202 Proceedings in the First-tier Tribunal: contempt
203 Tribunal Procedure Rules

Interpretation

204 Meaning of "health professional" and "social work professional"
205 General interpretation
206 Index of defined expressions

Territorial application

207 Territorial application of this Act

General

208 Children in Scotland
209 Application to the Crown
210 Application to Parliament
211 Minor and consequential provision

Final

212 Commencement
213 Transitional provision
214 Extent
215 Short title

Schedule 1 — Special categories of personal data and criminal convictions etc data

Part 1 — Conditions relating to employment, health and research etc
Part 2 — Substantial public interest conditions
Part 3 — Additional conditions relating to criminal convictions etc
Part 4 — Appropriate policy document and additional safeguards

Schedule 2 — Exemptions etc from the GDPR

Part 1 — Adaptations and restrictions based on Articles 6(3) and 23(1)
Part 2 — Restrictions based on Article 23(1): restrictions of rules in Articles 13 to 21 and 34
Part 3 — Restriction based on Article 23(1): protection of rights of others
Part 4 — Restrictions based on Article 23(1): restrictions of rules in Articles 13 to 15
Part 5 — Exemptions etc based on Article 85(2) for reasons of freedom of expression and information
Part 6 — Derogations etc based on Article 89 for research, statistics and archiving

Schedule 3 — Exemptions etc from the GDPR: health, social work, education and child abuse data

Part 1 — GDPR provisions to be restricted
Part 2 — Health data
Part 3 — Social work data
Part 4 — Education data
Part 5 — Child abuse data

Schedule 4 — Exemptions etc from the GDPR: disclosure prohibited or restricted by an enactment

Schedule 5 — Accreditation of certification providers: reviews and appeals

Schedule 6 — The applied GDPR and the applied Chapter 2

Part 1 — Modifications to the GDPR
Part 2 — Modifications to Chapter 2 of Part 2

Schedule 7 — Competent authorities
Schedule 8 — Conditions for sensitive processing under Part 3

Schedule 9 — Conditions for processing under Part 4

Schedule 10 — Conditions for sensitive processing under Part 4

Schedule 11 — Other exemptions under Part 4

Schedule 12 — The Information Commissioner
Schedule 13 — Other general functions of the Commissioner

Schedule 14 — Co-operation and mutual assistance

Part 1 — Law Enforcement Directive
Part 2 — Data Protection Convention

Schedule 15 — Powers of entry and inspection

Schedule 16 — Penalties

Schedule 17 — Review of processing of personal data for the purposes of journalism

Schedule 18 — Relevant records

Schedule 19 — Minor and consequential amendments

Part 1 — Amendments of primary legislation
Part 2 — Amendments of other legislation
Part 3 — Modifications
Part 4 — Supplementary

Schedule 20 — Transitional provision etc

Part 1 — General
Part 2 — Rights of data subjects
Part 3 — The GDPR and Part 2 of this Act
Part 4 — Law enforcement and intelligence services processing
Part 5 — National security certificates
Part 6 — The Information Commissioner
Part 7 — Enforcement etc under the 1998 Act
Part 8 — Enforcement etc under this Act
Part 9 — Other enactments

APPENDIX THREE
DEFINITIONS

DPA	*GDPR – Article 4*
'consent' *any freely given specific and informed indication of his wishes by which the data subject signifies his agreement to personal data relating to him being processed*	***'consent'*** *of the data subject means any freely given, specific, informed and unambiguous indication of the data subject's wishes by which he or she, by a statement or by a clear affirmative action, signifies agreement to the processing of personal data relating to him or her;*
"data controller" *means, subject to subsection (4), a person who (either alone or jointly or in common with other persons) determines the purposes for which and the manner in which any personal data are, or are to be, processed;*	***'controller'*** *means the natural or legal person, public authority, agency or other body which, alone or jointly with others, determines the purposes and means of the processing of personal data; where the purposes and means of such processing are determined by Union or Member State law, the controller or the specific criteria for its nomination may be provided for by Union or Member State law;*
"data processor"*, in relation to personal data, means any person (other than an employee of the data controller) who processes the data on behalf of the data controller;*	***'processor'*** *means a natural or legal person, public authority, agency or other body which processes personal data on behalf of the controller;*

*"**data subject**" means an individual who is the subject of personal data;*	*'**data subject**' means an identifiable natural person*
*"**personal data**" means data which relate to a living individual who can be identified -* *a. from those data, or* *b. from those data and other information which is in the possession of, or is likely to come into the possession of, the data controller,* *and includes any expression of opinion about the individual and any indication of the intentions of the data controller or any other person in respect of the individual;*	*'**personal data**' means any information relating to an identified or identifiable natural person ('data subject'); an identifiable natural person is one who can be identified, directly or indirectly, in particular by reference to an identifier such as a name, an identification number, location data, an online identifier or to one or more factors specific to the physical, physiological, genetic, mental, economic, cultural or social identity of that natural person;*
*"**relevant filing system**" means any set of information relating to individuals to the extent that, although the information is not processed by means of equipment operating automatically in response to instructions given for that purpose, the set is structured, either by reference to individuals or by reference to criteria relating to individuals, in such a way that specific information relating to a particular individual is readily accessible.*	*'**filing system**' means any structured set of personal data which are accessible according to specific criteria, whether centralised, decentralised or dispersed on a functional or geographical basis;*

*"**sensitive personal data**" means personal data consisting of information as to -* *a. the racial or ethnic origin of the data subject,* *b. his political opinions,* *c. his religious beliefs or other beliefs of a similar nature,* *d. whether he is a member of a trade union (within the meaning of the Trade Union and Labour Relations (Consolidation) Act 1992),* *e. his physical or mental health or condition,* *f. his sexual life,* *g. the commission or alleged commission by him of any offence, or* *h. any proceedings for any offence committed or alleged to have been committed by him, the disposal of such proceedings or the sentence of any court in such proceedings.*	*'**special categories**' processing of personal data revealing racial or ethnic origin, political opinions, religious or philosophical beliefs, or trade-union membership, and the processing of genetic data, biometric data for the purpose of uniquely identifying a natural person, data concerning health or data concerning a natural person's sex life or sexual orientation shall be prohibited.*

APPENDIX FOUR
TEMPLATE DATA PROTECTION IMPACT ASSESSMENT FORM

Sample DPIA template

Information Commissioner's Office

This template is an example of how you can record your DPIA process and outcome. It follows the process set out in our DPIA guidance, and you should read it alongside that guidance and the Criteria for an acceptable DPIA set out in European guidelines on DPIAs.

Start to fill out the template at the beginning of any major project involving the use of personal data, or if you are making a significant change to an existing process. Integrate the final outcomes back into your project plan.

Step 1: Identify the need for a DPIA

Explain broadly what the project aims to achieve and what type of processing it involves. You may find it helpful to refer or link to other documents, such as a project proposal. Summarise why you identified the need for a DPIA.

Step 2: Describe the processing

Describe the nature of the processing: how will you collect, use, store and delete data? What is the source of the data? Will you be sharing data with anyone? You might find it useful to refer to a flow diagram or another way of describing data flows. What types of processing identified as likely high risk are involved?

Describe the scope of the processing: what is the nature of the data, and does it include special category or criminal offence data? How much data will you be collecting and using? How often? How long will you keep it? How many individuals are affected? What geographical area does it cover?

Describe the context of the processing: what is the nature of your relationship with the individuals? How much control will they have? Would they expect you to use their data in this way? Do they include children or other vulnerable groups? Are there prior concerns over this type of processing or security flaws? Is it novel in any way? What is the current state of technology in this area? Are there any current issues of public concern that you should factor in? Are you signed up to any approved code of conduct or certification scheme (once any have been approved)?

Describe the purposes of the processing: what do you want to achieve? What is the intended effect on individuals? What are the benefits of the processing for you, and more broadly?

Step 3: Consultation process

Consider how to consult with relevant stakeholders: describe when and how you will seek individuals' views – or justify why it's not appropriate to do so. Who else do you need to involve within your organisation? Do you need to ask your processors to assist? Do you plan to consult information security experts, or any other experts?

Step 4: Assess necessity and proportionality

Describe compliance and proportionality measures, in particular: what is your lawful basis for processing? Does the processing actually achieve your purpose? Is there another way to achieve the same outcome? How will you prevent function creep? How will you ensure data quality and data minimisation? What information will you give individuals? How will you help to support their rights? What measures do you take to ensure processors comply? How do you safeguard any international transfers?

Step 5: Identify and assess risks

Describe the source of risk and nature of potential impact on individuals. Include associated compliance and corporate risks as necessary.	**Likelihood of harm**	**Severity of harm**	**Overall risk**
	Remote, possible or probable	Minimal, significant or severe	Low, medium or high

Step 6: Identify measures to reduce risk

Identify additional measures you could take to reduce or eliminate risks identified as medium or high risk in step 5				
Risk	**Options to reduce or eliminate risk**	**Effect on risk**	**Residual risk**	**Measure approved**
		Eliminated, reduced or accepted	Low, medium or high	Yes/no

Step 7: Sign off and record outcomes

Item	Name/date	Notes
Measures approved by:		Integrate actions back into project plan, with date and responsibility for completion
Residual risks approved by:		If accepting any residual high risk, consult the ICO before going ahead
DPO advice provided:		DPO should advise on compliance, step 6 measures and whether processing can proceed
Summary of DPO advice:		
DPO advice accepted or overruled by:		If overruled, you must explain your reasons
Comments:		
Consultation responses reviewed by:		If your decision departs from individuals' views, you must explain your reasons
Comments:		
This DPIA will be kept under review by:		The DPO should also review ongoing compliance with DPIA

APPENDIX FIVE
RESOURCES

There are two main places where information can be accessed and I summarise these below:

(i) ICO Main Website

www.ico.org.uk

There are a number of useful documents that can be accessed here:

Guide to the General Data Protection Regulation

https://ico.org.uk/for-organisations/guide-to-the-general-data-protection-regulation-gdpr/

This document is quoted from extensively throughout this book. There is an index available on the first page which can be used to navigate to the content that is of most interest to you.

Brexit Guidance

https://ico.org.uk/for-organisations/data-protection-and-brexit/

Register Entries

https://ico.org.uk/about-the-ico/what-we-do/register-of-data-controllers/

Self-assessment Toolkits

https://ico.org.uk/for-organisations/data-protection-self-assessment/

Enforcement Decisions

https://ico.org.uk/action-weve-taken/enforcement/

ICO Blog Posts

https://ico.org.uk/about-the-ico/news-and-events/news-and-blogs/

(ii) European Data Protection Board Website

https://edpb.europa.eu/

On this website you can access a number of relevant guidance notes that to date cover the following topics:

- Personal data breach notification
- Automated decision making and profiling
- Data Portability
- Data Protection Officers
- Lead Supervisory Authority

MORE BOOKS BY LAW BRIEF PUBLISHING

A selection of our other titles available now:-

'Ellis on Credit Hire – Sixth Edition' by Aidan Ellis & Tim Kevan
'A Practical Guide to Coercive Control for Legal Practitioners and Victims' by Rachel Horman
'A Practical Guide to Rights Over Airspace and Subsoil' by Daniel Gatty
'Tackling Disclosure in the Criminal Courts – A Practitioner's Guide' by Narita Bahra QC & Don Ramble
'A Practical Guide to the Law of Driverless Cars – Second Edition' by Alex Glassbrook, Emma Northey & Scarlett Milligan
'A Practical Guide to TOLATA Claims' by Greg Williams
'Artificial Intelligence – The Practical Legal Issues' by John Buyers
'A Practical Guide to the Law of Bullying and Harassment in the Workplace' by Philip Hyland
'How to Be a Freelance Solicitor: A Practical Guide to the SRA-Regulated Freelance Solicitor Model' by Paul Bennett
'A Practical Guide to Prison Injury Claims' by Malcolm Johnson
'A Practical Guide to the Small Claims Track' by Dominic Bright
'A Practical Guide to Advising Clients at the Police Station' by Colin Stephen McKeown-Beaumont
'A Practical Guide to Antisocial Behaviour Injunctions' by Iain Wightwick
'Practical Mediation: A Guide for Mediators, Advocates, Advisers, Lawyers, and Students in Civil, Commercial, Business, Property, Workplace, and Employment Cases' by Jonathan Dingle with John Sephton
'The Mini-Pupillage Workbook' by David Boyle
'Planning Obligations Demystified: A Practical Guide to Planning Obligations and Section 106 Agreements' by Bob Mc Geady & Meyric Lewis
'A Practical Guide to Crofting Law' by Brian Inkster

'A Practical Guide to Spousal Maintenance' by Liz Cowell
'A Practical Guide to the Law of Domain Names and Cybersquatting' by Andrew Clemson
'A Practical Guide to the Law of Gender Pay Gap Reporting' by Harini Iyengar
'A Practical Guide to the Rights of Grandparents in Children Proceedings' by Stuart Barlow
'NHS Whistleblowing and the Law' by Joseph England
'Employment Law and the Gig Economy' by Nigel Mackay & Annie Powell
'A Practical Guide to the General Data Protection Regulation (GDPR)' by Keith Markham
'A Practical Guide to Noise Induced Hearing Loss (NIHL) Claims' by Andrew Mckie, Ian Skeate, Gareth McAloon
'An Introduction to Beauty Negligence Claims – A Practical Guide for the Personal Injury Practitioner' by Greg Almond
'Intercompany Agreements for Transfer Pricing Compliance' by Paul Sutton
'Zen and the Art of Mediation' by Martin Plowman
'A Practical Guide to the SRA Principles, Individual and Law Firm Codes of Conduct 2019 – What Every Law Firm Needs to Know' by Paul Bennett
'A Practical Guide to Licensing Law for Commercial Property Lawyers' by Niall McCann & Richard Williams
'A Practical Guide to Adoption for Family Lawyers' by Graham Pegg
'A Practical Guide to Industrial Disease Claims' by Andrew Mckie & Ian Skeate
'A Practical Guide to Redundancy' by Philip Hyland
'A Practical Guide to Vicarious Liability' by Mariel Irvine
'A Practical Guide to Claims Arising from Delays in Diagnosing Cancer' by Bella Webb
'A Practical Guide to Applications for Landlord's Consent and Variation of Leases' by Mark Shelton
'A Practical Guide to Relief from Sanctions Post-Mitchell and Denton' by Peter Causton
'A Practical Guide to Equity Release for Advisors' by Paul Sams
'A Practical Guide to Unlawful Eviction and Harassment' by Stephanie Lovegrove

'A Practical Guide to the Law Relating to Food' by Ian Thomas
'A Practical Guide to the Ending of Assured Shorthold Tenancies' by Elizabeth Dwomoh
'A Practical Guide to Financial Services Claims' by Chris Hegarty
'The Law of Houses in Multiple Occupation: A Practical Guide to HMO Proceedings' by Julian Hunt
'A Practical Guide to Unlawful Eviction and Harassment' by Stephanie Lovegrove
'A Practical Guide to Solicitor and Client Costs' by Robin Dunne
'A Practical Guide to Wrongful Conception, Wrongful Birth and Wrongful Life Claims' by Rebecca Greenstreet
'Occupiers, Highways and Defective Premises Claims: A Practical Guide Post-Jackson – 2nd Edition' by Andrew Mckie
'A Practical Guide to Financial Ombudsman Service Claims' by Adam Temple & Robert Scrivenor
'A Practical Guide to the Law of Enfranchisement and Lease Extension' by Paul Sams
'A Practical Guide to Marketing for Lawyers – 2nd Edition' by Catherine Bailey & Jennet Ingram
'A Practical Guide to Advising Schools on Employment Law' by Jonathan Holden
'Certificates of Lawful Use and Development: A Guide to Making and Determining Applications' by Bob Mc Geady & Meyric Lewis
'A Guide to Consent in Clinical Negligence Post-Montgomery' by Lauren Sutherland QC
'A Practical Guide to Running Housing Disrepair and Cavity Wall Claims: 2nd Edition' by Andrew Mckie & Ian Skeate
'A Practical Guide to Holiday Sickness Claims – 2nd Edition' by Andrew Mckie & Ian Skeate
'Arguments and Tactics for Personal Injury and Clinical Negligence Claims' by Dorian Williams
'A Practical Guide to QOCS and Fundamental Dishonesty' by James Bentley
'A Practical Guide to Drone Law' by Rufus Ballaster, Andrew Firman, Eleanor Clot
'A Practical Guide to Compliance for Personal Injury Firms Working With Claims Management Companies' by Paul Bennett

www.ingramcontent.com/pod-product-compliance
Lightning Source LLC
LaVergne TN
LVHW052221200926
848481LV00001B/176